A Practical English Grammar

A. J. Thomson and A. V. Martinet

A Practical English Grammar

Second Edition

London
OXFORD UNIVERSITY PRESS

Oxford University Press, Ely House, London W.1

GLASGOW NEW YORK TORONTO MELBOURNE WELLINGTON
CAPE TOWN IBADAN NAIROBI DAR ES SALAAM LUSAKA ADDIS ABABA
DELHI BOMBAY CALCUTTA MADRAS KARACHI LAHORE DACCA
KUALA LUMPUR SINGAPORE HONG KONG TOKYO

ISBN 0 19 431323 9

FIRST PUBLISHED 1960
(as a Practical English Grammar for Foreign Students)
REPRINTED SEVEN TIMES
SECOND EDITION 1969
FIFTH IMPRESSION 1972

PRINTED AND BOUND IN ENGLAND BY
HAZELL WATSON AND VINEY LTD
AYLESBURY, BUCKS

Preface to the First Edition

This book deals with the construction of English from elementary to advanced level and is intended for intermediate and advanced students of English as a foreign language. Though written chiefly for adults it is suitable also for senior forms in schools. It is hoped also that teachers of English as a foreign language may find it useful as a reference book.

Special features of the book are:

1 A very comprehensive index, which should make this Grammar easy to use as a book of reference.
2 A very careful and detailed treatment of those points which students of English find particularly difficult, e.g. auxiliary verbs, the use of the present perfect and simple past tenses, the difference between certain similar words such as 'during' and 'for', &c.
3 A new treatment of the future.
4 Indication where necessary of the difference between ordinary conversational usage and strict grammatical form.
5 A list of over 300 of the more important of the verb + preposition/adverb combinations (e.g. give up, take off, &c.).
6 A chapter on spelling rules.
7 The use of the simplest possible English for all explanations so as to present the minimum difficulty to students who have not yet learned to read English easily.
8 Copious examples in good modern English.

Those using this Grammar as a textbook are warned that it is not a graded course, and that the chapters are not presented in order of difficulty. Difficult sections may therefore be met with in any part of the book, and intermediate students may prefer to omit these on the first reading. It is not, of course, necessary to study the chapters in the order given.

There are six booklets of exercises based on this grammar. The exercises are graded and can be had with or without key.

Preface to the Second Edition

Certain sections, e.g. the conditional, the gerund, the passive, participles and indirect speech, have been expanded so as to present a clearer and more comprehensive picture of each structure. Various other additions have also been made which we hope will be of assistance to teachers and students using this book. The paragraph structure of the first edition has been retained as far as possible.

London, July 1968 A.J.T., A.V.M.

Contents

1 Articles

The Indefinite Article

1 Form

The indefinite article is **a** or **an**. The form **a** is used before a word beginning with a consonant, or a vowel sounded like a consonant:

a man   a table   a university   a useful thing

The form **an** is used before words beginning with a vowel (**a, e, i, o, u**) or words beginning with a mute **h**:

an hour   an honourable man   an egg   an elephant   an apple

It is the same for all genders:

a man   a woman   an actor   an actress

2 The indefinite article, **a** or **an**, is used:

a Before a singular noun which is countable (i.e. of which there is more than one) when it is mentioned for the first time and represents no particular person or thing:

A dog is an animal.   I see a man.   A house has a roof.
A cat can catch a mouse.

b Before a singular countable noun which is used as an example of a class of things:

A cow has horns (i.e. All cows have horns).   An elephant never forgets.
A palm tree is usually very tall.

c With a noun complement. This includes names of professions:

He is a doctor.   She is a teacher.   He became a great man.
She is a good girl.

d In certain numerical expressions: a couple, a dozen, half a dozen, a score (20), a gross (144), a hundred, a thousand, a million, and a lot of, a great many of, a great deal of.

e In expressions of price, speed, ratio &c.:

sixpence a pound   a shilling a dozen   sixty miles an hour   four times a day
ten shillings a yard

(Note that **a** and **one** are not usually interchangeable. For the difference between them see **25**.)

f With **few** and **little**

a few = a small number, or what the speaker considers a small number

a little = a small amount, or what the speaker considers a small amount So that 'a little time' can mean days or years, depending on the speaker; and 'a few friends' can mean two or three, or twenty or thirty.

only placed first: 'only a few/only a little' emphasizes that the number/quantity really is small – in the speaker's opinion.

few and **little** can also be used without article but then have an almost negative meaning, and can usually be replaced by **hardly any**:

'We had little time for amusement' *implies that we were always busy.*
'Few people know this' = It is almost unknown.

g In exclamations before singular, countable nouns:

What a hot day! What a pretty girl! Such a pity!
but What pretty girls! What big dogs! (plural nouns, so no article. See **3**.)

h **a** can be placed before Mr/Mrs/Miss + surname:

a Mr Smith a Mrs Smith a Miss Smith

'a Mr Smith' means 'a man called Smith' and implies that he is a stranger to the speaker.

'Mr Smith', without **a**, implies that the speaker knows Mr Smith or knows of his existence.

(For the difference between **a/an** and **one** see **25**.)

3 The indefinite article is **not** used:

a Before plural nouns:

The indefinite article has no plural form. Therefore the plural of 'a dog' is 'dogs'.

b Before uncountable nouns:

i The following nouns are singular and uncountable in English: advice, information, news, baggage, luggage, furniture.
They are often preceded by: some, any, a little, a lot of, a piece of &c.

I'll give you a piece of advice. There isn't any news.
You need some more furniture.

Knowledge is also considered uncountable, but when used in a particular sense takes the article:

A knowledge of languages is always useful.
He has a good knowledge of mathematics.

Hair (all the hair on one's head) is considered uncountable, but if we consider each hair separately we say: a hair, two hairs &c.:

She has black hair. The fisherman used a hair to tie the feather to the hook

ii Materials: glass, wood, iron, stone, paper, cloth, wine, coffee, tea &c. are considered uncountable. But many of these nouns can also denote one particular thing, and then take an article:

Windows are made of glass *but* Have a glass of wine.
We write on paper *but* I've got a (news)paper.
Iron is a metal *but* I use an electric iron.

Some, any, a piece of, a lot of &c., are often used as shown in b(i) above:

Would you like some coffee? I want a piece of wood.

c Before abstract nouns: beauty, happiness, fear, hope, death &c., except when they are used in a particular sense:

He was pale with fear. Some children suffer from a fear of the dark.

d Before names of meals, except when preceded by an adjective:

We have breakfast at eight. He gave us a good breakfast.

The article is also used when it is a special meal given to celebrate something or in someone's honour:

I was invited to dinner (at their house, in the ordinary way)
but I was invited to a dinner given to welcome the new ambassador.

The Definite Article

The definite article is **the**. It is the same for singular and plural and for all genders:

the boy the boys the girl the girls

4 Use and omission of the definite article

a The definite article is used:

i Before nouns of which there is only one, or which are considered as one:

the earth the sea the sky the weather the North Pole

ii Before a noun which has become definite as a result of being mentioned a second time:

His car struck a tree; you can still see the mark on the tree.

iii Before a noun made definite by the addition of a phrase or clause:

the boy that I met the place where I met him the girl in blue
the man on the donkey

iv Before a noun which, by reason of locality, can represent only one particular thing:

Ann is in the garden (= the garden of this house).
He sent for the doctor (= his own doctor).
Please pass the wine (= the wine on the table).

v Before superlatives and **first/second** &c., and **only**, used as adjectives or pronouns:

Mont Blanc is the highest mountain in Europe.
Most people think that Monday is the worst day in the week.

vi Before singular nouns used to represent a class of objects:

The cuckoo is lazy (= all cuckoos are lazy).

vii Before an adjective used to represent a class of persons:

There is no peace for any but the dead.
The old and the young should be able to live together.

viii Before names of seas, rivers, chains of mountains, groups of islands and plural names of countries:

the Atlantic Ocean the Thames the Alps the U.S.A. the U.S.S.R. the Netherlands the Orkneys. *Note also* the Congo the Sudan.

ix Before musical instruments:

She learnt to play the flute.

x With the type of meal mentioned in **3d**:

The dinner given to celebrate their victory cost £200.

b The definite article is **not** used:

i Before countries, towns, proper names:

Mr Jones returned to Wales and bought a house in Swansea.

Exceptions:

the U.S.A. the Congo the Sudan the Netherlands the U.S.S.R.
the Mall the Strand (in London) the High Street.
the Smiths (= Mr and Mrs Smith and family) the Joneses (Mr and Mrs Jones) &c.

The Mr Smith would be possible in such sentences as:

I don't want the Mr Smith who works in the accounts office; I want the other one/the other Mr Smith.

ii Before abstract nouns except when they are used in a particular sense:

Men fear death *but* The death of the Prime Minister left his party without a leader.

iii After a noun in the possessive case, or a possessive adjective:

the uncle of the boy = the boy's uncle.
The (blue) book is mine = it is my (blue) book.

iv Before names of meals (but see **3d**):

The Scots have porridge for breakfast
but The wedding breakfast was held in her father's house.

v Before parts of the body and articles of clothing, as these normally prefer a possessive adjective:

Raise your right hand. He took off his coat.

But notice that sentences of the type:

She seized the child's collar. I patted his shoulder.
The brick hit John's face.

could be expressed:

She seized the child *by the* collar. I patted him *on the* shoulder.
The brick hit John *in the* face.

Similarly in the passive:

He was hit on the head. He was cut in the hand.

vi Note that in some languages the definite article is used before indefinite plural nouns but that in English **the** is never used in this way:

Women are expected to like housework (i.e. women in general).
Big hotels all over the world are very much the same.

If we put **the** before **women** in the first example, it would mean that we were referring to a particular group of women.

5 Omission of **the** before **home** and before **church, market, school, hospital** &c.

a home

When **home** is used alone, i.e. is not preceded or followed by a descriptive word or phrase, **the** is omitted:

He went home. She left home. They got home late.
They hurried home. They arrived home after dark.

Note that the preposition **to** is omitted and **at** is not used after **arrive.**

But when **home** is preceded or followed by a descriptive word or phrase it is treated like any other noun as regards articles and prepositions:

We went to *the bride's* home
For some years this was *the* home *of your queen.*
A mud hut was *the* only home *he had ever known.*

b chapel, church, market, college, school, hospital, court, prison, work, sea, bed

These nouns are used without **the** when they are visited or used for their primary purpose:

we go to church to pray	to market to buy or sell
to school to study	to hospital as patients
to college to study	to prison as prisoners
to bed to sleep	to court as litigants
to sea as sailors	to work as workers

Similarly we can be in prison/hospital/court/bed as prisoners/patients &c. and at church/work/sea/market as worshippers/workers &c.
We return from work/school/market/church. We get out of bed/leave hospital/escape from prison.
When these places are not visited for their primary purpose the article **the** is used:

I went to the church to see the carvings.
He comes to the school sometimes to speak to the headmaster.
He returned from the prison where he had been visiting his brother.
They are at the sea = at the seaside. *Compare this with*

They are at sea = in a ship (but not necessarily as sailors).
He went to the bed = walked over to it. *Compare with*
He went to bed = got into it and presumably went to sleep.

In contrast to the above list, the following very common nouns always take **the**: **cathedral, office, cinema, theatre**:

He is at *the* office (*but* at work).
She is going to *the* theatre.

2 Nouns

6 Kinds

There are four kinds of nouns in English:

1 Common nouns – dog, table, man
2 Proper nouns – Tom, France, Madrid, Mrs Smith
3 Abstract nouns – charity, beauty, fear, courage, joy
4 Collective nouns – swarm, team, crowd, flock, group

7 Gender

English genders are extremely simple, and in any case the gender of a noun only affects its pronoun and possessive adjective.
Men, boys and male animals are masculine.
Women, girls and female animals are feminine.
Inanimate things are neuter.
Exceptions: ships are normally considered feminine, and so are countries when referred to by name:

The ship struck an iceberg, which tore a huge hole in her bow.
Scotland lost many of her bravest men in two great rebellions.

Most nouns have the same form for masculine and feminine:

parent, child, cousin, author, painter, artist, rider, driver, cook, prisoner, singer, dancer, reporter, journalist

Some have different forms:

brother – sister   uncle – aunt   nephew – niece   lord – lady   duke – duchess
cock – hen   drake – duck   horse – mare

Some form the feminine from the masculine by adding **ess**. Note that words ending in **er** or **or** often drop the **e** or the **o**:

manager – manageress   actor – actress   conductor – conductress

8 Plurals

The plural of a noun is usually made by adding **s** to the singular:

dog, dogs   day, days   house, houses

Exceptions:

a Nouns ending in **o** or **ss**, **sh**, **ch**, or **x** form their plural by adding **es**:

tomato, tomatoes   kiss, kisses   brush, brushes   watch, watches
box, boxes

But foreign or abbreviated words ending in **o** add **s** only:

piano, pianos   dynamo, dynamos   photo, photos

b Nouns ending in **y** following a consonant form their plural by dropping the **y** and adding **ies**:

baby, babies   lady, ladies   country, countries   fly, flies

Nouns ending in **y** following a vowel form their plural by adding **s** only:

donkey, donkeys   boy, boys   day, days

c Twelve nouns ending in **f** or **fe** drop the **f** or **fe** and add **ves**. These nouns are: wife, life, knife, wolf, self, calf, shelf, leaf, loaf, thief, sheaf, half:

wife, wives   wolf, wolves   loaf, loaves   &c.

The nouns scarf, wharf, and hoof take either **s** or **ves** in the plural:

scarfs *or* scarves   wharfs *or* wharves   hoofs *or* hooves

Other words ending in **f** or **fe** add **s** in the plural in the ordinary way:

cliff, cliffs   handkerchief, handkerchiefs   fife, fifes

d A few nouns form their plural by a vowel change:

man, men   woman, women   foot, feet   mouse, mice   louse, lice
goose, geese   tooth, teeth

The plural of 'child' is 'children'.

The plural of 'penny' is either 'pennies' or 'pence'. 'Pennies' is used when referring to individual coins, and 'pence' when the amount only is being considered:

The ticket costs fourpence. If you have four pennies you can get it from the machine.

e A few names of fish and animals do not change in the plural: sheep, deer, salmon, trout, fish, grouse &c.:

one sheep, two sheep   one fish, six fish   &c.

Some measurements and numerals do not change either (see **301**, **305**).

f Words which retain their original Greek or Latin forms make their plurals according to the rules of Greek or Latin:

agendum, agenda
erratum, errata
radius, radii
crisis, crises
(/ˈkraisis/, /ˈkraisi:z/)
basis, bases
(/ˈbeisis/, /ˈbeisi:z/)
axis, axes
(/ˈaeksis/, /ˈaeksi:z/)
memorandum, memoranda
datum, data
phenomenon, phenomena
terminus, termini
appendix, appendices
oasis, oases
(/ouˈeisis/, /ouˈeisi:z/)
thesis, theses

Sometimes there are two plural forms with different meanings:

index, indexes (lists of contents of books)
indices (a mathematical term)
genius, geniuses (extraordinarily intelligent persons)
genii (supernatural beings)

But there is a tendency, particularly with fairly common Latin or Greek words, to make the plural according to the rules of English:

dogma, dogmas formula, formulas (though **formulae** is used by scientists)
gymnasium, gymnasiums

g Compound nouns

Normally the last word is made plural:

armchair, armchairs bookcase, bookcases

Where **man** or **woman** is prefixed, both parts are made plural:

manservant, menservants

Compound nouns formed with prepositions or adverbs make only the first word plural:

sister-in-law, sisters-in-law looker-on, lookers-on

Where the compound noun has an adjective as the last word, the first word is usually made plural:

court martial, courts martial (*but* **court martials** *is also heard*)

Words in **ful** usually make their plural in the ordinary way:

handful, handfuls armful, armfuls

9 Cases of nouns

a English nouns have no case endings except in the possessive case. We say, however, that they are in the nominative, accusative, or dative case according to the work that they do in the sentence.
A noun is in the nominative case when it is:

i the subject of a sentence:
Tom drove the car.

ii the complement of the verb **to be, to seem** &c.:
He is my *father.*

b A noun is in the accusative case when it:

i is the direct object of a verb:
We ate the *octopus.*

or **ii** follows a preposition:
We went to the *river.*

c A noun is in the dative case when it stands for **to** + noun or **for** + noun. We say that a noun in the dative case is the indirect object of a verb; i.e. in the first of the examples 'Mary' is the indirect object, and 'book' is the direct object:

I gave *Mary* a book. I bought *the child* a top. (See 77)

Possessive Case

10 The case endings for the possessive case

1 **'s** is used with singular nouns and plural nouns not ending in **s**:

Tom's book the boy's room the man's hat the men's hats
women's work St. James's Park

2 A simple apostrophe (') is used with plural nouns ending in **s**:

the girls' school the dogs' kennels

Classical names ending in s and also some less common English names add only the apostrophe:

Archimedes' Law Hercules' club Keats' poetry

Compounds are generally treated as one word:

my mother-in-law's house

Possessives of titles are formed as follows:

George the First's reign

11 Use of the possessive case

a Possession, when the possessor is a person or animal, is normally indicated by putting the possessor in the possessive case, not by using the preposition of:

The cat's bowl *not* the bowl of the cat
Tom's books my father's car

But when the possessor noun is immediately followed by a phrase or clause the of construction is used:

The boys rushed this way and that, obeying the directions of a man with a whistle.
'Novels are a waste of time,' was the opinion of my father, who had never read a novel in his life.

b Note that when the possessive case is used, the article before the person or thing possessed disappears:

the horns of the bull = the bull's horns

c When the possessor is a thing **of** is normally used:

the walls of the town   the legs of the table

But with many well-known combinations it is usual to put the two nouns together using the first noun as a sort of adjective. This is often done to indicate the position of something:

hall door   dining-room table   street lamp   kitchen sink

Similarly with names of towns and sometimes districts:

London transport.   Liverpool Cathedral.   Harris tweed

or when there is a connexion with time:

summer holidays   winter sports   autumn colours   spring fever
November fogs   Sunday dinner   birthday party

or to indicate the use of clothes, equipment, vehicles &c.:

golf clubs   tennis shoes   football ground   snow plough   shoe polish
coffee cup

and with kinds of stories:

detective stories   crime stories   murder stories   ghost stories
fairy stories   adventure stories

d The possessive form is used with expressions of time such as: second, minute, hour, day, night, week, fortnight, month, year:

a day's work   today's paper   a week's holiday   two years' pay

The nouns **money, shilling, half-crown,** and **pound** can be used in the possessive case when they are followed by **worth**:

a shilling's worth of parsley   five pounds' worth of orchids

3 Adjectives

12 Kinds

The main kinds of adjectives are:

1 of Quality – square, good, golden, fat, heavy, dry, clever
2 Demonstrative – this, that, these, those
3 Distributive – each, every, either, neither
4 Quantitative – some, any, no, few, many, much, one, twenty
5 Interrogative – which, what, whose
6 Possessive – my, your, his, her, its, our, your, their

13 Agreement

Adjectives in English have only one form, which is used with singular and plural, masculine and feminine nouns:

a good boy, good boys   a good girl, good girls

The only exceptions are the demonstrative adjectives **this** and **that**, which change to **these** and **those** before plural nouns:

this cat, these cats   that man, those men

14 Position of adjectives and the use of **and**

Adjectives in English usually come before their nouns:

a big town   a blue car   an interesting book

When there are two or more adjectives before a noun they are not usually separated by **and** except when the last two are adjectives of colour:

a big, square box   a tall young man   six yellow roses
but a black and white cap   a red, white, and blue flag

Adjectives of quality, however, can be placed after the verbs **be**, **seem**, **appear**, **look** (= seem, appear); **and** is then placed between the last two adjectives:

The house looked large and inconvenient.   It was cold, wet, and windy.

Comparison

15 There are three degrees of comparison:

1 Positive:	dark	tall	useful
2 Comparative:	darker	taller	more useful
3 Superlative:	darkest	tallest	most useful

a One-syllable adjectives form their comparative and superlative by adding **er** and **est** to the positive form:

bright brighter brightest   new newer newest

b Adjectives of three or more syllables form their comparative and superlative by putting **more** and **most** before the positive:

interesting more interesting most interesting
frightening more frightening most frightening

c Adjectives of two syllables follow one or other of the above rules. Those ending in **ful** or **re** usually take **more** and **most**:

doubtful more doubtful most doubtful
careful more careful most careful
obscure more obscure most obscure

Those ending in **er**, **y**, or **ly** add **er**, **est**:

pretty prettier prettiest (note that the **y** becomes **i**)
holy holier holiest
clever cleverer cleverest

d Irregular comparisons:

good	better	best
bad	worse	worst
little	less	least
many much	more	most
far	further	furthest (of distance and time)
	farther	farthest (of distance only)
old	older	oldest (of people and things)
	elder	eldest (of people only)

elder and **eldest** imply seniority rather than age. They are chiefly used for comparisons within a family:

his eldest boy/girl/nephew   my elder brother/sister

but **elder** cannot be placed before **than**, so **older** must be used here:

He is older than I (*elder* would not be possible).

Superlatives can be preceded by **the** and used as pronouns:

Tom is the cleverest. The eldest was only eight years old.

Comparatives can be used similarly:

His two sons look the same age. Which is the elder?

But this use of the comparative is considered rather literary. In informal English a superlative might be used here instead, i.e. we would say:

Which is the eldest?

16 Constructions with comparisons.

a With the positive form of the adjective, e.g. good, tall, clever (see **15**(1)), we use **as . . . as** in the affirmative

and **not as** / **not so** } . . . **as** in the negative:

A boy of sixteen is often as tall as his father.
Manslaughter is not so/as bad as murder.
Your coffee is not so/as good as the coffee my mother makes.

b With the comparative form of the adjective, e.g. better, taller (see **15(2)**), we use **than**:

A mountain is higher than a hill.
He isn't cleverer than you, but he is more careful and makes fewer mistakes than you do.

c Comparison of three or more persons or things is expressed by the superlative with

the . . . of
or **the . . . in** (of places):

Tom is the cleverest boy in the class.
St. Paul's isn't the highest cathedral in England.
She is the prettiest of them all.

d Parallel increase is expressed by

the + comparative . . . **the** + comparative:

The bigger the house is, the more money it will cost.
The more leisure he has, the happier he is.

e Gradual increase is expressed by two comparatives joined by **and**:

The weather is getting colder and colder.
He became more and more interested.

f Comparison of actions is made similarly:

Riding a horse is not as easy as riding a bicycle.
It is nicer to go with someone than to go alone.

When the infinitive is used after **than**, as in the above example, the **to** of the infinitive can be omitted:

It is nicer to go with someone than go alone.
It is sometimes quicker to walk than take a bus.

g Other examples of comparison:

You are as obstinate as a mule. This one is the better of the two.
Chinchilla is more expensive than mink.
Helen was the most beautiful woman in Greece.
In old stories the youngest of the family is always the hero.

17 than or as followed by a pronoun

When **than** or **as** is followed by a third person pronoun we usually repeat the verb:

He has more money than she *has.* We are taller than they *are.*
I am not as clever as he *is.*

When **than** or **as** is followed by a first or second person pronoun it is usually possible to omit the verb:

I am not as old as you. He has more time than I.

The pronoun, in formal English, remains in the nominative case as it is still considered to be the subject of the verb, even though the verb is not expressed.
In informal English, however, the pronoun is often put into the accusative case:

He has more time than me. They are wiser than us.

(This rule applies also when comparisons are made with adverbs. See **66**.)

18 Adjectives of quality used as nouns

Good/bad, poor/rich, healthy/sick, young/old, living/dead, and certain other adjectives describing human character or condition can be preceded by **the** and used to represent a class of persons:

the poor = poor people the dead = dead people
The poor are usually generous to each other.
After the battle they buried the dead.

These expressions have a plural meaning and are followed by a plural verb. If we wish to denote a single person we must add a noun:

The old receive pensions *but* An old man usually receives a pension.

Note that these expressions refer to a group or class of persons considered in a general sense only. If we wish to refer to a particular group it is necessary to add a noun:

The young are usually intolerant *is a general statement but* The young men are fishing *refers to particular young people.*

19 Use with the pronoun **one/ones**

Adjectives of quality can be used without their nouns if the pronoun **one** (singular), or **ones** (plural) is placed afterwards. This form is mainly used when there is some idea of selection or comparison:

I like those pencils; I'll take a blue one.
Small bananas are often better than big ones.

one is often omitted after **the** + superlative and **the** + comparative, which, as shown in **15**, can be used alone. It is also sometimes omitted after adjectives of colour:

I took the largest (one). I bought the more expensive (one) of the two.
Which do you like? I like the blue (one).

(For the other kinds of adjectives see the next chapter on Adjectives and Pronouns.)

4 Demonstrative, Distributive, and Quantitative Adjectives and Pronouns

Demonstrative Adjectives and Pronouns

20 Form

The demonstrative adjectives and pronouns are:

this (singular) **these** (plural)
that (singular) **those** (plural)

Demonstrative adjectives, as already mentioned, are the only adjectives that agree with their nouns, and they agree only in number:

this man, these men this girl, these girls
that cow, those cows that tree, those trees

Examples of use as pronouns:

This is my brother; these are my brothers.
That is my sister; those are my sisters. What is that? It is a rat.
What are those? They are melons.

21 Use with the pronoun **one/ones**

When there is some idea of comparison or selection the pronoun **one/ones** is often placed after these demonstratives, but this is not essential except when the demonstrative is followed by an adjective:

That chair is too big; I'll sit in this (one).
Don't buy those oranges; buy these (ones).
I want a cake. I'll buy this chocolate one.
You carry the heavy cases; I'll bring these light ones.

(**one/ones** is necessary in the last two examples but optional in the first two.)

Distributive Adjectives and Pronouns

22 **each, every, everyone, everybody, everything**

a **each** (adjective and pronoun) and **every** (adjective) both mean 'all' with the following slight difference:

each/every imply a number of persons/things considered individually. **all** implies a number of persons/things considered as a group. **each** and **every**

are followed by a singular verb. The only important differences between them are:

1 **each** can be used as a pronoun while **every** cannot.

2 **each** can be used for two or more persons/things while **every** is not normally used for very small numbers:

Two boys entered. Each (boy) was carrying a suitcase (**every** could not be used here).
Every (*or* Each) man carried a torch.

(For the reciprocal pronoun **each other** see **46**.)

b **everyone, everybody** (pronouns) mean 'all people' or 'all the people' and are normally used instead of these expressions. There is no difference in meaning between **everyone** and **everybody**. Both take singular verbs.
everything (pronoun) means 'all things' or 'all the things' and is normally used instead of them. It also takes a singular verb.
The expressions 'all people' and 'all things' are seldom heard; 'all the people'/'all the things' + a qualifying phrase or clause (see below) is possible; but **everyone/everybody** or **everything** is more usual:

Everyone likes him = All the people who know him like him.
Everybody clapped = All the people in the room clapped.
Everything that he said was true = All that he said was true.

23 either and neither (pronouns and adjectives)

either means any one of two persons or things:

I will take either. It doesn't matter which.
Do you like either of these? No, I don't like either.

neither + affirmative verb = **either** + negative verb:

I like neither = I don't like either.

neither is preferred at the beginning of a sentence and can also be used alone as a negative answer to a question:

Neither of them was any good. Which did you buy? Neither.

(For other uses of **neither** and **either** see **94** and **107c**.)

Quantitative Adjectives and Pronouns

24 These are all the numerals, together with: **a** (adj. only), **one**, **some**, **any**, **no** (adj. only), **none** (pronoun only), **much, many, little, few**.

Numerals (see **300–2**).
These present no difficulty. The same form is used for adjectives and pronouns:

He has six pens; I have six. Tom wrote ten letters; Joan wrote four.

The pronoun **one/ones** is added when the numeral is followed by an adjective alone:

Have you any apple trees? I have six *old ones.*

25 a and one

a The adjective **one** is not always interchangeable with **a** and **an**, because '**a** handkerchief' means any handkerchief, no particular handkerchief, while '**one** handkerchief', means no more than one:

A shotgun is no good (i.e. it is the wrong sort of thing).
One shotgun is no good (i.e. I need two or three).

Notice also the use of **one** with **other, others** &c., to emphasize a contrast:

One man said, 'Yes', the others said, 'No'. *but* A man showed me the way.

b As **a/an** cannot be used as pronouns, **one** is used instead:

One of my friends Reserve a table, and try to get *one* near the door.

one is used before **day, week, month** &c., to denote a particular time when something happened:

One day a telegram arrived. One night there was a terrible storm.
but A rainy day is very common in England. He spent a night in Paris.

26 some, any

some and **any** mean 'a certain quantity', and are used before plural or uncountable nouns. They can be pronouns or adjectives. **some** is used in affirmative sentences:

I'll cut you some bread, shall I? No thanks, I've still got some.

any is used

a In negative sentences:

I haven't any butter, and he hasn't any either. He hasn't any friends.

b After **hardly, scarcely,** and **barely** (which are almost negatives) (see 76):

I have hardly any money. There are scarcely any flowers in the garden.

c After interrogatives:

Have you any money? Did you see any swans?

But when the question is really an invitation or a request **some** is used:

Will you have some tea? Would you like some wine?
Will you carry some of these bottles for me, please?

some can also be used when the answer 'Yes' is expected:

I heard a knock; is there someone at the door?
Did he see some tall men with black beards? (I know that they were there, so feel sure that he saw them.)

d After **if** and in expressions of doubt:

I don't think that there is any milk in the house.
If I find any of your books I'll send them to you.
If you have any difficulty, ask me for help.

e To mean 'practically every', 'no particular (one)':

Any book about riding will tell you how to mount a horse.
Anybody will show you the way (i.e. everybody knows the way so that you can ask the first person you see).

27 **no** and **none**

no and **none** can be used with affirmative verbs to express a negative. They are therefore an alternative to the negative verb + **any** construction already mentioned.

Note that **any** can be pronoun or adjective,
while **no** is only an adjective
and **none** is always a pronoun:

{I haven't any apples. He hasn't any.	{He did not eat any nuts. He did not eat any.
{I have no apples. I have none.	{He ate no nuts. He ate none.

28 Compounds formed with **some**, **any**, and **no** follow the same rules:

someone	somebody	something
anyone	anybody	anything
no one	nobody	nothing

I know something.
Do you know anything?

{You do not know anything.
You know nothing.

29 **many** and **much**

many is used before plural countable nouns, **much** before uncountable nouns:

We haven't much money. He didn't make many mistakes.

Both can be used as pronouns:

You have plenty of petrol but I haven't much.
Tom gets lots of letters but Ann doesn't get many.

many is not often used as the object or part of the object of an affirmative verb, being normally replaced by **a lot (of)**:

She has a lot of hens *is much more usual than* She has many hens.

But when **many** is preceded by **a good/a great** it need not be replaced:

She has a good many hens/a great many hens.

much is not very often used with affirmative verbs, as almost always in the accusative and usually in the nominative, it is replaced by **a lot (of)/a great deal (of)**:

These cars use a great deal of petrol/a lot of petrol.
A lot of time/a great deal of time/much time was wasted.

30 little and few

little is used before uncountable nouns: little milk
few is used before plural countable nouns: few bottles
Both can also be used as pronouns. (For ***a*** **little/*a*** **few** see **2f.**)
little/few denote scarcity or lack and have almost the force of a negative.

There is little good agricultural land here = {there is not much good land. / there is hardly any good land.}

Few towns have such a splendid market place = {hardly any towns have .... / not many towns have ....}

This use of **little** and **few** is normally confined to written English and fairly formal speech. In ordinary conversation it is more usual to say **hardly any** or **not many/much** or to use a negative verb with **much/many**:

We saw little on account of the fog *would normally be replaced by*
We saw hardly anything/we didn't see much.
and Few people come this way *would normally be replaced by*
Hardly anyone comes this way/not many people come this way.

But **little** and **few** when preceded by **very, too, extremely, comparatively** &c., are often used in ordinary conversation:

I have very little time. We have too few holidays.

5 Interrogative Adjectives, Pronouns, and Adverbs

31 Interrogative adjectives and pronouns:

Form:

a for persons: Nom.: **who** (pro.)
Acc.: **whom, who** (pro.)
Poss.: **whose** (pro. and adj.)

b for things: Nom.: **what** (pro. and adj.)
Acc.: **what** (pro. and adj.)

c for persons or things when the choice is restricted:
Nom.: **which** (pro. and adj.)
Acc.: **which** (pro. and adj.)

what (adjective) can be used for persons also (see **33**).
All these adjectives and pronouns have the same form for singular and plural.

Examples of use:

a **who**

Who took my gun? Tom took it.
Who are those men? They are Tom's sons.

who/whom

Who (*or* whom) did you see? I saw the queen.
Who (*or* whom) did she pay? She paid Tom and me.
Who did they speak to? (i.e. to whom did they speak?) They spoke to Mary.

whose

Whose books are these? (adj.) They are Ann's.
Whose are these? (pro.) They are Ann's.
Whose car is this? (adj.) It is mine.

b **what**

(Nom.) What delayed you? (pro.) The storm delayed us.
(Acc.) What papers do you read? (adj.) I read *The Times*.
What did they eat? (pro.) They ate octopus.
What did they eat it with? (pro.) They ate it with chopsticks.

c **which**

(Nom.) Which of them is the eldest? Mary is the eldest.
(Acc.) Which do you like best? I like Tom best.
Which university did he go to, Oxford or Cambridge? He went to Oxford.

32 The accusative pronouns **who** and **whom**

a As direct objects

whom is the technically correct accusative form and is used in formal written and spoken English. In ordinary conversation, however, it is much more common to use **who** as the accusative form, so that we can say:

Whom did you meet? (formal) *or* Who did you meet? (informal)

There is no difference in meaning but the second is more usual than the first. Similarly we can say:

Whom did you help? *or* Who did you help?

b After prepositions

In formal English the preposition is immediately followed by **whom**:

With whom did you go?

But in ordinary spoken English it is more usual to move the preposition to the end of the sentence. The **whom** then normally changes to **who**:

Who did you go with?

33 **what** (adjective and pronoun)

a **what** is a general interrogative used for things:

What time is it? What street is this?
What did you say? What does he want?

When **what** is used with prepositions, the preposition is normally placed at the end of the sentence, as shown above:

What did you open it with? I opened it with my knife.

b **what . . . for? = why**

What did you do that for? = Why did you do it?

c **what + be . . . like?** is a request for a description and can be used for people or things:

What was the weather like? It was very wet and cold.

Used of people it may concern either appearance or character:

What is he like? He's a friendly sort of man.
or He's a tall man with a grey beard.

what does he/it look like? concerns appearance only, and can also mean 'What does he/it resemble?':

What does he look like? He is tall and thin.
He looks like a scarecrow.

What does it look like? It's white and puffy.
It looks like cotton wool.

Do not confuse the **What . . . like?** forms with **Who is he like?** and **Who does he look like?** Both of these mean 'Who does he resemble?' The first could refer to appearance or character, the second to appearance only.

d **what** is he? = what is his profession?

What was his father? He was a tailor.

what (adjective) used for persons is possible but not common:

What men are you talking about?

e **what** (adjective) is very common in questions about size:

What height is your room?

Note that the verb **to be** is always used here.

(Such questions can also be expressed by **how** with an adjective: How high is your room? See **36**.)

34 which compared with who and what

who is a general interrogative pronoun for persons.
what is a general interrogative pronoun and adjective used mainly for things.
which (pronoun and adjective) is used instead of **who** and **what** when the choice is restricted:

Mr A: Who do you want to speak to? (general inquiry)
Mr B: I want to speak to Mr Smith.
Mr A: We have two Smiths here; which do you want?
or Which Smith do you mean?
or Which of them do you want? We have two here.
What will you have to drink? (general inquiry)
but There's whisky, gin and sherry; which will you have?

35 An affirmative verb is used when the question concerns the subject of the sentence:

Who *saw* me? *The policeman* saw you.
What *woke* you up? *The thunder* woke me.
Which of them *won*? *Tom* won.

In other cases an interrogative verb must be used:

Who *did he see*? He saw *you*.
What *did he win*? He won a *silver cup*.
Who *did he go* with? He went *with his wife*.

36 Interrogative adverbs

These are: **why** **when** **where** **how**

why? means 'for what reason?' and is usually answered by 'because':

Why was he late? He was late because he missed the bus.

when? means 'at what time?':

When do you get up? I get up at 7 a.m.

where? means 'in what place?':

Where do you live? I live in London.

how? means 'in what way?':

How did you come? I came by plane.
How do you start the engine? You press this button.

how can also be used

a With adjectives, as an alternative to **what** followed by a noun (see 33):

How tall are you? I am six feet tall.
How high is Mount Everest? It is over five miles high.
How wide is the river? It is fifty yards wide.
How long does it take to fly from London to Paris?

b With **much** and **many**:

How much do you want? How many pictures did you buy?

c With adverbs:

How fast does he drive? He drives at fifty miles an hour.
How often do you go abroad? I go every year.
How quickly can you say 'Tottenham Court Road'?
I can say it in a quarter of a second.

Note that 'How is she?' is an inquiry about her health. A possible answer is, 'She is very well'.
But 'What is she like?' is a request for a description. A possible answer is 'She is tall and dark with green eyes'.

6 Possessive Adjectives, Personal and Other Pronouns

Possessive Adjectives and Pronouns

37 Form

Possessive adjectives	*Possessive pronouns*
my	mine
your	yours
his her its	his hers its
our	ours
your	yours
their	theirs

Note that no apostrophes are used here. Students should guard particularly against the common mistake of writing the possessive **its** with an apostrophe. **it's** (with an apostrophe) means **it is** (see **109**).
The old form of the second person singular, now no longer used in current English, can be found in the Bible and poetry:

thy thine

38 Agreement of possessive adjectives

Possessive adjectives in English refer to the possessor and not to the thing possessed. Everything that a man or boy possesses is **his** thing; everything that a woman or girl possesses is **her** thing:

Tom's father is *his* father *but* Mary's father is *her* father.
A boy loves *his* mother A girl loves *her* mother.

Everything that an animal or thing possesses is **its** thing:

A tree drops *its* leaves in autumn. A dog wags *its* tail when it is happy.

If there is more than one possessor, human or otherwise, **their** is used:

The boys are playing with *their* football. The girls are with *their* mothers.
Trees drop *their* leaves in autumn.

Notice that the possessive adjective remains the same whether the thing possessed is singular or plural:

my book, my books his aunt, his aunts

39 Possessive pronouns are used to replace possessive adjectives + nouns

a They follow the same rules as possessive adjectives:

This is *my pen* *or* This is *mine.*
This is *their house* *or* This is *theirs.*
It is *our room* *or* It is *ours.*
I have my pen; have you got *yours*?
Are those your books? No, they are *hers.*

b The expression **of mine** &c., means 'one of my':

a friend of mine = one of my friends a sister of hers = one of her sisters

Personal Pronouns

40 Form

		Nominative	*Accusative and dative*
Singular	1st person	I	me
	2nd person	you	you
	3rd person	he she it	him her it
Plural	1st person	we	us
	2nd person	you	you
	3rd person	they	them

The old form of the second person singular is:

thou (nom.) thee (acc. and dat.)

41 Use of the nominative, accusative, and dative forms

a Nominative pronouns are used:

i as subjects of a verb:

He knows. *We* were there. How many houses has *he*? *I* see it.

ii as complements of the verb **to be**:

It is *I*. Was it *they*?

In informal conversation, however, the accusative is often used after the verb to be:

It is *me*. Was it *them*?

But the nominative should be used if the pronoun is followed by a clause:

Surely the husband has the right to make the decisions since it is *he* who pays the bills.

b The accusative form is used:

i as direct object of a verb:

I saw *her.* Tom likes *them.*

ii after prepositions:

with *him* to *her* for *us* by *them*

c The dative form is used as indirect object, i.e. to replace **to** + noun/pronoun or **for** + noun/pronoun:

I gave *him* a book.

42 The position of accusative and dative pronouns

An indirect object comes before a direct object; i.e. dative before accusative:

I told him a story. (**him** here is dative.)
I bought them a ball. (**them** is dative.)

But if instead of a dative we use **to** or **for** with a noun or pronoun, these two words are placed *after* the direct object:

I told a story *to her*. I bought a ball *for them*.

to or **for** is usually used when the direct object is a pronoun:

I introduced her *to them*.
I gave it *to him*. ('I gave him it' would be very unusual.) (See **77**)

43 The pronoun **it**

it is the third person singular neuter pronoun and is used for things and often animals.
The same form, **it**, is used for nominative, accusative, and dative. The possessive form is **its** (see **38**). This should not be confused with **it's**, which is a contraction of **it is**. The plural form is **they/them**, as for people.
Examples of use:

Look at that bird. It always comes to this window.
Do you give it anything to eat? Yes, I always feed it.
What does this cloth cost? It costs five shillings a yard.
The mouse has gone back to its hole.

44 Other uses of **it**

a **it** is used in expressions of time, distance, weather, temperature &c.:

It is hot/cold/quiet/noisy in this room. What time is it? It is six o'clock.
How far is it to York? It is sixty miles.
It is raining/snowing/freezing. It is a fine day. What day is it? It is Monday.
What is the date? It is the third of March.

b **it** can also be used in sentences of the type:

It is better to be early. It is easy to criticize.

The infinitive is really the subject of this type of sentence, and the sentence could be rewritten:

To be early is better. To criticize is easy.

But the **it** construction is much the more usual.

c **it** can be used similarly to replace a clause at the beginning of a sentence. It would be possible, but most unusual, to say:

That he has not returned yet is strange.
That he will leave the village is hoped.

It is much better to place the **it** before the verb and move the clause to the end of the sentence:

It is strange that he has not returned yet.
It is hoped that he will leave the village.

d **it** also acts as subjects for impersonal verbs:

It seems. It appears &c.

45 The indefinite pronoun **one**

The indefinite pronoun **one** is not much used because **you** can also be employed as an indefinite pronoun and is more common:

One must be careful when driving a car *is possible, but*
You must be careful when driving a car *is much more usual.*

Note that **you** here applies to no particular person but merely replaces **one.**

The possessive adjective **one's** is much more often used:

It is easy to lose one's way in Venice.
It is a pity to spend all one's life in the same place.

Reflexive and Emphasizing Pronouns

These are: **myself, yourself, himself, herself, itself, ourselves, yourselves, themselves.**

Note the difference between the second person singular **yourself,** and the second person plural **yourselves.**
The indefinite reflexive/emphasizing pronoun is **oneself.**

46 Used as reflexive pronouns

myself, yourself &c., are used as objects of a verb when the action of the verb returns to the doer, i.e. when subject and object are the same person:

I cut myself. He shaved himself.
It is not always easy to amuse oneself on holiday.
Tom and Ann blamed themselves for the accident.

Note the change of meaning if we replace the reflexive pronoun by the reciprocal pronoun **each other:**

Tom and Ann blamed each other = Tom blamed Ann and Ann blamed Tom.

myself, yourself &c., are used similarly after a preposition:

He spoke to himself.
They looked at themselves in the looking glass. (Compare with: They looked at *each other* – a reciprocal action.)
He sat by himself (i.e. alone). I did it by myself (i.e. alone, without help).

47 As emphasizing pronouns

myself &c., can also be used to emphasize a noun or pronoun:

The king himself gave her the medal.

When used in this way the pronoun is never essential and can be omitted without changing the sense. It usually emphasizes the subject of the sentence and is then placed after the subject:

Ann herself opened the door. Tom himself went.

Alternatively it can be placed after the object if there is one:

Ann opened the door herself.

or after an intransitive verb:

Tom went himself.

If the intransitive verb is followed by a preposition + noun, the emphasizing pronoun can be placed after this noun:

Tom went to London himself *or* Tom himself went to London.

When it emphasizes another noun it is placed immediately after it:

I saw Tom himself. I spoke to the President himself.
She liked the diamond itself but not the setting.

48 so and not

so placed after the verbs *think, believe, hope, expect, suppose, am afraid* (= regret) can represent a whole clause. It is chiefly used to avoid repetition of a previous remark or question:

Will Mr Pitt be there? Yes, I think so (i.e. I think he will be there).
Is he going to pay you for this? I hope so (i.e. I hope he is going to pay me).
Do you think that he'll be very angry?
No, I don't suppose so (i.e. I don't suppose that he'll be very angry).

A negative clause can be expressed:

a by **not** placed after the affirmative form of the above verbs:

Is he going to tell the police? I hope not (I hope he won't).
Can you play bridge? I'm afraid not (I'm afraid I can't).
Will she get here before dark? I expect not.

or b except with **hope** and **be afraid** by **so** placed after the negative form of these verbs:

Do you think he'll be angry? I don't suppose so.

The negative verb + **so** is the more usual construction, but cannot be used with **be afraid** and **hope** because these two forms/verbs are not used in the negative in this sense.

7 Relative Pronouns

Relative pronouns introduce relative clauses. Relative clauses are of two kinds: 1. Defining 2. Non-defining.

Defining Relative Clauses

49 These describe the preceding noun in such a way as to distinguish it from other nouns of the same class. A clause of this kind is essential to the clear understanding of the noun:

The man *who told me this* refused to give me his name.

'Who told me this' is the relative clause. If we omit this, it is not clear what man we are talking about. Notice that there is no comma between a noun and a defining relative clause:

The noise *that he made* woke everybody up.

Relative Pronouns used in Defining Relative Clauses

50 Form

These relatives vary slightly according to whether they refer to persons or things and according to their case. They do not vary for singular or plural or masculine or feminine.

The forms are as follows:

For persons:	Nominative:	**who**	**that**	
	Accusative:	**whom**	**who**	**that**
	Possessive:	**whose**		
For things:	Nominative:	**which**	**that**	
	Accusative:	**which**	**that**	
	Possessive:	**whose**	**of which**	

It is sometimes essential to use **that** (see below).

51 Use for persons

a Nominative: **who** or **that**

who is normally used:

The man *who* robbed you is called Sykes.
The girls *who* serve in the shop are the owner's daughters.
The policeman *who* reported the accident has red hair.

that is much less usual than **who** in the nominative except after superlatives and after: **all, nobody, no one, somebody, someone, anybody** &c., when either **who** or **that** can be used:

All who/that heard him were delighted with him.
He was the best king who/that ever sat on the throne. (Compare with **52b.**)

b Accusative as object: **whom** or **who** or **that**

The technically correct accusative form is **whom**, but this is considered very formal and seldom used in spoken English. Instead of **whom**, therefore, in spoken English we use **who** or **that** (**that** being more usual than **who**), and it is still more common to omit the accusative relative pronoun altogether:

The man *whom* I saw was called Smith.
= The man *who* I saw is called Smith.
= The man *that* I saw . . .
= The man I saw . . . (relative pronoun omitted).

and The girls *whom* he praised were delighted.
= The girls *who* he praised . . .
= The girls *that* he praised . . .
= The girls he praised . . . (relative pronoun omitted).

c With a preposition: **whom** or **that**

In technically correct English the preposition is placed before the relative pronoun, which must then be put into the formal accusative form **whom**:

The man *to whom* I spoke. (This is formal but quite often used.)

In informal speech, however, it is more usual to move the preposition to the end of the clause. **whom** then is often replaced by **that**, but it is still more common to omit the relative altogether:

The man *from whom* I bought it told me to oil it.
The man *who(m)* I bought it *from* told me to oil it.
The man *that* I bought it *from* told me to oil it.
The man I bought it *from* told me to oil it.

d Possessive: **whose** is the only possible form:

People whose rents have been raised can appeal.

52 Relative pronouns for things

a Nominative: either **which** or **that**; **which** is the more formal:

This is the picture which/that caused such a sensation.
The stairs which/that lead to the cellar are rather slippery. (See also **b** below.)

b Accusative as object: **which** or **that**, or no relative at all:

The car which/that I hired broke down after five miles.
or The car I hired broke down after five miles.

which is hardly ever used after **all, much, little, everything, none, no** and compounds of **no,** or after superlatives. Instead we use **that,** or omit the relative altogether, if it is in the accusative case.

All the apples that fall are eaten by the pigs.
This is the best hotel (that) I know.

c Accusative with a preposition:

The formal construction is preposition + **which,** but it is more usual to move the preposition to the end of the clause, using **which** or **that** or omitting the relative altogether:

The ladder *on which* I was standing began to slip.
The ladder *which/that* I was standing *on* began to slip.
The ladder I was standing *on* began to slip.

d Possessive: **whose** + a clause is possible but can often be replaced by **with** + a phrase:

Living in a house whose walls were made of glass would be horrible.
Living in a house with glass walls would be horrible.

53 The relative pronoun **what**

what = the thing that/the things that &c.
The things that we saw astonished us = *What* we saw astonished us.
When she sees *the damage that* you have done she will be furious =
When she sees *what* you have done she will be furious.

what cannot be used as a connective relative (see **60**):

He said that he had no money. This was perfectly true. = He said that he had no money, **which** was perfectly true (not **what**).

54 An infinitive can sometimes replace a relative clause

a after **the first/second** &c., after **the last/only** and sometimes after superlatives:

The last man to leave the ship = The last man who left/leaves.
The only one to understand = The only one who understood/understands.

Notice that the infinitive here replaces a verb + nominative relative pronoun. It could not be used to replace a verb + accusative pronoun. For example the clause in 'The first man *that we saw*' could not be replaced by an infinitive, for 'The first man to see' would have a completely different meaning. If however we make **that** the subject of a passive verb, e.g. 'The first man that was seen,' we can replace the clause by a passive infinitive, e.g. 'The first man to be seen'.

b when there is some idea of purpose or permission:

He has a lot of books to read = a lot of books that he can read/must read
She had something to do = something that she could do/had to do
A garden to play in = a garden they can play in

Note that here the infinitive replaces a verb + *accusative* relative pronoun. It might be thought that these two uses of the infinitive would lead to confusion but in practice this is very rare as the meaning of the infinitive is made clear by the rest of the sentence. By itself the phrase 'The first man to see' could mean either 'The first man that we must see' (accusative use) or 'The first man who saw' (nominative use), but when it is part of a sentence we can see at once which meaning is intended:

The first man to see is Tom = the first man that we must see
while The first man to see me was Tom = the first man who saw me.

55 it is/was &c. + noun/pronoun + relative clause

It was Tom who paid.

This construction can be used instead of the simpler 'Tom paid' form when there has been some query or misapprehension about the subject of an action. It often follows a question about this or a mis-statement by a previous speaker:

Peter: One of the players is being carried off the field.
James: I think it is the referee who is being carried off.

Similarly 'It is always Ann who makes the tea' implies that there are other girls who could do it but don't, and 'It was the second bomb that did the damage' implies that the first one hadn't exploded.

Non-defining Relative Clauses

56 Non-defining relative clauses are placed after nouns which are definite already. They do not therefore define the noun, but merely add something to it by giving some more information about it. Unlike defining relative clauses, they are not essential in the sentence and can be omitted without causing confusion. Also unlike defining relatives, they are separated from their noun by commas. This construction is fairly formal and more common in written than in spoken English.

Relative Pronouns used in Non-defining Relative Clauses

57 Form

These relatives do not vary for singular or plural, masculine or feminine:

		Nominative	*Accusative*	*Possessive*
a	for persons:	**who**	**whom, who**	**whose**
b	for things:	**which**	**which**	**of which, whose**

58 Use for persons

a Nominative: **who**

Only **who** can be used. Note the commas:

My gardener, *who* is very pessimistic, says that there will be no apples this year.
Tom, *who* is incurably romantic, has just got engaged for the fourth time.

b Accusative as object: **whom, who**

The accusative must always be used and cannot be omitted: **whom** is the correct form though **who** is sometimes used in conversation:

His employer, *whom* he heartily dislikes, says that he is not suited to the work.
She introduced me to her husband, *whom* I hadn't seen before.

c Accusative with a preposition: **whom**

The preposition is normally placed before the relative, **whom**, though it is possible in conversation to use **who(m)** and move the preposition to the end of the clause as in defining relative clauses:

Mary, *with whom* I drove home, has a Rolls Royce
or Mary, *who* I drove home *with*, has a Rolls Royce.

Just note that:

Mary, with whom I drove home yesterday *will become*
Mary, who I drove home with yesterday.

(The adverb of time will remain at the end.)

d Possessive: **whose**

Chopin, *whose* works are world-famous, composed some of his music here.
Rousseau, *whose* paintings are extraordinarily interesting, was by profession a Customs Officer.

59 Use for things

a Nominative: **which**

His old car, *which* breaks down every few miles, is dearer to him than his wife.
His new house, *which* is absolutely enormous, has no running water.

b Accusative as object: **which**

The oak tree near the house, *which* I intended to cut down anyway, was struck by lightning last night.
'Julius Caesar', *which* you are going to see tomorrow, was written by Shakespeare.

which must always be used, as there is no alternative pronoun. It cannot be omitted.

c With a preposition: **which**

The preposition can be placed before the relative pronoun **which**, or at the end of the clause (but see **58c**):

This sherry, *for which* I paid 25/-, is awful.
or This sherry, which I paid 25/- for, is awful.

d With a verb + preposition/adverb combination

A verb + preposition/adverb combination such as: look forward to, run out of, look after, put up with, give up &c. (see **298**), should be treated as a whole, i.e. the preposition/adverb should not be separated from the verb:

This machine, *which* I have *looked after* for thirty years, is as good as new.
Your inefficiency, *which* I have *put up with* since you came to this office, is beginning to be unbearable.

e Possessive: **whose** or **of which**

whose can be used, especially of animals, and **of which** for things:

My bitch, *whose* temper is very uncertain, often bites the judges at important dog shows.
His thesis, *of which* the last hundred pages are absolute nonsense, will probably win him a lot of notoriety.

But such constructions are avoided wherever possible, and it would be more usual to say:

My bitch has a very uncertain temper and often bites the judges.
and His thesis will probably win him a lot of notoriety although (*or* because) the last hundred pages are nonsense.

Non-defining relative clauses are usually avoided in spoken English. This is done by using two simple sentences or a conjunction such as **and, but, because** &c.:

That well, *which* they began digging on Monday, is now thirty feet deep
is more likely to be expressed in spoken English as
They began digging that well on Monday. It is thirty feet deep now.

60 The connective relatives are **who** and **which**

I met Mary. She gave me this *could be combined as*
I met Mary *and she* gave me this.
or I met Mary, *who* gave me this.

Similarly:

I bought this map. It helped me a lot.
= I bought this map, *which* helped me a lot.

which can refer to a whole clause:

He said that he had never seen her before, *which* was not true.
Rats ran about the attic all night, *which* kept her awake.
We had to sleep in our wet clothes, *which* was most uncomfortable.

Notice that commas are used with connective relatives.

what cannot be used as a connective relative, and neither can **that.**

61 Relative adverbs

The relative adverbs **when, where,** and **why** are used to replace a preposition + the relative pronoun **which.**

when replaces **in/on which**, used for time
where replaces **in which** or **at which**, used for place
why replaces **for which**, used for reasons

the year *in which* he died = the year *when* he died.
the day *on which* she arrived = the day *when* she arrived.
the house *in which* he lived = the house *where* he lived.

Similarly:

Finland, *where* he spends his holidays, has lots of lakes.
The reason *why* he came is not very convincing.

62 The importance of commas in relative clauses

Remember that a defining relative clause is written without commas. Notice how the meaning changes when commas are inserted:

i The travellers who knew about the floods took another road.
ii The travellers, who knew about the floods, took another road.

In (i) we have a defining relative clause, which defines or limits the noun 'travellers'. This sentence therefore tells us that *only the travellers who knew about the floods* took the other road, and implies that there were other travellers who did not know and who took the flooded road.
In (ii) we have a non-defining clause, which does not define or limit the noun it follows. This sentence therefore implies that all the travellers knew about the floods and took the other road.

8 Adverbs

63 Kinds

There are seven kinds of adverbs:

1 of manner: e.g. quickly, bravely, happily, hard, fast, well
2 of place: e.g. here, there, everywhere, up, down, near, by (see **90**)
3 of time: e.g. now, soon, yet, still, then, today
4 of frequency: e.g. twice, often, never, always, occasionally
5 of degree: e.g. very, fairly, rather, quite, too, hardly
6 interrogative: e.g. when? where? why? (see **36**)
7 relative: e.g. when, where, why (see **61**)

64 The formation of adverbs from adjectives

a Most adverbs of manner and some adverbs of degree are formed by adding **ly** to the corresponding adjectives:

slow, slowly   grave, gravely   immediate, immediately

Spelling notes:

i a final **y** changes to **i**: ga*y* ga*i*ly

ii a final **e** is retained:

extreme, extremely   sincere, sincerely

Exceptions:

true due whole *become* truly duly wholly

Adjectives ending in **able/ible** drop the final **e** and add **y**:

sensible, sensibly   capable, capably

iii Adjectives ending in a vowel + **l** follow the usual rule and add **ly**:

final, finally   beautiful, beautifully

b Exceptions:

i The adverb of **good** is **well.**

ii With the exception of **leisurely** and **kindly**, adjectives ending in **ly** e.g. friendly, lovely, lonely, likely, lowly, have no adverb form. To supply this deficiency we use a similar adverb or an adverb phrase:

likely (adj.)   probably (adv.)
friendly (adj.)   in a friendly way (adverb phrase)

iii **high, low, deep, near, far, fast, hard, early, late, much, little, leisurely, kindly** can be used as adjectives or adverbs:

as adjectives	*as adverbs*
a high mountain	The bird flew high.
a fast train	The train went fast.
the near bank (the one nearest us)	Don't come near, this may explode.
The work is hard (tiring or difficult).	They worked hard (energetically).

iv The forms **highly, lowly, deeply, nearly, hardly, lately** exist, but have a narrower meaning than their corresponding adjectives:

highly is used only in an abstract sense:

He was highly placed = he had an important office.
They spoke very highly of him = they praised him, recommended him.

lowly is an adjective meaning **humble**; **nearly** = **almost**
lately = **recently** (for **hardly** see 76)
deeply is used chiefly in an emotional sense:

He was deeply hurt = his feelings were very much hurt.

v **warmly, hotly, coolly, coldly, presently, shortly, scarcely** and **barely** also differ in meaning from their corresponding adjectives:
warmly, hotly, coolly and **coldly** are used mainly in an emotional sense:

He denied the accusation hotly (indignantly).
They behaved very coolly in a dangerous situation (calmly, courageously).
She welcomed me warmly (in a friendly way).
We received them coldly (in an unfriendly way).

presently = **soon, shortly** = **briefly** or **soon** (for **scarcely, barely** see 76)

The Comparison of Adverbs

65 The comparative and superlative forms

a With adverbs of two or more syllables the comparative is formed by putting **more** before the adverbs, and the superlative by putting **most** before the adverb:

Positive	*Comparative*	*Superlative*
quickly	more quickly	most quickly
fortunately	more fortunately	most fortunately

Single-syllable adverbs, however, and the adverb **early**, add **er est**:

hard	harder	hardest
high	higher	highest

b Irregular comparisons:

well	better	best
badly	worse	worst
late	later	last
little	less	least
much	more	most
far	farther	farthest (of distance only)
	further	furthest (used of distance, time, and in an abstract sense).

66 Constructions with comparisons

a With the positive form we use **as . . . as** with an affirmative verb, and **as/so . . . as** with a negative verb:

He worked as slowly as he dared. He doesn't snore as/so loudly as you do.

b With the comparative form we use **than**:

i They arrived earlier than she did/than her. (See **17**.)
ii He eats more than I do/than me.
iii She danced more gracefully than the other girls.
iv He went further than the other explorers.

c With the superlative it is possible to use **of** + noun:

He went the furthest of the explorers.

But this construction is not very common and such a sentence would normally be expressed by a comparative, as shown above (**b** iv).
A superlative adverb + **of all** is quite common:

He ran fastest of all.

But **of all** here very often refers to other actions by the same subject:

He likes swimming best of all = better than he likes anything else.
She works best of all when she is alone = better than at other times.

of all can be omitted:

He likes swimming best.

d **most** placed before an adverb or adjective can also mean **very**:

She behaved most generously. They were most apologetic.

The Position of Adverbs

67 Adverbs of manner (kindly, badly, well &c.)

These answer the question 'How?'. They are usually placed after the direct object if there is one, otherwise after the verb:

He spoke English *well.* They walk *quickly.*

They must never be placed between a verb and its direct object.

68 Adverbs of place (here, there &c.)

Like adverbs of manner they are usually placed after the direct object if there is one, otherwise after the verb:

She painted that picture *here.* I looked *everywhere.*

If there is also an adverb of manner, the adverb of place comes after it:

He played well *there.*

somewhere, anywhere are used in the same way as **some** and **any** (see **26**):

I saw your hat *somewhere.* Did you see my hat *anywhere*?
I didn't see your hat *anywhere.*

nowhere is chiefly used in short answers:

Where are you going? *Nowhere* (i.e. I'm not going anywhere).

69 Adverbs of time (then, yet, still, now, soon &c.)

a These adverbs and the frequency adverbs **once, twice** &c., are normally placed at the very beginning or at the very end of a clause or sentence, the end position being the more usual:

He is coming *tomorrow.* He is working *now.*
I have been there *three times.* *Then* we went home.

b **yet** and **still**, used as adverbs of time, have slightly different position rules. **yet** should be placed at the end of a sentence. **still** is usually placed before the verb, though after the verb **to be**:

He hasn't finished *yet.* ('He hasn't *yet* finished' is also possible but is a less usual order.)
She *still* dislikes him. She is *still* in her bath.

Note the difference in meaning:

yet means 'up to the time of speaking'. It is chiefly used with the negative or interrogative. It is not normally used with the affirmative:

He left home at six and hasn't returned *yet.*
The shop isn't open *yet.* We'll come back at nine.
Aren't you ready *yet*? (Used with the negative interrogative **yet** usually expresses surprise or impatience.)

still emphasizes that the action continues:

He is *still* in bed.

If the **still** is stressed in speech it expresses surprise or irritation. **still** is chiefly used with the affirmative but it can be used with the negative also to emphasize the continuance of a negative action. Used in this way it is sometimes a possible alternative to **yet**:

He *still* doesn't understand. (The negative action of 'not understanding' continues.)
He doesn't understand *yet.* (The positive action of 'understanding' hasn't yet started.)

But it is on the whole safer to use **still** with the affirmative only.

Both these words can also be used as conjunctions:

You knew that the bridge was dangerous. *Yet* you didn't repair it.
I know that you aren't a doctor. *Still* (i.e. nevertheless) you could have bandaged his cuts.

70 Adverbs of frequency (sometimes, seldom, rarely, always, ever &c.)

These adverbs have more complicated position rules:

a They are placed after the simple tenses of **to be**:

He is always in time for meals.

b but before the simple tenses of all other verbs:

They sometimes stay up all night.

c With tenses consisting of more than one verb, they are placed after the first auxiliary:

I have *hardly* begun. He can *never* understand.
You have *often* been told not to do that.

Exceptions:

i **used to** and **have to** prefer the adverb in front of them:

You *hardly ever* have to remind him; he always remembers.

ii Frequency adverbs are often placed before auxiliaries when these are used alone, in additions to remarks or in answers to questions:

Can you park your car near the shops? Yes, I *usually* can.
He expects me to be ready when he comes, but I very *rarely* am.
I know I should take exercise but I *never* do.

iii When, to give emphasis to a compound verb, the auxiliary is stressed, the adverb of frequency is usually placed before the auxiliary:

I never 'can remember. She hardly ever 'has met him.

Similarly when **do** is added for emphasis:

But I always 'do arrive in time.

Note however that emphasis could also be given by stressing the frequency adverb and leaving it in its usual position after the auxiliary:

You should 'always check your oil before starting.

71 Adverbs of degree (almost, nearly, quite, just, too &c.)

a An adverb of degree modifies an adjective or another adverb. It is placed before the adjective or adverb:

It was *too* hot to work. I know him *quite* well.
The film was *fairly* good. He played *extremely* badly.

b The following adverbs of degree can also modify verbs: almost, nearly, quite, hardly, scarcely, barely, and just. They are then placed before the main verb, i.e. they obey the rules in **70 b** and **c** above:

I *quite* understand. He can *nearly* swim. I am *just* going.

c **enough** follows its adjective or adverb:

He didn't work quickly *enough*. The box isn't big *enough*.

(For **too/enough** + infinitive see **248.**)

d **only** is supposed to be placed next to the word to which it applies, preceding verbs, adjectives, and adverbs and preceding or following nouns and pronouns:

i He had *only* six apples (i.e. not more than six).
ii He *only* lent the car (i.e. he didn't give it).
iii He lent the car to me *only* (i.e. not to anyone else).
iv I believed *only* half of what he said.

But in spoken English, people usually put it before the verb, obtaining the required meaning by stressing the word to which the **only** applies:

He only had 'six apples *is the same as (i) above, and is more usual.*
He only lent the car to 'me *is the same as (iii) above.*
I only believed 'half &c. *is the same as (iv).*

72 Inversion of the verb after certain adverbs

a Certain adverbs and adverb phrases, mostly with a restrictive or negative sense, can for emphasis be placed first in a sentence and are then followed by the inverted (i.e. interrogative) form of the verb. The most important of these are: **never, seldom, scarcely, ever, scarcely . . . when, no sooner . . . than nowhere, in no circumstances, on no account, only by, only then, only when, only in this way, not only, so, neither, nor**:

Never before had I been asked to accept a bribe. = I had never before been asked (less emphatic form).
On no account must this switch be touched. = This switch must not be touched on any account.
Only by shouting at the top of his voice was he able to make himself heard.
No sooner had he left the shelter than the storm broke.

b The adverbs **in, out, up, down, round, over, back, forward &c.**, when placed at the beginning of a sentence are followed by verb + subject in that order.

In came Tom. Up jumped two large dogs. Down fell half a dozen apples.

But if the subject is a pronoun no inversion is necessary:

In he came. Back he went again.

The Meaning of Certain Adverbs of Degree

73 fairly and rather

a Both can mean 'moderately', but **fairly** is chiefly used with 'favourable' adjectives and adverbs (e.g. good, bravely, well, nice &c.), while **rather** is chiefly used in this sense before 'unfavourable' adjectives and adverbs (e.g. bad, stupidly, ugly &c.):

Tom is fairly clever, but Peter is rather stupid.
He is fairly rich, but she is rather poor.
You did fairly well in your exam, but Ann did rather badly.
This case is rather heavy, but that one is fairly light.

The indefinite article can be placed before or after **rather**:

This is rather a silly book *or* a rather silly book.

With **fairly** the article must come first:

a fairly interesting lecture

With adjectives/adverbs such as: fast, slow, thin, thick, hot, old &c., which are not in themselves either 'favourable' or 'unfavourable', the speaker can express approval by using **fairly** and disapproval by using **rather**:

This soup is fairly hot *implies that the speaker likes hot soup*
while This soup is rather hot *implies that it is a little too hot for him.*

b **rather** can be used before **alike, like, similar, different** &c., and before comparatives. It then means **a little** or **slightly**:

Siamese cats are rather like dogs in some ways.
The weather was rather worse than I had expected.

fairly cannot be used before comparatives.

c **rather** can be used before certain 'favourable' adjectives/adverbs such as **good, well, pretty, clever, amusing**, but its meaning then changes; it becomes nearly equivalent to **very**, and the idea of disapproval vanishes:

She is rather clever *is nearly the same as* She is very clever.

rather used in this way is obviously much more complimentary than **fairly.** For example the expression, 'It is a fairly good play,' would, if anything, discourage others from going to see it. But, 'It is rather a good play', is definitely a recommendation.
Occasionally **rather** used in this way conveys the idea of surprise:

Ann: I suppose the house was filthy.
Tom: No, as a matter of fact it was rather clean.

d **rather** can also be used before **enjoy, like** and sometimes before **dislike, object** and some similar verbs:

I rather like the smell of petrol.
Most people dislike driving on icy roads, but he rather enjoys it.
When he finally persuaded me to try oysters I found that I rather liked them.

rather here is chiefly used to express a liking which is a surprise to others or to the speaker himself.
It can also be used, as in **c** above, to strengthen the verb:

I rather like Tom *would normally imply greater interest than* I like Tom.

But **rather** is this sense should be used sparingly.
For **would rather** see **229, 272.**

74 quite

This is a confusing word because it has two meanings.

1 It means completely when it is used with a word or phrase which can express the idea of completeness: e.g. **full, empty, finished, wrong, right, all right, sure, certain, determined, ready** &c., and when it is used with a very strong adjective/adverb such as **perfect, amazing, horrible, extraordinary**:

The bottle was quite empty. You're quite wrong.
It's quite extraordinary; I can't understand it at all.

2 When used with other adjectives/adverbs, **quite** has a slightly weakening effect, so that **quite good** is less complimentary than **good**. **quite** used in this way has approximately the same meaning as **fairly** but its strength can vary very much according to the way it is stressed:

'quite good' (weak **quite**, strong **good**) is very little less than 'good'
'quite good' (equal stress) means 'moderately good'
'quite good' (strong **quite**, weak **good**) is much less than 'good'.

75 much

In the affirmative **much** is usually preceded by **very**:

I liked it very much/I enjoyed it very much. Thank you very much.

But **much** does not need very in the negative:

I don't like it much. I don't much like it.

much can also be an adverb of degree used with comparatives:

It is much better to say nothing.

76 hardly, barely, scarcely

These three are very similar. They are almost negative in meaning.

hardly is chiefly used with **any**, **ever**, or the verb **can**.
hardly any = very, very little/few.
hardly ever = very, very seldom.
hardly used with **can** means 'only with difficulty':

I have hardly any money (i.e. very, very little money).
I hardly ever go out (i.e. I very, very seldom go out).
I can hardly see the mark (i.e. the mark is difficult to see, or it is dark, or I have bad sight).

barely means 'no more than' and is often used with adjectives such as 'enough' and 'sufficient':

He had barely enough to eat (implying that he was often hungry).
He was barely sixteen (i.e. only just sixteen, no older).
I can barely see it (i.e. I can hardly see it).

scarcely combines the meanings of **hardly** and **barely**.

9 Prepositions

77 Omission of to and for before indirect objects

Instead of:	He gave the book to Tom	*and*	I'll find a job for Ann
we can say:	He gave Tom a book	*and*	I'll find Ann a job

i.e. we can put the indirect object before the direct object and omit the preposition.
We can use this construction after **take, bring, give, send, lend, promise, pay, offer, hand, pass, throw, tell, show, sing, play** (piano etc.), **tell**, instead of the construction with **to** as in (a) above;
and after **get, find, keep, reserve, book, make, build, knit, buy, order** (meals etc.), **fetch**, instead of the construction with **for** as in (b) above.

i.e. we can say:	I showed the map to Ann	*or*	I showed Ann the map
	She sent £5 to Tom	*or*	She sent Tom £5
	They kept a seat for Bill	*or*	They kept Bill a seat
	She made a coat for me	*or*	She made me a coat

The construction without preposition is the more common of the two, but it is not used when the direct object is a pronoun.

i.e. we can say:	He offered the job to Anne	*or*	He offered Ann the job
but	He offered it to Ann		(no alternative)
similarly	He bought a book for us	*or*	He bought us a book
but	He bought it for us		(no alternative)

Tell, show, promise, read, write, sing, can also be used with indirect object only; **tell, show, promise,** without **to:**

Tell Tom. Show me. He promised me.

Read, write, sing, play, with **to:**

Read to us. I'll write to him. He sang to them. (Sing/play **for** someone is also possible).

78 Prepositions of time and date

a **at** a time e.g. at six o'clock, at noon, at midnight
on a day e.g. on Monday, on July 21st., on Christmas Day
in a period e.g. in August, in 1914, in summer, in the morning, in the afternoon

Exceptions:

at night
at Christmas/at Easter (the period generally, not the day only)
on the morning/afternoon/evening of a certain date:

The battle started on the morning of the 24th.

b **on time** = at the time arranged
in time = not late:

The 10 a.m. train started on time (= at 10 a.m.).
We were in time for the train (= we arrived before 10.0).

in time can also mean **in the end/eventually**:

You'll get used to it in time.

c **at** 6 a.m., **at** noon &c. = at that time precisely
by 6 a.m., **by** noon &c. = at that time or before it, usually before it:

Tom: I'll be finished at six (= I'll be working up to that time).
Ann: I'll be finished by six (= almost certainly before six; so Ann will be finished before Tom).

d **at the beginning (of)** = literally at the beginning
at the end (of) = literally at the end:

at the beginning of the book = in the first few pages/on the first page
at the end (of the book) = in the last few pages/on the last page

in the beginning/at first (**of** is not normally used) = in the early stages, and implies a change later on:

In the beginning/At first we used knives; later we used axes.

in the end/at last = eventually/after some time:

At first he opposed the marriage but in the end he gave his consent.

79 Prepositions of travel and movement

We travel **from** our starting point **to** our destination.
We travel **by** bus/car/train/boat/sea/plane/air.
We travel **on** horseback, **on** foot, **on** a bicycle or **by** bicycle.
We arrive **in** a country or town. We arrive **in** or **at** a village.

We arrive **at** any other destination e.g. an address, a hotel, theatre, station, meeting point, bus-stop, river, bridge, cross-roads.
We get **to** any destination = arrive at it. (**into** can be used here, but only of towns and villages.)
We get **in** = arrive at/in a destination. This is chiefly used of trains arriving at stations. The destination is understood but not mentioned. (**in** here is an abverb, not a preposition.)

But we travel/go/return etc. **home** (without **to**) and we get **home** (without **to**) and arrive **home** (without **at**) except when **home** is preceded or followed by a descriptive word/phrase:

We went to Jack's home. I arrived at Ann's home. (See **5**)

We get **in/into** a public or private vehicle (= enter it).
We get **on/onto** a public vehicle, a horse, a bicycle (= enter or mount).
We get **out of** a public or private vehicle (= alight).
We get **off** a public vehicle, a horse &c. (= alight, dismount).

Notice also **get in/out/on/off** used without objects, i.e. as adverbs. **Get on/off** is used for public vehicles only.
get in/into/out/out of can also be used to mean **enter/leave** buildings, institutions, countries &c. but usually implies that there is some difficulty: e.g. 'We went into the house' implies that we went in by the door but 'We got into the house' might imply that we forced the lock or climbed in through a window:

The stairs are on fire! How are we to get out?
It's quite difficult to get into a university these days.

80 Use and omission of the preposition **to** before the person addressed

Verbs of communication used with the object + infinitive construction (see **238, 239**) are followed by the person addressed *without* **to:**

He asked us to wait. I warned them to wear gloves.

Some of these verbs can also be used with other constructions and then the person addressed may be optional or omitted. But it is still used *without* **to:**

He asked (me) some questions. He asked (us) for £5.

except after **tell** (= **relate**) and **recommend** in constructions of the type

He told lies to the police (see **77**).

Read, write, sing, speak, say, talk, whisper, mutter, murmur, shout, call (= **shout**), **complain, grumble, explain, suggest** etc. need **to** before the person addressed. It is not, however, essential to mention this person:

He complained (to me) about the food. Tom suggested the plan (to Peter).

But **read, write** and **sing** can be used with or without **to** as shown in **77.**

He read me the letter.

Telephone, phone, wire, cable, can be used with or without **to:**

He phoned (to) the hotel.

81 **at** and **in**

We can be **at** a small village, an address, a certain point (e.g. a cross-roads a bridge, a bus-stop), at home, at work:

He stayed at home yesterday. I live at 9 York Street.

We can be **in** a country, a town, a village, a square, a street, a room, a forest, a wood, a field or any other enclosed space. But we could say 'We are **at** a village/square/street/field', meaning 'We have reached it'.

We can be **at** or **in** a river/lake/swimming-pool etc. and **at** or **in** the sea. **At** here means 'beside'; **in** means 'actually in the water'. But **at sea** (without **the**) means 'on a ship' (see **5**).

We can be **at** or **in** a building. **At** means inside or just outside or in the grounds of the building. **In** means inside only.

If I am 'at the station' I could be 'in the street just outside' or 'in the station building' or 'in the waiting room/at the bookstall/on the platform.'

Note that we say **at home** (without **the**). **In** cannot be used in this way. **In a/the home** is possible, but is better avoided, as **home** used in this way would probably be taken to mean institution.

82 **in** and **into**

in is used for position as shown above:

The milk is in the saucepan. The boys are in bed.
She is in the house/in the swimming-pool.

into is used with a verb of motion to indicate entrance:

I poured the milk into the saucepan. The boys got into bed.
She went into the house/fell into the swimming-pool.
He went into the army (= became a soldier).

83 **to** and **till/until**

to can be used for place and time, **till/until** for time only.

a **to** and **till** used of time:

We work from 8.0 to 6.0 *or* from 8.0 till 6.0.

If there is no **from** we put **till** (not **to**) before the final time:

Let's start now and work till dark.

till is often used with a negative verb to emphasize lateness:

We didn't get home till 2 a.m.
There's no hurry; I don't have to be back till midnight.

till can also be used as a conjunction of time:

Wait till I come back.

b **to** used for place:

He walks to his office every day.
Go to the cross-roads.

till could not replace **to** in the above sentences, though we could say:

Go on till you get to the cross-roads.

84 from and since

from can be used for time and place:

He waited from 6.0 till 6.30.
I went from Westminster Bridge to the Tower of London.

since is used for time, never for place, and means, 'from that time to the time of speaking':

I've been here since Monday (from Monday till now).
He left on Sunday and we haven't seen him since/since then/since he left.

since can also be a conjunction, meaning 'seeing that':

Since you don't trust him why do you ask his opinion?

85 for and since (see also 183)

for is used with a period of time:

for six years   for two months   for ever

since is used with a point in time. The action either began at this point and continued to the time of speaking, or occurred in the period between this point and the time of speaking:

He has been here *since* six o'clock.   I've seen him twice since May.

since can also be a conjunction of time, without change of meaning:

I have done nothing *since* I arrived.

86 during and for

a **for** is used for a period of time, definite in length but otherwise indefinite. It is usually followed by a singular noun preceded by **a**, a plural noun, an adjective of quantity, or **ever**:

for a long time   for years   for five days   for ever

It implies that the action continues for the whole period.
Either **for** or **during** can be used before **the whole**. Neither is used before **all**:

He worked for the whole day. = He worked all day.

b **during** is placed before known periods of time, i.e. those known by name, such as: Lent, Easter &c., or those previously defined. It is, therefore, usually followed immediately by the name of a period or by **the, this, that, these** or **those**:

During the summer   during 1941   during the Middle Ages   during that time
during my holidays   during his childhood

The action can either last the whole period or occur at some time within the period:

It rained all Monday but stopped raining during that night (i.e. at some time on Monday night).
I was ill for a week and during that week I ate nothing.

c **for** is, however, often used before known periods of time with actions which are intended to last for the whole period. These actions are usually planned in advance and there is sometimes an idea of purpose. The verbs *go*, *come*, *be*, *stay*, *rent*, *hire*, and *lend* are often used with **for** in this way:

I went there for July (i.e. to spend July). He stayed with me for Christmas.
They hired a car for their holidays.

during used instead of **for** above would remove any idea of purpose and imply that the action probably did not last for the whole period.

87 **after** (preposition) and **afterwards** (adverb)

after must be followed by a noun, pronoun or gerund. If there is no noun pronoun or gerund we use **afterwards** or **then**:

It is unwise to bathe immediately *after a meal/after eating.*
It is unwise to have a meal and bathe immediately *after it.*
but It is unwise to have a meal and bathe immediately *afterwards.*
After finding a hotel we went to look at the town.
but We found a hotel and *then* (*or* *afterwards*) went to look at the town.

88 Gerunds after prepositions

When a verb is placed immediately after a preposition the gerund form is used:

I am tired of waiting (see **254**).

Exceptions are **but** and **except**, which are followed by the infinitive without **to**:

They did nothing but complain.
I would do anything for her except eat what she cooks.

But when **but** is used as a conjunction a verb placed after it could be either a gerund or a full infinitive:

To complain/Complaining after you are hurt is reasonable, but to complain/complaining before you are hurt is ridiculous.

but used as a conjunction is not replaceable by **except.**

89 **like** (adjective + preposition)

like can be treated like a preposition and followed immediately by noun, pronoun or gerund:

He is not like me; he is like his father.
The windows are all barred. It's like being in prison.

Note the expression **feel like** = feel inclined (for):

Do you feel like a walk? Do you feel like walking the next ten miles?
I was so angry that I felt like throwing something at him.

90 prepositions/adverbs

a Some words can be used as either prepositions or adverbs, i.e. they can be followed immediately by a noun/pronoun/gerund or used alone:

He fell **through** the ice (**through** used as a preposition).
The ice broke and he fell **through** (**through** used as an adverb).

The most important words of this type are: **in, on, up, down, off, near, through, along, across, over under, round.**

He climbed **up** the rope. (preposition)
He went **up** in the lift. (adverb)
She ran **along** the passage. (preposition)
Come **along**; we're late already. (adverb)

b These prepositions/adverbs and some other prepositions and adverbs are often placed after certain verbs so as to give these verbs a variety of meanings (see **298**). When such combinations are followed by a verb object, the gerund form of the verb must be used:

His plans **fell through** = came to nothing.
He **gave up** trying = stopped trying.

See also **51c, 52c, 245, 31, 32b** for alternative positions of pronouns and **255** for **to** (preposition) and **to** (part of the infinitive).

10 Conjunctions

Conjunctions which introduce adverb clauses are dealt with in the paragraphs on the various types of adverb clause (see Chapter 20 for conditional clauses and Chapter 29 for clauses of purpose, comparison, reason, time, result and concession).
Pairs or groups of clauses which are sometimes confused with each other are dealt with below.

91 **though/although, nevertheless, however** and the phrase **in spite of**

These, and the conjunction **but**, can be used to combine two opposing or constrasting statements. The difference between them is best seen by example. We could combine the following two sentences:

He was angry.
and He listened to me patiently.

in the following ways:

i with **but** or **though/although**

He was angry, but he listened to me patiently.
Though (although) he was angry he listened to me patiently.
He listened to me patiently though he was angry.

ii with **in spite of** + noun/pronoun/gerund

In spite of being angry he listened to me.
In spite of his anger he listened.

iii with **nevertheless**, which means **in spite of this/that,** or with **however,** which can also have this meaning:

He was angry, nevertheless/however he listened to me.

(See also clauses of concession **295**.)

92 **like** and **as**

like is placed before nouns/pronouns in the simpler types of comparison:

He fought like a madman.

But if the noun/pronoun is followed immediately by a verb, i.e. if there is a clause of comparison, **as** not **like**, should be used:

Can you pour wine straight down your throat, as they do in Spain?
When in Rome, do as the Romans do.

as can also be used with a noun alone, in the same way as **like**, but there is some difference in meaning:

I worked *as* a slave = I *was* a slave.
I worked *like* a slave = I worked very hard (but I was a free man).
He used his umbrella *as* a weapon = he defended himself with it. (See also **95**.)

93 for and because

These conjunctions have nearly the same meaning and very often either can be used. It is, however, safer to use **because**, as a clause introduced by **for** (which we will call a '**for**-clause') has a more restricted use than a clause introduced by **because**:

a A **for**-clause cannot precede the verb which it explains:

Because it was wet he took a taxi (**for** is not possible).

b A **for**-clause cannot be preceded by **not**, **but** or any conjunction:

He stole not because he wanted the money but because he liked stealing (**for** not possible).

c A **for**-clause cannot be used in answer to a question:

Why did you do it? I did it because I was angry (**for** not possible).

d A **for**-clause cannot be a mere repetition of what has been already stated, but always includes some new piece of information:

He spoke in French. She was angry because he had spoken in French (**for** not possible).

but She was angry, for she didn't know French (here **for** is correct; **because** is also possible).

The reason for these restrictions is that a **for**-clause does not tell us why a certain action was performed, but merely presents a piece of additional information which helps to explain it.
Some examples of **for**-clauses:

The days were short, for it was now December.
He took the food eagerly, for he had eaten nothing since dawn.
When I saw her in the river I was frightened. For at that point the currents were dangerous &c.

In speech a short pause is usually made before a **for**-clause and in written English this place is usually marked by a comma, and sometimes, as in the last example above, by a full stop.
because could be used in the above sentences also, though **for** is better.

94 both, either, neither, nor and so

We can express emphatically a combination of two things (nouns, verbs, adjectives &c.) by using **both . . . and**:

He has both the time and the money to play polo.
She both built and endowed the hospital.
It was both cold and wet.

We express two alternatives emphatically by **either . . . or** for the affirmative or interrogative:

We can have either tripe or liver. Can you eat either tripe or liver?

and by using **either . . . or** + a negative verb or **neither . . . nor** + an affirmative verb for the negative:

I can't eat either tripe or liver. = I can eat neither tripe nor liver.

b **either, neither, nor** and **so**, in additions to remarks

When a negative verb is repeated with a new subject, **either** may be placed at the end of the sentence:

He didn't go and she didn't go either.

But this can be more neatly expressed by using **neither/nor** + auxiliary verb (affirmative) + subject:

He didn't go and neither did she.

The same construction can be used in the affirmative with **so**:

I went and she went also. = I went and so did she. (See also **107a, c.**)

95 as, when, while

a Used with simple tenses to express time

when is used:

i When one action occurs at the same time as another or in the span of another:

When it is wet the buses are crowded.
When we lived in town we often went to the theatre.

ii When one action follows another:

When she pressed the button the lift stopped.

as is used:

iii When the second action occurs before the first is finished:

As I left the house I remembered the key.

This implies that I remembered the key before I had completed the action of leaving the house; I was probably still in the doorway. 'While I was leaving' would have the same meaning here, but 'When I left' would give the impression that the act of leaving was complete and the door shut behind me.

iv For parallel actions (these are usually by the same subject, or one is the result of the other):

As the sun rose the fog dispersed. He sang as he worked.
As it grew darker it became colder (= The darker it grew, the colder it became).

If we used **when** here we would lose all idea of simultaneous progression or development.

v **as** can mean **while** (= during the time that):

As he stood there he saw two men enter the bar.

But there is no particular advantage in using **as** here, and **while** is safer.

as is chiefly used with verbs of **doing** and **becoming** rather than verbs of **being**. It is not therefore normally used with auxiliary verbs, or, except when there is an idea of development, with verbs of emotion or of the senses, or verbs of knowing and understanding. **as** used for time must be kept within its proper limits because otherwise there is danger or confusion with **as** meaning **because**:

As he was tired he sat down *could only mean* Because he was tired.
As she loved him she let him stay *could only mean* Because she loved him.

But **as** + noun could mean either **when** or **because**:

As a student he had lived on bread and water = when he was a student.
As a married man he has to think of the future = because he is a married man/being a married man.

b as, when, while used to mean **because/since, although, seeing that**

as can mean **because/since**, as shown above:

We had to walk all the way as we had no money for fares.

as + noun can mean **because/since**:

As an old customer I have a right to better treatment than this.

as can mean **although** but only in the combination adjective + **as** + subject + **to be/to seem/to appear**:

Tired as he was he offered to carry the child (although he was tired).

while can mean **but** and is used to emphasize a contrast:

'At sea' means 'on a ship', while 'at the sea' means 'at the seaside'.
Some people waste food while others haven't enough.

while can also mean **although** and is then usually placed at the beginning of a sentence:

While I sympathize with your point of view I cannot accept it.

when can mean **seeing that/although**. It is therefore very similar to **while**, but is chiefly used to introduce a statement which makes another action seem unreasonable. It is often, though not necessarily, used with a question:

How can you expect your children to be truthful when you yourself tell lies?
It's not fair to expect her to do all the cooking when she has had no training or experience.

11 Introduction to Verbs

96 There are two classes of verbs in English:

a The auxiliary verbs (auxiliaries): **to be, to have, to do, to dare, to need, to be able (can), may, must, will, shall, ought**, and **used** (see **102** for function of auxiliaries).

b All other verbs, which we may call ordinary verbs:

to work   to sing   to pray

Note that English verbs are normally known by their infinitives:

to work   to be   to have

but some of the auxiliaries have no infinitive and are known by the form used for their present tense:

may   must   will   shall   &c.

Before studying auxiliaries it may be helpful to look briefly at the form of the ordinary verbs.

Ordinary Verbs

97 These are all conjugated the same way. There are a certain number of irregular verbs but these are irregular only in the form of their simple past tense and past participle (see **296**). Regular and irregular verbs form their simple present tense as shown in the next paragraph, and their simple past tense as shown in paragraph **99**. All other tenses are formed with an auxiliary + a participle or an infinitive.

All tenses will be dealt with fully in the chapters on tenses, but for the convenience of students the simple present, simple past, and future tenses are given below.

98 The simple present tense

This has the same form as the infinitive (without **to**), **s** being added for the 3rd person singular. The simple present tense of the verb **to work** is:

I work   you work   he (she, it) work*s*   we work   you work   they work.

The negative is formed with **does not** + infinitive (without **to**) for the 3rd person singular, and **do not** + infinitive (without **to**) for all other persons:

I do not work   you do not work   he (she, it) *does* not work   we do not work   you do not work   they do not work.

do not is usually contracted to **don't**, and **does not** to **doesn't**.

The interrogative is formed with **does** + subject + infinitive (without **to**) for the 3rd person singular, and **do** + subject + infinitive (without **to**) for all other persons:

Do I work? do you work? *does* he (she, it) work? do we work?
do you work? do they work?

Note that the same form is used for the 2nd person singular and the 2nd person plural, i.e. 'you work' can refer to one person or to more than one. There is a 2nd person singular pronoun, **thou**, but it is not used in modern English.

99 The simple past tense

In all regular verbs this is formed by adding **ed** (or **d** when the verb ends in **e**) to the infinitive. It is the same for all persons:

I worked you worked he worked we worked you worked they worked.

In irregular verbs the simple past form varies so that the simple past form of the verb **to speak** is **spoke**, of the verb **to eat** is **ate**, of the verb **to do** is **did** (see also **296**). These forms must be learnt, but once this is done there is no other difficulty, as the same form is used for all persons:

I spoke you spoke he spoke we spoke you spoke they spoke.

The negative (regular and irregular) is formed with **did not** + infinitive (without **to**). It is the same for all persons:

I did not work you did not work he did not work &c.
I did not speak you did not speak he did not speak &c.

The interrogative (regular and irregular) is formed with **did** + subject + infinitive (without **to**). It is the same for all persons:

Did I work? did you work? did he work? &c.
Did I speak? did you speak? did he speak? &c.

100 The future tense

This is formed with **shall** + infinitive (without **to**) for the 1st person and **will** + infinitive (without **to**) for the other persons:

I shall work you will work he will work we shall work they will work.

The negative is formed with **shall/will not** + infinitive:

I shall not work you will not work he will not work we shall not work
you will not work they will not work.

The interrogative is formed with **shall/will** + subject + infinitive:

Shall I work? will you work? will he work? shall we work? will they work?

101 The past participle and the perfect infinitive

The past participle of regular verbs is the same as the simple past form. The past participle of irregular verbs varies and must be learnt (see list **296**):

	Infinitive and present tense	*Past tense*	*Past participle*
Regular verbs:	work	worked	worked
	live	lived	lived
Irregular verbs:	speak	spoke	spoken
	eat	ate	eaten
	do	did	done

The perfect infinitive is formed with **to have** and the past participle:

to have worked to have spoken to have lived to have eaten to have done

Auxiliary Verbs

102 List of auxiliary verbs with their principal parts

	Infinitive	*Present tense*	*Past tense*	*Past participle*
be	to be	am, is, are	was, were	been
have	to have	have, has	had	had
do	to do	do, does	did	done
can	to be able	can, *or* am/is/are able	could, *or* was/were able	been able
may	..	may	might	..
must	(to have to)	must	had to	had to
need	to need	need	didn't need	needed
will	..	will	would	..
shall	..	shall	should	..
ought	..	ought	ought	..
dare	to dare	dare	dared	dared
used	..	..	used	..

These are called auxiliary verbs because:

i They help to form tenses, being combined with the present participle, the past participle or infinitive:

I am waiting. They will be there. He would like to come.

ii They are used with infinitives to indicate possibility, permission, ability, obligation, deduction &c. as will be seen in the following paragraphs:

He may come tomorrow (possibility). I can type (ability).
We must stop now (obligation).

In the following pages we shall deal with each of the auxiliaries in the above list with the exception of **will** and **shall**, which will be dealt with separately. (See **199–236** or index.)

103 Rules applicable to all auxiliaries

a All auxiliaries except **be, have,** and **do** are uninflected, i.e. all persons have the same form:

I can you can he can we can &c.
I must you must he must we must &c.

b The negative is formed by putting **not** after the auxiliary:

I must not. He has not. They do not.

(But **do not** + infinitive is sometimes used also. See **117–20, 123.**)

c The interrogative is formed by inverting subject and verb:

Can he? May we? Must I?

(But **do** + subject + infinitive is also sometimes used. See **117–20, 123.**)

d Auxiliaries are not normally used in the continuous tenses except for **be** when used in the passive voice. But see **have, 118, 120,** and **do, 123.**

e Auxiliaries are followed by infinitives (**be** and **have** can also be followed by other parts of the verb).

be, have, ought, and **used** are followed by the infinitive *with* **to:**

He is *to go.* I have *to work.* Tom ought *to write* to her.
She used *to know* Greek.

do, can, may, must, will, and **shall** are followed by the infinitive *without* **to:**

He doesn't *read.* She can *swim.* You may *go.* I must *see* it.
He will *help* you.

need and **dare** take the infinitive without **to** except when they are conjugated with **do:**

He need not *go* *but* He doesn't need *to go.*
How dare you *borrow* it without my permission!
He didn't dare *to say* anything.

f Auxiliaries are usually contracted in conversation:

be, have, had, would, will, and **shall** can be contracted in the affirmative.

had and **would** have the same contraction: **'d:**

I'm here. We've seen it. They'll go.
I'd seen it (= I had seen it). I'd go (= I should or would go).

But affirmative contractions cannot be used at the end of a sentence:

I'm not French but *he is* ('he is' here could not be contracted).

All auxiliaries can be contracted in the negative.

Use of Auxiliaries in Short Answers, Agreements &c.

Auxiliaries are extremely important in conversation because in short answers, agreements, disagreements with remarks, additions to remarks &c., we use auxiliaries instead of repeating the original verb.

104 Auxiliaries in short answers

Questions requiring the answer 'Yes' or 'No', i.e. questions such as, 'Do you smoke?' or 'Can you ride a bicycle?', should be answered by 'Yes' or 'No' and the auxiliary only. The original subject, if a noun, is replaced by a pronoun:

Do you smoke?	Yes, I do (*not* Yes, I smoke).
Can he cook?	No, he can't.
Did you win anything?	No, we didn't.
Has Tom a car?	Yes, he has.
Will Mr and Mrs Pitt be there?	Yes, they will.
May I go?	Yes, you may.
Do you eat snails?	No, I don't.
Did you put garlic in it?	Yes, I did.
Must he go?	Yes, he must *or* No, he needn't (see **147**).

105 Agreements and disagreements with remarks

a Agreements with affirmative remarks are made similarly, with 'Yes', 'So', or 'Of course'. If there is an auxiliary in the first verb this auxiliary is repeated; if there is no auxiliary, **do/does** is used in the present and **did** in the past:

It is very cold in here.	Yes, it is.
The fire has gone out.	So it has.
Bill smokes too much.	Yes, he does.
Those shoes are too small for you.	Yes, they are.
He may give us some champagne.	Yes, he may.
Avocado pears are fattening.	Yes, they are.
Mr and Mrs Pitt go abroad every year.	Yes, they do.
The boys left home yesterday.	Yes, they did.
Your chimney is on fire.	So it is.
There is a mosquito inside your mosquito-net.	Oh, so there is.

so used instead of **yes** expresses surprise.

b Agreements with negative remarks are made with 'No' and negative auxiliaries:

Her husband isn't rich.	No, he isn't.
Mr Pitt doesn't play golf well.	No, he doesn't.
We haven't much time.	No, we haven't.
My parents didn't like it.	No, they didn't.
I oughtn't to do that.	No, you oughtn't.

c Disagreement with affirmative remarks is made with 'No' or 'Oh, no' and the auxiliary. **do, does,** and **did** are used as above. 'But' may be used in disagreeing with questions and assumptions:

She is very pretty.	No, she isn't.
I have finished my work.	Oh, no, you haven't.
The boy will hurt himself.	No, he won't.
Why did you go to York yesterday?	But I didn't.
Your sister lent you the money.	No, she didn't.
Mr Pitt beats his wife.	No, he doesn't.

d Disagreement with negative remarks is made with 'Yes' or 'Oh, yes' and the auxiliary in the affirmative:

She won't come.	Oh, yes, she will.
Alex doesn't like you.	Oh, yes, he does.
You can't do it.	Yes, I can.
That horse hasn't won any races.	Oh, yes, it has.
The boat didn't capsize.	Oh, yes, it did.

106 Question tags

These are short additions to sentences, asking for agreement or confirmation. When the sentence is affirmative the question tag is made by repeating the auxiliary (or **do/does/did** if there is no auxiliary) in the negative interrogative form. This is always used in the contracted form and expects the answer, **yes.** The subject of the question tag is always a pronoun, never a noun.

He is always late, isn't he?
Jean went to Spain, didn't she?
Agnes can cook well, can't she?
There are plenty of taxis in Rome, aren't there?
Mrs Pitt likes crème de menthe, doesn't she?
Mr Pitt should take more exercise, shouldn't he?
I can borrow your car, can't I?
She will have to go with him, won't she? (Where there is more than one auxiliary in the main verb, only the *first* is repeated in the tag.)

When the sentence is negative the question tag is made by repeating the auxiliary in the ordinary interrogative form:

Spanish women don't wear hats much, do they?
She is not so stupid as she looks, is she?
You won't be late, will you?
You shouldn't drive so fast, should you?
Mr Pitt doesn't like oysters, does he?
Pythons don't make good pets, do they?

107 Additions to remarks

a Affirmative additions to affirmative remarks are made by using **so** + the auxiliary (or **do/does/did** if there is no auxiliary) + the subject, in that order. Instead of saying:

Bill likes tennis and Tom likes tennis too

we can say:

Bill likes tennis and *so does Tom.*

Similarly:

Men smoke in England and so do women.
I read *The Times* and so does Mr Pitt.
You can come in my car and so can your dog.
Shakespeare wrote plays and so did Lope de Vega.

b Affirmative additions to negative remarks are made with **but** + subject + auxiliary:

Bill can't ride that horse but Diana can. I didn't eat lobster but she did.
He won't go but they will.

c Negative additions to negative remarks are made with **nor** or **neither** + auxiliary + subject:

She didn't give anything and neither did he.
The men were not well dressed. Nor were the women.
She hasn't much time and neither have I.

d Negative additions to affirmative remarks are made with **but** + subject + auxiliary (or **do**/**does**/**did**) in the negative:

He likes Picasso but I don't. Henry can come but George can't.
The Pitts will accept but the Browns won't. My cat caught rats but yours didn't.

108 Auxiliaries used in comparisons

Auxiliaries can be used similarly with comparisons:

Tom runs faster than I do. I can ride better than he can.
She is taller than he is. She doesn't drive as well as he does.

The auxiliary, however, is often omitted (see **17**).

12 The Auxiliaries 'Be' and 'Have'

To be

109 Form

Principal parts: be – was – been

Present Tense:

Affirmative	*Negative*	*Interrogative*
I am (I'm)	I am not (I'm not)	am I?
you are (you're)	you are not (aren't)	are you?
he is (he's)	he is not (isn't)	is he?
she is (she's)	she is not (isn't)	is she?
it is (it's)	it is not (isn't)	is it?
we are (we're)	we are not (aren't)	are we?
you are (you're)	you are not (aren't)	are you?
they are (they're)	they are not (aren't)	are they?

The interrogative is not contracted.
Alternative negative contractions are: you're not, he's not &c.
The negative interrogative form is: am I not? (with contraction: aren't I?), are you not (aren't you?), is he not? (isn't he?) &c.

Past Tense:

Affirmative	*Negative*	*Interrogative*
I was	I was not (wasn't)	was I?
you were	you were not (weren't)	were you?
he/she/it was	he/she/it was not (wasn't)	was he/she/it
we were	we were not (weren't)	were we?
you were	you were not (weren't)	were you?
they were	they were not (weren't)	were they?

The negative interrogative form is: Was I not? (wasn't I?), were you not? (weren't you?) &c.
Other tenses of **to be** follow the rules for ordinary verbs. But **be** is not normally used in the continuous forms except (i) in the passive and, (ii), as shown in **114a**.

'To be' used as an Auxiliary

110 In the formation of tenses

be is used in continuous active forms:

He is working/will be working &c.

and in all passive forms:

He was followed/is being followed.

Note that **be** can be used in the continuous forms in the passive:

Active: They are carrying him.
Passive: He is being carried.

Active: She was towing the car.
Passive: The car was being towed. (See also **273**.)

111 Used with the infinitive

The **be** + infinitive construction, e.g. 'I am to go', is extremely important and can be used in the following ways:

a To convey orders or instructions:

No one is to leave this building without the permission of the police (= no one must leave).
He is to stay here till we return (= he must stay).

This is a rather impersonal way of giving instructions and is chiefly used with the third person. When used with *you* it often implies that the speaker is passing on instructions issued by someone else. The difference, between (i) 'Stay here, Tom' *or* 'You must stay here, Tom' and (ii) 'You are to stay here, Tom', is that in (i) the *speaker* wishes Tom to stay while in (ii) he may be merely conveying to Tom the wishes of another person.
This distinction disappears of course in indirect speech, and the **be** + infinitive construction is an extremely useful way of expressing indirect commands, particularly when the introductory verb is in the present tense:

He says, 'Wait till I come'. = He says that we are to wait till he comes.

or when there is a clause in front of the imperative:

He said, 'If I fall asleep at the wheel wake me up'. = He said that if he fell asleep at the wheel she was to wake him up.

It is also used in reporting requests for instructions:

'Where shall I put it, sir?' he asked. = He asked where he was to put it. (See also **279, 281**.)

b To convey a plan:

She is to be married next month.
The expedition is to start in a week's time.

This construction is very much used in newspapers:

The Prime Minister is to make a statement tomorrow.

In headlines the verb **be** is often omitted to save space:

Prime Minister to make statement tomorrow.

Past forms: i. He was to go (present infinitive).

ii. He was to have gone (perfect infinitive).

The first of these doesn't tell us whether the plan was carried out or not. The second is used for an unfulfilled plan, i.e. one which was not carried out:

The Lord Mayor was to have laid the foundation stone but he was taken ill last night so the Lady Mayoress is doing it instead.

c **be about** + infinitive expresses the immediate future:

They are about to start = They are just going to start.
They are on the point of starting.

just can be added to make the future even more immediate:

They are just about to leave.

Similarly in the past:

He was just about to dive when he saw the shark.

d **be** + infinitive can also be used to express a more remote future, usually a future in the past:

He received a blow on the head. It didn't worry him at the time but it was to be very troublesome later (= turned out to be/proved troublesome).
They said goodbye, little knowing that they were never to meet again (= were never destined to meet).

'To be' used as an Ordinary Verb

112 To denote existence

a **to be** is the verb normally used to denote the existence of, or to give information about, a person or thing:

Tom is a carpenter.	The dog is in the garden.
Malta is an island.	The roads were rough and narrow.
Gold is a metal.	Peter was tall and fair.

b **there is, there are**

When a noun representing an indefinite person or thing is the subject of the verb **to be**, we usually put **there** before the verb and the noun after it:

It is possible to say	A man is in the hall.
But it is more usual to say	There is a man in the hall.
Similarly we can say	There is an egg in that nest.
	There are eggs in that nest.

Notice that, though **there** appears to be the subject, the real subject is the noun that follows the verb, and if this noun is plural the verb must be plural also:

There is a cigarette in that box.	There are cigarettes in that box.
There has been a storm.	There have been storms.
There was a queue at the station.	There were queues at the station.

Negative and interrogative examples:

There isn't any milk. There won't be a queue for that film.
Are there any apples? Is there a doctor in the house?

This construction is not used in general statements such as:

Gold is a metal. Hurricanes are terrible things. A snake is a reptile.
Parachutes are useful. Mosquitoes are a nuisance.

113 it is/there is

For **it is** see **44**, **55**, **114** and **247**.

Some examples may help to prevent confusion between these two forms.

a i There was a storm/a lot of rain last night.
ii It was stormy/very wet last night.

b i There was a hard frost last winter.
ii 'What killed these plants? Was it the slugs?'
'No, it was the frost that killed them.' (See **55**.)
i There is a policeman at the door (= a policeman is there).
ii 'Surely whoever saw you won't report you?'
'Unfortunately it was a policeman who saw me.' (See **55**.)

c i It is time for you to go home (i.e. you have to be home by six and it is five-thirty now).
ii There is time for you to go home and come back here again before we start (this amount of time exists; we'll start at eight and it is five-thirty now, so you will have time to go and return).
i It is a long way.
ii There is a long way to go still (a large part of our journey is still in front of us).

d i It is easy to criticize (= to criticize is easy, see **44**).
ii It is not known where he was on the night of the crime (where he was is not known, see **44**).
i It is enough to know that he is out of danger (as above see **44**).
ii There is enough for everyone (enough food/drink/petrol &c. exists).

e i It is nothing to do with you (= this matter doesn't concern you).
ii There is nothing to be done (= nothing can be done).

114 Other uses of **to be**

to be is used to express:

a Physical or mental condition:

I am hot/cold furious/delighted well/ill

Note the use of the continuous form of **be** with certain (usually uncomplimentary) adjectives such as *stupid*, *silly*, *obstinate*, *absurd*, *unreasonable*, *funny*, to imply that the subject is showing this quality *at this time only*. It often implies that the subject is deliberately pretending to be clever/stupid &c.
Compare: 'He is being stupid,' which often means, 'He is just pretending not to understand,' with: 'He is stupid,' which would imply permanent stupidity. 'He is being funny', often means, 'He is only joking; don't believe him'.

b Age:

I am thirty/I am thirty years old (*but not* 'I am thirty years').
How old are you? How old is that tower?
That church is 400 years old ('old' must be added when speaking of the age of *things*).

c Size and weight:

How tall are you? I am five feet six inches.
How high is that tower? It is a hundred feet high.
This room is fifteen feet by twenty feet.
The river is twenty miles long. I am ten stone (i.e. I weigh ten stone).

d Distance (**it** is usually the subject):

How far is it to Canterbury? It is sixty miles.
It is not far to the next village.

e Price:

How much is it? (i.e. What does it cost?) It is two pounds.
Is it expensive to go to Rome?

f Weather (**it** is usually the subject):

It is hot/cold/wet/windy. It will be foggy tomorrow.
It has been a very bad summer.

g Time and date (**it** is usually the subject):

What time is it? It is eleven o'clock. What is the date? It is December 8.

To have

115 Form

Principal parts: have – had – had

Present Tense:

Affirmative	*Negative*	*Interrogative*
I have (I've)	I have not (haven't)	have I?
you have (you've)	you have not (haven't)	have you?
he has (he's)	he has not (hasn't)	has he?
she has (she's)	she has not (hasn't)	has she?
it has (it's)	it has not (hasn't)	has it?
we have (we've)	we have not (haven't)	have we?
you have (you've)	you have not (haven't)	have you?
they have (they've)	they have not (haven't)	have they?

(The 3rd person singular affirmative contractions for **be** and **have** are the same, i.e. **'s** in both cases.)

Alternative negative contractions are: I've not, you've not &c.

The interrogative is not contracted.

The negative interrogative form is: have I not? (haven't I?), have you not? (haven't you?), has he not? (hasn't he?) &c.

Past Tense:

Affirmative	*Negative*	*Interrogative*
I had (I'd)	I had not (hadn't)	had I?
you had (you'd)	you had not (hadn't)	had you?
he had (he'd)	he had not (hadn't)	had he?
she had (she'd)	she had not (hadn't)	had she?
it had (it'd)	it had not (hadn't)	had it?
we had (we'd)	we had not (hadn't)	had we?
you had (you'd)	you had not (hadn't)	had you?
they had (they'd)	they had not (hadn't)	had they?

The interrogative is not contracted.

Alternative negative contractions are: I'd not &c., but these are less common.

(The contraction **'d** is also used for **should** and **would**.)

The negative interrogative form is: had I not? (hadn't I?), had you not? (hadn't you?) &c.

All other tenses follow the rules for ordinary verbs.

'To have' used as an Auxiliary

116 In the formation of tenses

have is used with the past participle to form the following tenses:

1 the present perfect e.g. I have worked.
2 the past perfect e.g. I had worked.
3 the future perfect e.g. I shall have worked.
4 the perfect conditional e.g. I should have worked.

117 With the infinitive to express obligation (see also 135)

have with the infinitive expresses obligation, having nearly the same meaning as **must**:

I have to go = I must go.

had with the infinitive expresses past obligation, and is considered as the past form of **must**, which has no past form of its own:

I had to buy some new shoes last week.

Note that the verb **have** is followed by the infinitive *with* **to**. To remind students of this, **have**, when used with an infinitive, is usually referred to as **have to**, with **had to** as its past form. **have to/had to** always express obligation, as **have** is not used with the infinitive in any other way.
In conversation it is often possible to use **have to/had to** alone, the infinitive being understood but not mentioned:

Why do you wear glasses? I have to (wear them). I am very short-sighted.
I didn't want to stop but I had to (stop) as I needed petrol.

The negative and interrogative of **have to** can be formed in either of the two ways: according to the rule for auxiliaries or according to the rule for ordinary verbs (i.e. with **do**).
got (the past participle of **get**) is often added to **have to** in the affirmative, and in the negative and interrogative forms when these are not made with **do**. This makes no difference to the meaning. **have** when used with **got** is usually contracted.
The negative and interrogative forms are as follows:

	Affirmative		*Negative*		*Interrogative*	
Present Tense:	have (got) to		haven't (got) to		have I (got) to?	&c.
		or	don't have to	*or*	do I have to?	&c.
Past Tense:	had to		hadn't (got) to		had I (got) to?	&c.
		or	didn't have to	*or*	did I have to?	&c.

There is no difference between the form with **do** and the forms with **got**, but in the present tense the form with **do** is the better one to use when we wish to express a habitual obligation:

Do you have to work on Saturdays?

118 The '**have** + object + past participle' construction

a This construction can be used to express more neatly sentences of the type 'I employed someone to do something for me'; i.e. instead of saying: 'I employed someone to clean my car,' we can say 'I had my car cleaned', and instead of 'I got a man to sweep my chimneys' (**got** here = **paid/persuaded** &c.), we can say 'I had my chimneys swept'.

Note that this order of words, i.e. **have** + object + past participle, must be observed as otherwise the meaning will be changed:

He had his hair cut = He employed someone to do it.
but He had cut his hair = He cut it himself some time before the time of speaking (past perfect tense).

When **have** is used in this way the negative and interrogative of its present and past tenses are formed with **do**:

Do you have your windows cleaned every month?
I don't have them cleaned; I clean them myself.
He was talking about having central heating put in. Did he have it put in in the end?

And it can be used in the continuous tenses:

I can't ask you to dinner this week as I am having my house painted at the moment and everything is upside down.
While I was having my hair done the police towed away my car.
He says that the house is too small and that he is having a room built on.

get can be used in exactly the same way as **have** above but is more colloquial. **get** is also used when we mention the person who performs the action:

She got him to dig away the snow = she paid/persuaded him to do it.

(**have** with infinitive without **to** can be used in the same way: 'She had him dig away the snow', but the **get** construction is much more usual.)

b This **have** + object + past participle construction can also be used colloquially to replace a passive verb, usually one concerning some accident or misfortune:

His fruit was stolen before he had a chance to pick it *can be replaced by*
He had his fruit stolen before he had &c.

and Two of his teeth were knocked out in the fight *can be replaced by*
He had two of his teeth knocked out.

It will be seen that, whereas in **118a** the subject is the person who orders the thing to be done, in **118b** the subject is the person who suffers as a result of the action.
In **b** the subject could be a thing:

The houses had their roofs ripped off by the gale.

get can replace **have** here also:

The cat got her tail singed through sitting too near the fire
= The cat's tail was singed.

'Have' as an Ordinary Verb

119 **have** meaning **possess**

This is the basic meaning of **have**:

He has a black beard. She will have £100 a year when she is twenty-one.
I have had this car for ten years.

The negative and interrogative can be formed in either of the two ways:

		Affirmative		*Negative*		*Interrogative*
Present Tense:		have (got)		haven't (got)		have I got? &c.
	or	have	*or*	don't have	*or*	do you have? &c.
Past Tense:		had		hadn't (got)		had you (got)? &c.
			or	didn't have	*or*	did you have? &c.

have is conjugated with **do** for habitual actions:

Customer: Do you ever have pineapples?
Shopkeeper: We don't have them very often.

When there is not this idea of habit, the **have not**/ **have you** forms are more usual in England, though other English-speaking countries use the **do** forms here also.
An American might say, 'Can you help me now? Do you have time?' where an Englishman would probably say, 'Can you help me now? Have you got time?'

do forms can therefore be used safely throughout, but students living in England should practise the other forms as well.

120 **have** meaning 'take' (a meal), 'give' (a party) &c.

have can also be used in the following ways:

a to mean 'take' (a meal/food or drink/a bath/a lesson &c).
b to mean 'give' (a party), 'entertain' (guests).
c to mean 'encounter' (difficulties/trouble).
d to mean 'experience', 'enjoy', usually with an adjective, e.g. good.

We have lunch at one. They are having a party tomorrow.
Did you have trouble with the Customs? I hope you'll have a good holiday.

have when used as above, obeys the rules for ordinary verbs:

1 It is never followed by **got**.
2 Its negative and interrogative are made with **do**.
3 It can be used in the continuous tenses.

I usually have some champagne at eleven (habit).
We are having breakfast early tomorrow (near future).
She is having twenty people to dinner next Monday (near future).
I can't answer the telephone, I am having my bath (present).
How many English lessons do you have a week? I have six.
Do you have coffee or tea for breakfast? I have coffee.
Will you have some more wine/a cup of tea/a cigarette? (This is an invitation. We can also omit the 'Will you' and say: Have some more wine. Have a cigarette &c.)
In Spain they don't have dinner till ten.
Did you have a good time at the theatre? (i.e. Did you enjoy yourself?)
Have a good time! (i.e. Enjoy yourself!)
I am having a wonderful holiday.
I didn't have a very good journey. I had a lot of trouble with my luggage.

13 The Auxiliaries 'Do', 'May', and 'Can'

Do

121 Form

Principal parts: do – did – done

Present Tense:

Affirmative	*Negative*	*Interrogative*
I do	I do not (don't)	do I?
you do	you do not (don't)	do you?
he does	he does not (doesn't)	does he?
she does	she does not (doesn't)	does she?
it does	it does not (doesn't)	does it?
we do	we do not (don't)	do we?
you do	you do not (don't)	do you?
they do	they do not (don't)	do they?

The negative interrogative form is: do I not? (don't I?) &c.

Past tense: **did** for all persons, negative **did not (didn't)**, interrogative **did I?** &c., negative interrogative **did I not? (didn't I?)** &c.

do is followed by the infinitive without **to**:

I don't know. Did you see it? He doesn't like me.

122 **do** used as an auxiliary

a **do** is used to form the negative and interrogative of the present simple and past simple tenses of ordinary verbs:

e.g. *Affirmative*:	he works	he worked
Negative:	he *doesn't* work	he *didn't* work
Interrogative:	*does* he work?	*did* he work?

b It is possible to use **do/did** + infinitive in the affirmative also when we wish to add special emphasis. It is chiefly used when another speaker has expressed doubt about the action referred to:

'You didn't see him.' 'I 'did see him.'
(The 'did' is strongly stressed in speech. This is more emphatic than the normal 'I saw him'.)
'I know that you didn't expect me to go, but I 'did go.'

c **do** is used to avoid repetition of a previous ordinary verb:

i in short agreements:

'Tom speaks a lot.' 'Yes, he does.'
'She sang well.' 'Yes, she did.'
'He didn't go.' 'No, he didn't.'

ii in short disagreements:

'Your dog barks a lot.' 'No, he doesn't.'
'You eat too much.' 'No, I don't.'

iii in additions:

He likes wine and so do we (note inversion).
He doesn't like caviar and neither do I.
He lives at home but I don't. He doesn't drive a car but I do.

iv in question tags:

He lives here, doesn't he? He didn't see you, did he? (See also **106**.)

d **do** is used in short answers to avoid repetition of the main verb:

Do you smoke?	Yes, I do (*not* 'Yes, I smoke').	No, I don't.
Did you see him?	Yes, I did.	No, I didn't.
Does he love you?	Yes, he does.	No, I'm afraid he doesn't.

e **do** is placed before the imperative to make a request or invitation more persuasive:

'ˈDo come with us' (more persuasive than 'Come with us').
'ˈDo work a little harder.' 'ˈDo help me, please.'

f It can similarly be used as an approving or encouraging affirmative answer to someone asking for approval of, or permission to do, some action:

'Shall I write to him?' 'Yes, do' *or* 'Do' *alone*.

123 do used as an ordinary verb

do, like **have**, can be used as an ordinary verb. It then forms its negative and interrogative in the simple present and simple past with **do** and **did**:

I do not do	do you do?	don't you do?
he does not do	does he do?	doesn't he do?
I did not do	did he do?	didn't he do? &c.

It can be used in the continuous forms, or simple forms:

What are you doing (now)? I'm doing my homework.
What's he doing tomorrow? (near future).
What does he do in the evenings? (habit).
How did you do it? I did it with my little axe.

'How do you do' is said by both parties after an introduction:

Hostess: Mrs Day, may I introduce Miss Knight? Miss Knight, Mrs Day.
Mrs Day: How do you do?
Miss Knight: How do you do?

Originally this was an inquiry about the other person's health. Now it is merely a formal greeting, used only at introductions.

May

124 Form

may for all persons in the present and future
might for all persons in the past and conditional
Negative: **may not (mayn't), might not (mightn't)**
Interrogative: **may I?** &c. **might I?** &c.
Negative interrogative: **may I not (mayn't I)? mightn't I?** &c.

may is followed by the infinitive without **to.**

may is chiefly used to express permission or possibility.

125 may used to express permission

may is chiefly used when we grant, refuse or request permission. Except with the first person it is not normally used to express the idea of having permission:

I/we may go *means* I/we have permission to go
but He/you/they may go *normally means* I allow him/you/them to go (i.e. it expresses the speaker's authority).

To make these sentences past we use **allow** (not **might**):

I may go today *becomes* I was allowed to go yesterday.
He may go today *becomes* I allowed him to go yesterday.

But **might** is of course used when the main verb is in the past:

He said, 'She may go today' = He said that she might go that day.

Formal permission is always expressed by **may**, but **may** can also be used informally as an alternative to **can**. It is fairly common in polite requests:

'**May** I use your phone?' is more polite than '**Can/could** I use your phone?' **might I?** (conditional) could also be used here with a present meaning. **might I?** is more diffident than **may I?** and indicates greater uncertainty about the answer. **might** (past) must of course be used when the main verb of the sentence is in the past tense:

He said, 'May I bring my dog?' = He asked if he might bring his dog.

126 may/might expressing possibility

a **may/might** + present infinitive expresses possibility in the present or future, i.e. at or after the time of speaking:

He may come today/tomorrow (perhaps he will come).
He might come/today/tomorrow (perhaps he will come).
She may/might not know that you are here (perhaps she doesn't know).

might must be used when the main verb of the sentence is in a past tense:

He said, 'I may/might be late tonight.'
but He said that he might be late that night.
and We think that he may/might be hiding in the woods.
but We thought that he might be hiding in the woods.

Otherwise either **may** or **might** may be used. **might** makes the possibility seem a little more remote.

may/might is not used in the interrogative to express probability. Instead we use such phrases as **do you think?** + present/future tense or **is he likely?** + an infinitive:

Are we likely to meet any snakes? Do you think she knows we are here? Do you think it will rain?

b **may/might** + perfect infinitive is used in speculations about past actions:

He may/might have gone = it is possible that he went.

might must be used, as shown above, when the main verb is in a past tense:

He said/thought that she might have missed the plane.

might, not **may**, must be used when the uncertainty no longer exists:

He came home alone. You shouldn't have let him do that; he might have got lost (but he didn't get lost).

So in the sentence:

You shouldn't have drunk the wine: it may/might have been drugged

it may have been drugged would indicate that we are still uncertain whether it was drugged or not.

it might have been drugged could have the same meaning but could also mean that we now know that it wasn't drugged.

might, not **may**, is also used when the matter was never put to the test, as in:

Perhaps we should have taken the other road. It might have been quicker.
and It's a good thing you didn't lend him the money. You might never have got it back.

Sentences of this kind are very similar to the third type of conditional sentence:

If we had taken the other road we might have arrived earlier.

c **may/might** can be used in conditional sentences instead of **will/would** to indicate a possible instead of a certain result:

If he sees you he will stop (certain). If he sees you he may stop (possible).

Similarly:

If you poured hot water into it it might crack.
and If you had left it there someone might have stolen it. (See **218e.**)

127 may/might can also be used (in the affirmative only) in the following ways:

a In the expression **may/might as well**:
I may/might as well + infinitive is a very unemphatic way of expressing an intention. **may/might as well** can be used with other persons to suggest or recommend an action:

I may/might as well start at once. You may/might as well come with me. He said that I might as well apply for the job.

might just as well means 'it would be equally good to' and is used to suggest an alternative action. It usually implies disapproval of a previously suggested action:

Tom: I'll go on Monday by the slow train.
Ann: You might just as well wait till Tuesday and go on the fast one.

b **you might** can express a very casual command. It indicates that the speaker is quite certain that he will be obeyed, and is roughly equivalent to an imperative + **will you**:

You might post these for me = Post these for me, will you.

This form should only be used between friends.

c **might** can also be used for persuasive requests, or requests which indicate that the speaker is annoyed that the action in question has not been performed already:

You might tell me what he said *can mean* please tell me/do tell me
or I am annoyed that you haven't told me already/you should have told me.

might can be also used with other persons to express this sort of irritation:

He might pay us *can mean* We are annoyed that he doesn't pay us/hasn't paid us.

Similarly, **might** + perfect infinitive can express irritation at, or reproach for the non-performance of an action in the past:

You might have warned us that the bull was dangerous *means* We think that you should have warned us (but you didn't).

Note that when **might** + infinitive expresses invitation the infinitive is strongly stressed in speech.

d **may** + infinitive can be used in expressions of faith and hope:

May you be happy! (= I hope you will be happy).

For **may/might** in purpose clauses see **289.**

Can

can used for permission, possibility and ability

128 **can** used to express permission

Form:

can for all persons in the present and future
could in the past and conditional
Negative: **cannot (can't), could not (couldn't)**
Interrogative: **can I?** &c. **could I?** &c.
Negative interrogative: **can I not** (**can't I**)?, **could I not** (**couldn't I**)? &c.
can has no participles, so all other tenses have to be supplied by **allow** or **permit**:

I've been allowed to smoke ever since I left school.

can is followed by the infinitive without **to.**

Use:

can used for permission is an informal alternative to **may**.
But it has a wider use than **may** for it can be used not only to grant, refuse or ask for permission, but also with all persons to express the idea of having permission:

You can't leave till six (*this could mean either* I don't allow it *or* your father/employer &c. doesn't allow it).
Can I/could I borrow your car? Yes, of course you can.
No, I'm afraid you can't.
He said we could park outside his house.

Both **can I?** and **could I?** can be used for requests. **Could** is the more polite.

could can mean 'was/were allowed to':

On weekdays we had to get up early but on Sundays we could stay in bed till nine.
The junior clerks couldn't (weren't allowed to) use the front door.

But when a particular action was permitted and performed
was allowed to is better:

Each child was allowed to take one book home. Mary chose 'Robinson Crusoe'.

129 **can** used to express possibility

you/one can can mean **it is possible**, i.e. circumstances permit (this is quite different from the kind of possibility expressed by **may**):

You can ski on the hills (there is enough snow).
You can't bathe here on account of the sharks (it isn't safe to bathe).
You couldn't bathe there on account of the sharks (it wasn't safe to bathe).

can cannot be used in this way in a future sense. To express a future possibility of this type we have to use **it will be possible** or people/you/we &c. **will be able**:

When the new tunnel is ready we'll be able to get to the town much more easily.

130 can expressing ability. can and be able

can here is used in conjunction with **to be able** (the verb **be** + the adjective **able**), which supplies the missing parts of **can** and provides an alternative form for the present and past tenses. We have therefore the following forms:

Infinitive: to be able
Past participle: been able

		Affirmative		*Negative*		*Interrogative*
Present:		can		cannot		can I?
	or	am able	*or*	am not able	*or*	am I able?
Past:		could		could not		could I?
	or	was able	*or*	was not able	*or*	was I able?
Future:		I shall be able		I shall not be able		shall I be able?
	or	he will be able	*or*	he will not be able	*or*	will he be able?

There is only one future form, for **can** is not used in the future except to express permission. In the conditional, however, we have two forms: **could** and **would be able**.

All other tenses are formed with **be able** according to the rules for ordinary verbs:

e.g. *present perfect:* have been able
past perfect: had been able.

Negative interrogatives are formed in the usual way:

couldn't you/weren't you able? won't you be able? &c.

can, be, will, shall not and **have** can be contracted in the usual way:

I wasn't able to he won't be able to I'd been able to

can is followed by the infinitive without **to**.
be able is followed by the infinitive with **to**.

131 can/am able, could/was able

a can and **be able**

i shall/will be able is the only future form:

Our baby will be able to walk in a few weeks.

ii Either **can** or **am able** may be used in the present. **can** is the more usual:

Can you/are you able to type?
I can't pay you today. Can you wait till tomorrow? (See also **b** below.)

iii For the present perfect, however, we must use the **be able** form:

Since his accident he hasn't been able to leave the house.

b could

i **could** can be used with a present meaning when there is an idea of condition:

Could you run the business by yourself (if this was necessary)?
Could he get another job (if he left this one)?
I could get you a copy if you want one.

In the first two examples **could** is replaceable by **would be able.**

ii **could you?** is a very good way of introducing a request. It is an alternative to **would you** and a little more polite:

Could you show me the way/lend me £5/wait half an hour?
Could you please send me an application form?

couldn't you? is also useful:

Householder: Could you come round and mend a leak in my hot water tank?
Plumber: Would sometime next month suit you?
Householder: Couldn't you come a little earlier?

c could and **was able** used for past ability:

i For ability only, either can be used:

When I was young I could/was able to climb any tree in the forest.

ii For ability + a particular action use **was able**:

Although the pilot was badly hurt he was able to explain what had happened (he could and *did* explain).
The boat capsized quite near the bank so the children were able to swim to safety (they could and *did* swim).

This rule, however, is relaxed in the negative and with verbs of the senses:

He read the message but he couldn't understand it.
or wasn't able to understand it.
I could/was able to/see him through the window.

d had been able is the past perfect form:

He said he had lost his passport and hadn't been able to leave the country.

(For **can/could** in reported speech see **287**.)

132 could + perfect infinitive is used for past ability, when:

a the action was not performed:

He could have stopped the train (but he didn't).
I could have lent you the money. Why didn't you ask me?

or b we don't know whether it was performed or not:

The money has disappeared! Who could have taken it?
Tom could have (taken it); he was here alone yesterday.

Compare:

i He was able to send a message (= he sent it).
ii He could have sent a message (= he didn't send it *or* we don't know whether he sent it or not).

133 **can't** and **couldn't** used to express negative deduction

i Negative deduction about a present event can be expressed by **can't** or **couldn't** with the present infinitive of the verb **be**:

Ann: He says he is still reading 'The Old Man and the Sea'.
Tom: He can't be still reading it. I gave it to him ages ago and it's quite a short book.

Child: Can I have some sweets? I'm hungry.
Mother: You can't be hungry. You've just had dinner (**couldn't** would also be possible here).

Ann: There's an aeroplane hovering over our house.
Tom: Then it can't be an aeroplane. It must be a helicopter.

ii Negative deduction about a past event is expressed by **can't/couldn't** + the perfect infinitive of any verb:

Ann: Who brought the grand piano upstairs?
Mary: Perhaps it was Tom.
Ann: He can't/couldn't have done it by himself.

Tom: A man answered the phone. I suppose it was her husband.
Ann: No, It couldn't have been her husband. He's been dead for ages.

We can use the same construction with statements which are suppositions rather than true deductions, but here it is better to use **can't** only, not **couldn't**:

Tom: I feel terribly ill this morning.
Ann: The meat you had for dinner last night can't have been good (= the meat probably wasn't good).

couldn't, however, must be used when the supposition or deduction forms part of a sentence whose main verb is in the past tense:

Ann said that the meat couldn't have been good.

14 'Must', 'Have To', and 'Need'

Positive Obligation

134 must

The form **must** is used for all persons in the present and future tenses. The negative is **must not (mustn't)** and the interrogative is **must I?** &c. **must** has no infinitive and no past tense. It is followed by the infinitive without **to** and is used to express obligation or very emphatic advice:

You must go = I want you to go. It is your duty to go. Go! (imperative).
When you are in London you must visit the National Gallery (emphatic advice).
Father to son: You must tell the truth.

135 must and have to

to have + infinitive with **to** (normally referred to as **have to**, see **117**) also expresses obligation and is normally used in combination with **must**. **have to** supplies the deficiencies of **must** and also provides an alternative form for the present and future tenses.
The two verbs taken together provide the following forms:

Infinitive: to have to
Past participle: had to

		Affirmative		*Interrogative*
Present Tense:		must		must I? &c.
	or	have/has to	*or*	have I (got) to? (see also **137**)
Future Tense:		must		must I?
	or	shall/will have to	*or*	shall I have to? will he have to? &c.
Past Tense:		had to		had I (got) to? &c. (see also **137**)

Negative forms will be treated later. All other tenses are formed from **have to** according to the ordinary tense rules.
There is a slight difference between **must** and the various **have to** forms. This will be dealt with in the next paragraphs.

136 Difference between the must and have to forms in the affirmative

Both express obligation but **must** expresses an obligation imposed by the speaker while **have to** expresses an external obligation, i.e. one imposed by external authority or circumstances:

You must clean your own boots (these are my orders).
You will have to clean your own boots when you join the army (the army will oblige you to do it).

That boy has to practise the piano every day (his parents insist).
Mr Pitt has to work very hard (circumstances make this necessary).

If the speaker adds his support or approval to the existing external authority he may use **must**:

Children must obey their parents (the speaker approves).
Children have to obey their parents (the speaker merely states the fact).

In the 1st person this difference is less important and very often either form is possible, though **have to** should be used for habits and **must** for an important or urgent obligation:

I have to be at my office at nine every day (habit).
We have to water this cactus twice a month (habit).
I must be at the station at ten. It's most important.

137 Difference between the **must** and **have to** forms in the interrogative

It is always safe to use a **have to** form here.

have to must be used for external obligations in the future:

Shall I have to obey the teachers when I go to school? Yes; they will be very angry if you don't obey them.
Will Mr Pitt have to cook his own meals when his wife is away? Yes, I expect he will.
Will you have to read Spinoza when you go to college? Yes, it is one of the set books.

It should also be used in the 3rd person for external obligations in the present:

Has that man got to carry all those parcels by himself?
Does she have to do it by hand?

Otherwise either form can be used, though **have to** is better for habits (see below):

Child: Must I clean my teeth tonight?/Have I got to clean them?
When must I do it?/When have I got to do it?
{Must you go now or can you wait a little longer?
{Have you got to go now?

have to has alternative interrogative forms (see **117**), i.e. in the present we can say: 'Have I got to?' or 'Do I have to?' There is no difference in meaning but 'Do I have to?' &c., is better for habits:

Do you have to wind your watch every day?

In the past we have: 'Had I (got) to?' and 'Did I have to?' &c. There is no difference but 'Did I have to?' &c., is more usual:

Did you have to pay customs duty on that?

138 Some more examples (all persons and tenses)

Mother to son: You must change your socks if they get wet (obligation imposed by speaker).
Railway notice: Passengers must cross the line by the footbridge (obligation imposed by the railway company).
Notice in a church: Ladies must cover their heads in church (obligation imposed by the church authorities).
I will have to go/must go in a few minutes. I don't want to miss my train.
I always have to wash up afterwards. I must tell you something very important.
Angry father: If Tom comes in after midnight he must come in quietly; he woke me up last night.
You must get your hair cut (I think it is too long).
You will have to get your hair cut when you join the army (The army will make you cut it).
You must come and have dinner with me some time (quite a usual way of expressing a casual invitation).
We must celebrate your engagement (a casual way of expressing an intention).
He must be here in time tomorrow; I can't wait for him.
He has to be at his office in time; his employer is very angry if he's late.
If there are no taxis we shall have to walk.
If your father was a poor man you would have to work.
Have you got to finish that tonight?
Did you have to clean the house yourself? (For **must/have to** in reported speech see **286**.)

139 Negative obligation: **must not**

must not expresses negative obligation in the present or future. Like **must** it implies the speaker's authority or very strong advice:

'You must not move' = 'I forbid you to move' 'don't move' *or* 'I very strongly advise you not to move'.
Railway notice: Passengers must not walk across the railway line.
Zoo notice: Visitors must not feed these giraffes.
Mother to child: You mustn't play with matches.
You mustn't miss that film, it is extraordinarily good.
We mustn't be late for the opera.
You must not speak like that to your mother.

Absence of Obligation

140 need

When this verb is used as an auxiliary, the same form, **need**, is used for all persons in the present and future tenses. **need** is chiefly used in the interrogative and negative. In the negative it expresses absence of obligation:

You need not go = It is not necessary for you to go.
Teacher to class: You need not write more than 200 words on this subject.
Mother to child: If it is very foggy tomorrow you need not go to school.

Negative and interrogative forms
The negative and interrogative forms of the past tense are: **did not (didn't) need** and **did I &c., need?**
In the present and future tenses the negative and interrogative can be formed in either of the two ways:

		Negative		Interrogative
Present Tense:		need not (needn't)		need I? &c.
	or	don't/doesn't need	*or*	do I need? does he need? &c.
Future Tense:		need not		need I?
	or	shan't/won't need	*or*	shall I need? will he need?

There is a slight difference between these two forms.
need not is used when the speaker gives authority for the non-performance of some action.
don't/won't need is used when external authorities or external circumstances do not require the action to be performed.
need can be used in the affirmative in expressions of doubt and after a negative verb:

I wonder if I need bring my mosquito-net. I don't think I need go just yet.

need and **need not** are followed by the infinitive without **to**. All other forms of **need** are followed by the infinitive with **to**.

141 Do not confuse **need not** and **must not**

'You *must not* see him', implies that it would be wrong or stupid of you to see him. 'You *need not* see him', means merely that it is not necessary for you to see him. If you did go to see him it would not be wrong or stupid, but probably a waste of time:

You *need not* light a match; I can see well enough.
You *must not* light a match; the room is full of gas.

142 The negative forms of **have to** (see also **117**)

have to in the negative also expresses absence of obligation.
have to has two negative forms in the present tense: **haven't (got) to** and **don't have to.** The future negative form is **shan't/won't have to.** The past tense has two negative forms: **hadn't to** and **didn't have to.**
From this and the preceding paragraph it will be clear that there are several ways of expressing absence of obligation. These will be discussed in the following paragraphs.

143 Present forms: **needn't, don't need to, haven't (got) to, don't have to**

needn't is used when the speaker gives authority for the non-performance of some action.

needn't
or **haven't (got) to**
or **don't need to**
} can be used when an external authority is involved, i.e. when external authority or external circumstances do not require the performance of the action.

don't have to is used when an external authority is involved and a habitual action is referred to.

144 From the above the following simplified rule may be evolved

Absence of obligation in the present can be expressed by **don't have to** when an external authority is involved and a habitual action is referred to, and **needn't** in every other case:

You needn't clean the kitchen today. The sweep is coming tomorrow.
He has to be at his office by 9.0, but as he lives close by he doesn't have to leave his house till 8.45.
The party starts at 8.0, but we needn't be there till 8.30.

145 Future forms: **needn't, won't have to, won't need to**

needn't is used when the speaker's authority is involved.

won't have to
won't need to
} are used when an external authority is involved.

Schoolmaster: You needn't bring your books to class tomorrow; we are going to listen to a wireless programme.
Boy to friend: You won't have to work hard when you come to my school; the lessons are very easy.
Doctor to patient: You needn't take any more pills after next Monday.
Ann to Mary: You needn't bring any food with you tomorrow. I'll have enough for us all.

146 Past forms: **didn't have to, didn't need to, hadn't (got) to**

There is no difference in meaning between these forms. **Didn't have to** is perhaps the most usual:

When I last crossed the frontier I didn't need to show my passport.
We didn't have to wait long. A bus came along at once.
I didn't have to pay the telephone bill last year. My brother was here then and he paid it.

147 **must, have to,** and **need** in the interrogative

For **must** and **have to** see 135, 137.

need I? &c., can be used instead of **must I?** &c., except when **must** follows an interrogative word (i.e. When? Where? Who? What? &c.), because **need?** cannot be used after interrogatives: in the sentence, 'Where must I put it?' **need** could not be used.

Both **need?** and **must?** imply that the person addressed is the authority concerned. **need?** also implies that the speaker is hoping for a negative answer: 'Must I go, mother?' and 'Need I go, mother?' mean the same but in the second question the speaker is hoping that his mother will say, 'No'. The other interrogative form of **need**, Do I need? &c., can be used similarly. Note possible answers:

Question	*Affirmative answer*	*Negative answer*
Shall I have to go?	Yes, you will.	No, you won't.
Have I got to go?	Yes, you have.	No, you haven't.
Does he have to go?	Yes, he does.	No, he doesn't.
Need I go?	Yes, you *must*.	No, you needn't
Must I go?	Yes, you must.	No, you *needn't*.

148 **must, have to,** and **need** in tabular form

	Obligation	*No obligation*	*Negative obligation*
Present Tense:	must	needn't	must not
	have (got) to	haven't (got) to	
		don't have to	
		don't need to	
Future Tense:	must	needn't	must not
	shall/will have to	shan't/won't have to	
Past Tense:	had to	hadn't (got) to	
		didn't have to	
		didn't need to	

'Needn't' + Perfect Infinitive

149 **needn't** + perfect infinitive is used to express an unnecessary action which was nevertheless performed:

I needn't have written to him because he phoned me shortly afterwards (but I did write, thus wasting my time).
You needn't have brought your umbrella for we are going by car (but you have brought your umbrella, unnecessarily).
He needn't have left home so early; the train won't be here for an hour (but the man is already at the station and so will have an hour to wait).

150 **needn't have (done)** compared with **didn't have to (do)**

a **needn't have done** – no obligation but action performed (unnecessarily), i.e. waste of time.

b **didn't have to do** – no obligation, and no action.

You needn't have watered the flowers, for it is going to rain (you wasted your time).
I didn't have to cut the grass myself. The gardener did it (no obligation and no action).
You needn't have written such a long essay. The teacher only asked for 300 words, and you have written 600.

He needn't have bought such a large house. His wife would have been quite happy in a cottage (waste of money).
I didn't have to translate it for him for he understands Latin.
You needn't have carried all these parcels yourself. The shop would have delivered them if you had asked them.

151 need as an ordinary verb

need, which we have seen as an auxiliary, can also be used as an ordinary verb, meaning 'require'. As such it is perfectly regular, and has the following forms:

Infinitive: to need
Present: I need you need he needs (note the **s** in the regular verb) we need you need they need
Past: I needed you needed &c.

Negative and interrogative are formed in the usual way with **do** and **does** for the present and **did** for the past:

I didn't need the money. Did he need help?
You don't need a new car; this one goes very well.

Auxiliaries used to Express Deduction

152 must

must + infinitive (without **to**) can express a deduction.

Mother: Hugh never does any work but he is always at the top of his class.
Friend: He must be a very clever boy.
That is an enormous animal; it must weigh a ton.

The past form of this construction is **must** + perfect infinitive. This expresses a present deduction about a past action:

Hercules killed two snakes that crawled into his cot. He must have been a very strong baby.
The prisoner must have escaped this way, for here are his footprints.

153 can't/couldn't

Negative deductions, however, are normally made with **can't** or **couldn't** + the present infinitive of **to be** or the perfect infinitive of any verb:

He was terribly tired after walking four miles. He can't be at all strong.
Tom can't have written this because it is in French and he doesn't know French (present deduction about a past action).
Jones couldn't have caught the 9.0 train for he only left his house at 9.15.

Either **can't** or **couldn't** can be used when the deduction is made in the present. **couldn't**, however, must be used when the deduction is made in the past:

He knew that she couldn't have stolen it as she hadn't been in the house at the time.

15 The Auxiliaries 'Ought', 'Dare', and 'Used'

154 Ought

ought has no infinitive and no inflexions (i.e. the same form is used for all persons). **ought** can be used as a present, past, or future tense, and is followed by the infinitive *with* **to**. The negative is **ought not (oughtn't)** and the interrogative **ought I?, ought you?, ought he?** &c.:

They ought to do it tomorrow. Ought we to do it at once?
He ought to get up earlier. I knew that I ought not to open the letter.

In conversation either **ought** or **ought to** can often be used alone, the infinitive being understood but not mentioned:

'You ought to paint your hall door.' 'Yes, I know I ought (*or* ought to).'

155 ought compared to must, have to, and should

a **ought** expresses the subject's obligations or duty. But here there is neither the speaker's authority (as with **must**), nor an outside authority (as with **have to**). The speaker is only reminding the subject of his duty, or giving advice or indicating a correct or sensible action. It is usually said without much emphasis.

should can be used in exactly the same way (see **233**) and questions or remarks with **ought** can be answered with **should**:

'You ought to (*or* should) finish your work before going out.' 'I know I should.'
You ought to obey your parents.
'You oughtn't to eat between meals; it will make you fat.' 'I know I oughtn't to.'

Compare with **have to** and **must**:

You have to obey Mr Pitt (Mr Pitt insists on it).
You must obey Mr Pitt (the speaker insists on, or approves of, Mr Pitt's authority).
Tom, you ought to obey Mr Pitt (neither the speaker's authority nor Mr Pitt's is involved here, but the speaker thinks that obeying Mr Pitt is advisable or part of Tom's duty).
You have to take these blue pills (the doctor insists on it).
You mustn't drink this; it is poison.
You oughtn't to smoke so much; you are wasting your money.

b Like **must**, **ought** can also be used in giving advice, but it is much less forceful than **must**:

You ought to go to Paris *is much less emphatic than* You must go to Paris.

156 **ought** and the perfect infinitive

This construction is used to express an unfulfilled duty or a sensible action that was neglected:

I ought to have taken those books back to the library last week. Now they are overdue and I shall have to pay a fine.
You ought to have told him that the paint on that seat is wet.
You ought to have waited till the lights were green before crossing the road.
You oughtn't to have crossed the road when the lights were red.

should with the perfect infinitive is used in exactly the same way.

157 **dare**

In the affirmative **dare** is conjugated like an ordinary verb, i.e. **dares/dare** in the present, **dared** in the past. But in the negative and interrogative it can be conjugated either like an ordinary verb or like an auxiliary:

Negative present:	do/does not dare	dare not
past:	did not dare	dared not
Interrogative present:	do you/does he dare?	dare you/he?
past:	did you/did he dare?	dared you/he?

Infinitives after **dare**
Negative and interrogative forms with **do/did** are in theory followed by the infinitive with **to**, but in practice the **to** is often omitted:

He doesn't dare (to) say anything.
Did he dare (to) criticize my arrangements?

Negative and interrogative forms without **do/did** are followed by the infinitive without **to**:

Dare we interrupt? They dared not move.

In the affirmative he/she/it **dares** is followed by the infinitive with **to**. With other persons either form of the infinitive can be used. **dare** however is not much used in the affirmative except in the expression: **I daresay.** **I daresay** (or **I dare say**) has two idiomatic meanings:

i I suppose:

I daresay there'll be taxis at the station.
I daresay there'll be a restaurant car on the train.

ii I accept what you say (but it doesn't make any difference):

English tourist: But I drive on the left in England!
Swiss policeman: I daresay you do, but you must drive on the right here.

Traveller: But the watch was given to me; I didn't buy it.

Customs officer: I daresay you didn't, but you'll have to pay duty on it all the same.

dare say is used in this way with the first person singular only.

how dare(d) you? how dare(d) he/they? can express indignation:

How dare you open my letters? (= I am angry with you for opening them).
How dared he complain? (= I am indignant because he complained).

dare is also an ordinary transitive verb meaning **challenge** (but only to deeds requiring courage). It is followed by object + infinitive with **to**:

Mother: Why did you throw that stone through the window?
Son: Another boy dared me to (throw it).

158 used (to)

used is the past tense of a defective verb which has no present tense. It has the same form for all persons: the affirmative is **used**, the negative is **used not (usedn't)**, the interrogative **used you?** &c. and the negative interrogative **usedn't you?** &c.
In conversation the forms: **didn't use (to), did you use (to)?, didn't you use (to)?** are fairly common, but the student must avoid **didn't used (to)**, which is also heard but is considered incorrect.
used is followed by the infinitive *with* **to**:

i His hair used to be black; but it's white now.
ii 'Usedn't she to be a concert pianist?'
'Yes, she did (*or* Yes, she used to) but she gave it up when she got married.
iii 'I thought you didn't like Tom?' 'I usedn't to (like him) but I do now.'

In (ii) and (iii) above the second infinitive is represented by its **to** to avoid repetition of a verb already mentioned (see **250**).

used to can express (1) a discontinued habit, as in the above examples or (2) a past routine, not necessarily discontinued:

It was very hot in the middle of the day and most people used to spend the early afternoon in bed. (They did this when we were there; very likely they still do it.)
Sometimes the fishermen used to speak to each other but mostly they sat there silently/used to sit there silently.

used here is replaceable by **would**, which is the more common form:

They would spend the afternoon in bed.
Sometimes the fishermen would speak.

But **would** cannot replace **used** when it expresses a discontinued habit, as in (i), (ii), and (iii) above.

Remember that **used** has no present tense and cannot therefore be used for a present habit, which is normally expressed by the simple present tense:

I ring the bell at nine every day (see **169, 170, 171**).

Do not confuse **used to** with the ordinary verb **to use** (jouz), meaning **employ**.

159 **used** as an adjective meaning **accustomed**

When employed in this way, **used** is preceded by **be/seem/get/become &c.** and followed by the preposition **to** + noun, pronoun or gerund: Note that here we are concerned not with the action itself, but with the effect it has had on the subject:

I'm used to the noise = I don't mind it/it doesn't worry me.
You'll soon get used to standing in queues = it will soon cease to annoy you.
I'm used to a very tidy office, so an untidy office gets on my nerves.

16 The Present Tenses

There are two present tenses in English

1 The Present Continuous: I am working.
2 The Simple Present: I work.

The Present Continuous

160 Form

The present continuous tense is formed with the present tense of the auxiliary verb **to be** + the present participle (the infinitive + **ing**):

I am working   you are working   he is working   &c.

The negative is formed by putting **not** after the auxiliary:

I am not working   you are not working   he is not working   &c.

The interrogative is formed by inverting subject and auxiliary:

Am I working?   are you working?   is he working?   &c.

Negative interrogative:

Am I not working?   are you not working?   is he not working?   &c.

161 The present continuous tense of the verb **to work**

Affirmative	*Negative*	*Interrogative*
I am working	I am not working	am I working?
you are working	you are not working	are you working?
he is working	he is not working	is he working?
we are working	we are not working	are we working?
you are working	you are not working	are you working?
they are working	they are not working	are they working?

Contractions: **to be** can be contracted in the present affirmative, negative and negative interrogative as shown in **109**, so the present continuous tense of any verb can be contracted:

I'm working   you're working   he's working
I'm not working   he isn't working   you aren't working
he's not working   you're not working
Aren't I working?   aren't you working?   isn't he working?

Note the irregular contraction for **am I not.**

162 Note on the spelling of the present participle

a When a verb ends in a single **e**, this **e** is dropped before **ing**:

Love, loving   hate, hating   argue, arguing

This does not happen when the verb ends in **ee**:

Agree, agreeing   see, seeing

b When a verb of one syllable has one vowel and ends in a single consonant, this consonant is doubled before **ing**:

Hit, hitting   run, running   stop, stopping

Verbs of two or more syllables whose last syllable contains only one vowel and ends in a single consonant, double this consonant if the stress falls on the last syllable:

be'gin, beginning   pre'fer, preferring   ad'mit, ad'mitting
but enter, entering (stress not on the last syllable)

A final **l** after a single vowel is, however, always doubled:

Travel, travelling   signal, signalling

163 The present continuous tense is used:

a for an action happening now:

It is raining (now). I am not wearing a coat as it isn't cold.
Why are you sitting at my desk?
What is the baby doing? He is tearing up a £5 note.

b for an action happening about this time but not necessarily at the moment of speaking:

I am reading a play by Shaw (this may mean 'at the moment of speaking' but may also mean 'now' in a more general sense).
He is teaching French and learning Greek (he may not be doing either at the moment of speaking).

When two continuous tenses, having the same subject, are joined by **and**, the auxiliary may be dropped before the second verb, as in the above example. This applies to all pairs of compound tenses.

c for a definite arrangement in the near future (and is the most usual way of expressing one's immediate plans):

I'm going to the theatre tonight (this would almost certainly imply that the tickets have been bought).
A: Are you doing anything tonight?
B: Yes, I'm going to my judo class and (I'm) meeting my brother afterwards.

Note that the time of the action must always be mentioned, as otherwise there might be confusion between present and future meanings. **go** and **come**, however, can be used in this way without a time expression.

164 Other possible uses of the present continuous:

a With a point in time to indicate an action which begins before this point and probably continues after it:

At 6.0 I am bathing the baby (i.e. I start bathing him before 6.0).

It can be used similarly with a verb in the simple present:

They are flying over the desert when one of the engines fails.

The present continuous is rarely used in this way except in descriptions of daily routine and in dramatic narrative, but with the past continuous such combinations are very useful. (See **176**.)

b With **always** for a frequently repeated action, often one which annoys the speaker or seems unreasonable to him:

Tom is always going away for weekends.

This implies that he goes away very often, probably too often for my taste; but it does not necessarily mean that he goes away every weekend. It is not a literal statement. Compare with:

Tom always goes away at weekends (simple present tense) =
Tom goes away every weekend (a literal statement).

Similarly, compare:

He is always doing homework (implying that he spends too much time on it in the speaker' opinion).

and *He always does his homework* (simple present tense), which merely means that he does it regularly.

Sometimes, especially when used with the first person, **always** with the continuous tense implies that the action is accidental, while **always** with a simple tense would imply a deliberate action:

I always do that *would imply a deliberate, routine action but* I am always doing that *would usually imply an accidental action.*

165 The following verbs are not normally used in the continuous form:

a Verbs of the senses e.g. *see, hear, smell, notice, recognize*

b Verbs of emotion e.g. *want, desire, refuse, forgive, wish, care, live, hate, adore, like, dislike*

c Verbs of thinking e.g. *think* (when an opinion is expressed) *feel* (= think), *realize, understand, know, mean, suppose, believe, expect, remember, recollect, forget, recall, trust* (= believe), *mind*

d Verbs of possessing e.g. *own, owe, belong, possess*

e The auxiliaries except **be** and **have** in certain uses (see **167**)

f *seem, signify, appear* (= seem), *contain, consist, keep* (= continue), *concern, matter.*

These therefore have only one possible present tense, the simple present:

I *don't believe* what you are saying. It's raining; I *want* to go home.
A: I *smell* something burning.
B: I *think* it's coming from Ann's room. She is probably ironing.

See **166** and **167** for some exceptions to the above rules.

166 Verbs implying *deliberate* use of the senses can be used in the continuous form

listen, look and **watch** are deliberate actions; and **smell** can be deliberate, though it is usually involuntary:

Someone's coming; I hear footsteps (involuntary action).
Don't disturb him now; he *is listening* to a radio play (deliberate).
Why *are you looking* at that car? It's far too expensive. I *see* one in the corner that would suit you much better.
Why *are you smelling* (sniffing) the fish? Do you think it has gone bad?

look is normally used with a stationary object; **watch** is used when there is movement, or when movement is expected. **watch** normally implies that the observation continues for some time:

The child is looking at the illustrations.
His mother is watching him turning over the pages.
The police are watching the house (expecting someone to enter or leave it).
We are looking at the house as we are thinking of buying it.

167 Some of the verbs listed in 165 can be used in the continuous tenses in certain cases

see meaning *meet by appointment*, *interview*:

The director is seeing the applicants this morning.
I'm seeing my solicitor tomorrow (definite future arrangement, see **163c**).

see = *visit*, used chiefly of places and in connexion with tourists:

Tom is seeing the sights; he'll be back later.
Let's go sightseeing.

see about = *make arrangements or inquiries*:

Tom is seeing about tickets for tonight (asking about tickets/getting them).
We are seeing about a work permit for you (trying to arrange this).

see to = *arrange*, *put right*, *deal with*:

Normally when we go on holiday I see to the food and packing and he sees to the travelling arrangements; but this year I'm seeing to everything as he's too busy.
The plumber's here. He's seeing to that leak in our tank.

hear = receive news of or from:

I've been hearing all about his accident (= He has been telling me).

think when no opinion is given or asked for:

A: What are you thinking about.
B: I'm thinking about that play we saw last night.
but *A*: What do you think of it? (opinion asked for).
B: I don't think much of it (opinion given).
A: Tom is thinking of emigrating. What do you think of the idea?
B: I think it is a stupid idea. He should stay where he is.

be as part of a passive tense:

The house opposite our college is being pulled down.

be used to imply that the subject is temporarily exhibiting some quality:

You're being very clever today *would indicate that this was unusual.*
The children are being very quiet; I wonder what they're up to (**114**).

have except when it means possession or obligation:

I can't open the door; I'm having a bath.
We are having a wonderful time (= enjoying ourselves).
I'm having a tooth (taken) out tomorrow.

like meaning *enjoy*:

How are you liking this hot weather?
but How do you like this hot weather? *could be equally usual.*

It is just possible to use **love** and **hate** in the affirmative and in the same way:

Are you liking this nice trip on the sea?
No, I'm hating it *or* Yes, I'm loving it.

but it would be safer for the student to use the verb 'enjoy' here:

No, I'm not enjoying it particularly *or* Yes, I'm enjoying it very much.

expect when it means 'await':

I am expecting a letter today.
She is expecting a baby in January.

feel in the medical sense can take either form:

How do you feel? I feel well.
or How are you feeling? I'm feeling well.

feel meaning 'think' can never be used in the continuous form:

I *feel* that it is going to be a success (*never* I am feeling &c.).

The Simple Present Tense

168 Form

(This has already been dealt with in the introduction to auxiliaries but will be repeated here for the convenience of students.)

The simple present has the same form as the infinitive but adds an **s** for the third person singular:

infinitive: to work
simple present: I work you work he (she, it) works &c.

The negative is formed with the present tense negative of the verb **to do** + the infinitive (without **to**) of the main verb:

I do not work you do not work he (she, it) does not work &c.

The interrogative is formed with the present tense interrogative of **to do** + the infinitive (without **to**) of the main verb:

Do I work? do you work? does he (she, it) work? &c.

The simple present tense of irregular verbs is formed in exactly the same way.

169 a The simple present tense of the verb **to work**

Affirmative	*Negative*	*Interrogative*	*Negative interrogative*
I work	I do not work	do I work?	do I not work?
you work	you do not work	do you work?	do you not work?
he works	he does not work	does he work?	does he not work?
we work	we do not work	do we work?	do we not work?
you work	you do not work	do you work?	do you not work?
they work	they do not work	do they work?	do they not work?

b *Contractions.* The verb **to do** is normally contracted in the negative and negative interrogative (see **121**):

I don't work he doesn't work don't I work? doesn't he work?

c *Spelling note*
Verbs ending in: **ss, sh, ch, x,** and **o,** add **es,** instead of **s** alone, to form the third person singular:

I kiss, he kisses I rush, he rushes I watch, he watches
I box, he boxes I go, he goes I do, he does

Verbs ending in **y** following a consonant, change the **y** into **i** and add **es**:

I carry, he carries I hurry, he hurries

but verbs ending in **y** following a vowel, obey the usual rule:

I obey, he obeys I say, he says

170 The simple present used to express habitual action

The main use of the simple present tense is to express habitual actions:

He smokes dogs bark cats drink milk birds fly.

This tense does not tell us whether or not the action is being performed at the moment of speaking, and if we want to make this clear we must add a verb in the present continuous tense:

I *usually wear* a coat but I *am not wearing* one today as it isn't cold (the first verb refers to a habit, the second to a present action).
My neighbour is practising the violin; she usually practises at about this time.
My dog barks an awful lot, but he isn't barking at the moment.

The simple present tense is often used with adverbs or adverb phrases such as: often, usually, sometimes, never, always, occasionally, on Mondays, twice a year, every week &c.:

I go to church on Sundays.
It rains in winter.
I never eat tripe.
(never + affirmative = negative).
Birds don't build nests in the autumn.
How often do you wash your hair?
She goes abroad every year.

171 Other uses of the simple present tense

a It is used to introduce quotations:

Rabelais says, 'Appetite comes with eating.'

b It can be used for dramatic narrative. This is particularly useful when describing the action of a play, opera &c., and is often used by radio commentators at sports events, public functions &c.

When the curtain rises, Juliet is sitting at her desk. The phone rings. She picks it up and listens quietly. Meanwhile the window opens and a masked man enters the room.

c It can be used for a planned future action or series of actions, particularly when these refer to a journey. Travel agents use it a good deal:

We leave London at 10 a.m. next Tuesday and arrive in Paris at 1.0 o'clock. We spend two hours in Paris and leave again at 3.30. We arrive in Rome at 7.30, spend four hours in Rome &c.

d It must be used instead of the present continuous with those verbs which cannot be used in the continuous form, e.g. love, see, believe &c., so that we can say, 'I love you' but not 'I am loving you'.

e It is used in conditional sentences, type 1 (see **216**).

f It is used in time clauses (see **201c**, **293**).

17 The Past and Perfect Tenses

The Simple Past Tense

172 Form

a The simple past tense in regular verbs is formed by adding **ed** to the infinitive:

infinitive: to work   simple past: worked

Verbs ending in **e** add **d** only:

infinitive: to love   simple past: loved

There are no inflexions, i.e. the same form is used for all persons:

I worked   you worked   he worked   &c.

The negative of regular and irregular verbs is formed with **did not** and the infinitive (without **to**):

I did not work   you did not work   he did not work   &c.

The interrogative of regular and irregular verbs is formed with **did** + subject + infinitive (without **to**):

Did I work?   did you work?   &c.

The simple past tense of the verb **to work**

Affirmative	*Negative*	*Interrogative*	*Negative interrogative*
I worked	I did not work	did I work?	did I not work?
you worked	you did not work	did you work?	did you not work?
he worked	he did not work	did he work?	did he not work?
we worked	we did not work	did we work?	did we not work?
you worked	you did not work	did you work?	did you not work?
they worked	they did not work	did they work?	did they not work?

b *Contractions*: **did not** is normally contracted in the negative and negative interrogative:

I didn't work   didn't I work?   &c.

c *Spelling note*. The rules about doubling the final consonant when adding **ing** (see **162**) apply also when adding **ed**:

stop, stopped   admit, admitted   travel, travelled

Verbs ending in **y** following a consonant change the **y** into **i** before adding **ed**:

carry, carried   *but*   obey, obeyed (**y** following a vowel does not change).

173 Irregular verbs

These vary considerably in their simple past form:

infinitive:	to speak	to eat	to see	to leave
simple past:	spoke	ate	saw	left

The simple past form of each irregular verb must therefore be learnt, but once this is done there is no other difficulty, as irregular verbs (like regular verbs) have no inflexions in the past tense:

The simple past tense of the verb **to speak** is **spoke** for all persons.
The negative is **did not speak** for all persons.
The interrogative is **did I speak?** &c.

A list of irregular verbs will be found in **296**.

174 The simple past is the tense normally used for the relation of past events

a It is used for actions completed in the past at a definite time. It is therefore used:

i for a past action when the time is given:

I met him yesterday.

ii or when the time is asked about:

When did you meet him?

iii or when the action clearly took place at a definite time even though this time is not mentioned:

The train was ten minutes late. I bought this car in Montreal.
How did you get your present job?

iv Sometimes the time becomes definite as a result of a question and answer in the present perfect:

Where have you been? I've been to the opera.
Did you enjoy it? (See **184** for further examples.)

b The simple past tense is used for an action whose time is not given but which (i) occupied a period of time now terminated, *or* (ii) occurred in a period of time now terminated.

These may be expressed diagrammatically thus:

i
ii
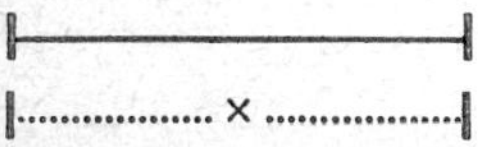

Examples of type (i):

He worked in that bank for four years (but he does not work there now).
She lived in Rome for a long time (but is not living there now).

Examples of type (ii):

My mother once saw Queen Victoria.
Did you ever hear Caruso sing?

These will be clearer when compared with the present perfect (see **181, 182**).

c The simple past tense is also used for a past habit:

He always carried an umbrella. They never drank wine.

(For **used to** used for past habits see **158**.)

d The simple past is used in conditional sentences, type 2 (see **216**). (For use after **as if, as though, it is time, if only, wish, would sooner/rather**, see 271, 272.)

The Past Continuous Tense

175 Form

The past continuous tense is formed by the past tense of the verb **to be** + the present participle:

Affirmative	*Negative*	*Interrogative*
I was working	I was not working	was I working?
you were working	you were not working	were you working?
he was working	he was not working	was he working?
we were working	we were not working	were we working?
you were working	you were not working	were you working?
they were working	they were not working	were they working?

Contractions: **was not** is usually contracted in the negative, so that we have:

I wasn't working you weren't working wasn't he working? &c.

Remember that some verbs cannot be used in the continuous tenses (**165–7**).

176 The past continuous is chiefly used for past actions which continued for some time but whose exact limits are not known and not important.

It might be expressed diagrammatically thus: 

a Used without a time expression it can indicate gradual development:

It was getting darker. The wind was rising.

b Used with a point in time, it expresses an action which began before that time and probably continued after it:

At 8.0 he was having breakfast *implies that he was in the middle of breakfast at 8.0*, i.e. *that he had started it before 8.0.*
(He had breakfast at 8.0 *would imply that he started it at 8.0.*)

c If we replace the time expression with a verb in the simple past tense:

When I *arrived* Tom *was 'talking* on the telephone

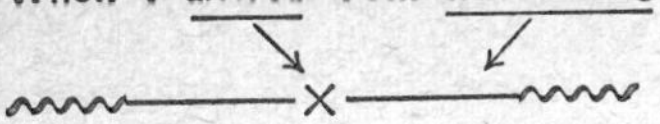

we convey the idea that the action in the past continuous started before the action in the simple past and probably continued after it. The diagram may help to show this relationship. The action in the simple past is indicated by X. Compare this combination with a combination of two simple past tenses, which normally indicates successive actions:

When he saw me he put the receiver down.

d We use the continuous tense in descriptions. Note the combination of description (past continuous) with narrative (simple past):

A wood fire was burning on the hearth, and a cat was sleeping in front of it. A girl was playing the piano and (was) singing softly to herself. Suddenly there was a knock on the door. The girl stopped playing. The cat woke up.

177 The past continuous used in indirect speech, for the future in the past, and with **always**. Here, as in **176**, this tense is used as a past equivalent of the present continuous:

a direct speech: He said, 'I am living in London.'
indirect speech: He said he was living in London.

b Just as the present continuous can be used to express a definite future arrangement:

I am going to the theatre tonight; I've got the tickets

so the past continuous can express this sort of future in the past:

He was busy packing, for he was leaving that night (the decision to leave had been made some time previously).

c The past continuous with **always**:

He was always ringing me up

expresses a frequently repeated past action, which often annoys the speaker (see **164b**).

178 The past continuous can be used as an alternative to the simple past to indicate a more casual, less deliberate action:

I was talking to Tom the other day.

The past continuous here gives the impression that the action was in no way unusual or remarkable. It also tends to remove responsibility from the subject. In the above example it is not clear who started the conversation, and it does not matter. Note the contrast with the simple past tense, 'I talked to Tom', which indicates that I took the initiative.
Similarly:

From four to six Tom was washing the car.

This would indicate that this was a casual, possibly routine action. Compare with:

From four to six Tom washed the car (implying a deliberate action by Tom).

Note that continuous tenses are used only for apparently continuous, uninterrupted actions. If we divide the action up, or say how many times it happened we must use the simple past:

I talked to Tom several times. Tom washed both cars.

But we may of course use the continuous for apparently parallel actions:

Between one and two I was doing the shopping and walking the dog.

This tense is normally used in this way with a time expression such as: today, last night, in the afternoon, which could either be regarded as points in time or as periods. Periods can also be indicated by exact times as shown above.

In questions about how a period was spent, the continuous often appears more polite than the simple past:

What were you doing before you came here? *sounds more polite than*
What did you do before you came here?

On the other hand

What were you doing in my room?

could indicate a feeling that I think you had no right to be there, but

What did you do in my room?

could never give this impression.

The Present Perfect Tense

179 a Form

The present perfect tense is formed with the present tense of **to have** + the past participle:

I have worked

The past participle in regular verbs has exactly the same form as the simple past, i.e. loved, walked &c. (see spelling rules **306**).

In irregular verbs the past participles vary (see **296**).
The negative is formed by adding **not** to the auxiliary. The interrogative is formed by inverting the auxiliary and subject. These forms are shown below:

Affirmative	*Negative*
I have worked	I have not worked
you have worked	you have not worked
he has worked	he has not worked
we have worked	we have not worked
you have worked	you have not worked
they have worked	they have not worked
Interrogative	*Negative interrogative*
have I worked?	have I not worked?
have you worked?	have you not worked?
has he worked?	has he not worked?
have we worked?	have we not worked?
have you worked?	have you not worked?
have they worked?	have they not worked?

Contractions: **have** and **have not** can be contracted (see **115**):

I've worked   you haven't worked   haven't I worked?   &c.

b Use

This tense may be said to be a sort of mixture of present and past. It always implies a strong connexion with the present and is chiefly used in conversations, letters, newspapers, and wireless reports.

180 The present perfect tense is used with **just** to express a recently completed action

He has just gone out = he went out a few minutes ago.

This is a special idiomatic use of this tense. **just** must be placed between the auxiliary and the main verb. This combination is used chiefly in the affirmative, though the interrogative form is possible:

Has he just gone out?

It is not normally used in the negative.

181 The present perfect is used for past actions whose time is not given and not definite

a for recent actions when the time is not mentioned:

I have read the instructions but I don't understand them.
Have you had breakfast? No, I haven't had it yet.

Compare with:

I read the instructions last night (time given, so simple past).

and Did you have breakfast at the hotel? (i.e. before you left the hotel – simple past).

Note possible answers to questions in the present perfect:

Have you seen my stamps? Yes, I have/No, I haven't.
Yes, I saw them on your desk a minute ago.

Have you had breakfast? Yes, I have/No, I haven't had it yet.
Yes, I had it at seven o'clock.
Yes, I had it with Mary (time implied).

b It can also be used for actions which occur further back in the past, provided the connexion with the present is still maintained, that is that the action could be repeated in the present. 'I have seen wolves in that forest' implies that it is still possible to see them, and 'John Smith has written a number of short stories' implies that John Smith is still alive and can write more.

If however the forest has been cut down and John Smith is dead we would say, 'I saw wolves in that forest once/several times' or 'I used to see wolves here' and 'John Smith wrote a number of short stories'.

Note also that when we use the present perfect in this way we are not necessarily thinking of any one particular action (the action may have occurred several times) or of the exact time when the action was performed. If we are thinking of one particular action, performed at a particular time we are more likely to use the simple past.

c It can be used with **lately, recently, yet**:

There have been a lot of changes recently. He hasn't finished yet.

or with a word or phrase denoting an incomplete period of time e.g. **today/this week/month/year** &c. It is chiefly used in this way in the interrogative or negative and conveys the idea that the action happened (or didn't happen) at some undefined time within the mentioned period:

Have you seen him today? (= at any time today).
No, I haven't seen him this week (= at any time during this week).

But the affirmative is possible:

We've had a lot of storms this winter (at various times during the winter).
I've been very busy lately.

When the present perfect is used in this way there is no clear idea of when within the period the action happened or of how many times. If there is a clear idea of when it happened we use the simple past:

He went back to work this morning. They arrived today.

(Students may prefer to consider that negative sentences of this kind and sentences formed with **has/have been** belong to the type shown in **182**.) Note that the present perfect can be used with **this morning** only up to about one o'clock, because after that **this morning** becomes a completed period and actions occurring in it are put into the simple past:

(at 11 a.m.) He has rung up three times this morning already.
(at 2 p.m.) He rang up three times this morning.

Similarly **this afternoon** could be used with the present perfect only up to about 5 p.m.

182 The present perfect can be used with a time expression

a for an action beginning in the past and still continuing:

He has been in the army for two years (he is still in the army).
I have smoked since I left school (I still smoke).
He has lived here all his life (he still lives here).
I have never seen an armadillo.
I have always written with my left hand.

This type of action might be expressed by diagram thus: |————
Compare the above sentences with:

He was in the army for two years (he is not in the army now).
I smoked for six months (and then stopped smoking).
He lived here all his life (presumably he is now dead).

In each of the last three examples we are dealing with a completed period of time |————|, so the simple past tense is used (see **174**).

b However the present perfect can sometimes be used for an action which begins in the past and finishes at the moment of speaking. It is chiefly used in this way with the verb **be** and with negative verbs:

(on meeting someone) I haven't seen you for ages (but I see you now).
This room hasn't been cleaned for months (but we are cleaning it now).
It has been very cold lately but it's beginning to get a bit warmer.

This type of action could be expressed by diagram thus: |————|

c Verbs of **knowing, believing, understanding** &c. cannot be used in the present perfect except as shown in **182a**:

I have known him for a long time.
We have always believed that this is not possible.

Actions of the type shown in **181** must be expressed by the simple past tense of verbs of **knowing** &c.:

Have you heard that he is going to be married?
but Did you know that he is going to be married? (**do you know** would also be possible here).
and Hello! I didn't know you were in London. How long have you been here?

d Note that questions/answers such as

Q: How long have you been here? *A*: I've been here six months.

will normally be followed by general inquiries in the present perfect about actions occurring within the period mentioned, which is regarded as an incomplete period of time |———— because the action of staying, being &c., is not yet finished:

Have you been to the Zoo/the theatre/the museums/the casino?
Have you enrolled in a school/found a job/met many people?

The answers will be in the same tense if no time is mentioned, otherwise they will be in the simple past tense:

Yes, I have (been to the Zoo &c.) *or* Yes, I went there last week.
No, I haven't enrolled yet *or* Yes, I enrolled {on Monday. / this morning.}

183 for and since used with the present perfect

for is used with a period of time:

for six days   for a long time

for used with the simple past tense denotes a terminated period of time:

We *lived* there for ten years (but we don't live there now).

for used with the present perfect denotes a period of time extending into the present:

We *have lived* in London for ten years (and still live there).

for can sometimes be omitted:

We've been here an hour.

since is used with a point in time and means 'from that point to the time of speaking'. It is always used with a perfect tense:

She has been here since six o'clock (and is still here).

since can never be omitted.

Note that there is a rather confusing difference between **last** and **the last**. We say 'I have been here *since last* week (month, year &c.)', but 'I have been here *for the last* week'. In the first sentence 'last week' means a *point* in time about seven days ago. In the second sentence 'the last week' means the *period* of seven days that has just finished.

184 Further examples of the use of the present perfect and simple past

a Have you ever seen a dinosaur?
I've seen one in a museum. I've never seen a live one; they've been extinct for millions of years.

b *Tom*: (visiting Philip for the first time): I didn't know you lived in a houseboat.
Philip: I've always lived in a houseboat. I was born in one.

c I didn't know you were in England. When did you arrive?
I arrived last week.
Did you have a good journey?
No, I came by air and it was very bumpy.

d Have you found a job yet?
Yes, I've just had an interview for a post and I think I've got it.

e Note that a conversation about a past action often begins with a question and answer in the present perfect, but normally continues in the simple past, even when no time is given. This is because the action first mentioned has now become definite in the minds of the speakers:

Where have you been?
I've been to the theatre.
What was the play?
Hamlet.
Did you like it/did you have a good seat/was the theatre crowded?

f *Husband*: Where have you been?
Wife: I've been at the sales.
Husband: What have you bought/what did you buy? (either could be used).
Wife: I have bought/I bought you some yellow pyjamas.
Husband: Why did you buy yellow? I told you never to buy yellow for me.
Wife: I couldn't resist it. They were very much reduced.

g The present perfect is often used in letters:

I am sorry I haven't written for such a long time, but I've been very busy lately as my partner has been away and I have had to do his work as well as my own. However he came back this morning (*or* has just come back) so things are a bit easier now.

My colleagues and I have carefully considered the important issues raised in the report which you sent me on April 26, and we have decided to take the following action.

h The present perfect is often used in newspapers and broadcasts to introduce an action which will then be described in the simple past tense. The time of the action is very often given in the second sentence:

Thirty thousand pounds' worth of jewellery has been stolen from Jonathan Wild and Company, the jewellers. The thieves broke into the flat above some time during Sunday night and entered the shop by cutting a hole in the floor.

The Prime Minister has decided to continue with his plan to build X-type aircraft. This decision was announced yesterday and was received with mixed feelings. (Notice that **has been received** would be used if the reporter wished to cover comments made between then and the time of speaking.)

i But even if the time of the action is not given the past tense will normally be used in the second sentence:

Two prisoners have escaped from Dartmoor. They *used* a ladder which had been left behind by some workmen, climbed a twenty-foot wall and got away in a stolen car.

The Present Perfect Continuous Tense

185 Form

This tense is formed by the present perfect of the verb **to be** + the present participle:

affirmative: I have been working he has been working &c.
negative: I have not (haven't) been working.
interrogative: have you been working?
negative interrogative: haven't you been working?

186 Use

This tense is used for an action which began in the past and is still continuing |————, or has only just finished, |————|:

I've been waiting for an hour and he still hasn't turned up.
I'm so sorry I'm late. Have you been waiting long?

Remember that a number of verbs are not normally used in the continuous form (see **165**), but that some of these can be used in this form in certain cases (**167**). We can therefore say:

Tom has been seeing about a work permit for you.
She has been having a tooth out.
I've been thinking it over. I've been hearing all about his operation.

In addition, the verb **want** is often used in this tense, and **wish** is also possible:

Thank you so much for the binoculars. I've been wanting a pair for ages.

But the participle **being** is not normally part of the present perfect continuous, so this tense is not normally used in the passive. The nearest passive equivalent of a sentence such as 'They have been repairing the road' would normally be 'The road has been repaired lately', which is not exactly the same thing.

187 Comparison of the present perfect simple and continuous

a The simple present perfect can also express an action which began in the past and still continues, or has only just finished. When used in this way it is very like the present perfect continuous, and often either form can be used:

He has lived here for six weeks. He has been living here for six weeks.
How long have you learnt English? How long have you been learning English?
I've wanted to throw something at him for a long time.
I've been wanting to throw something at him for a long time.

This is not of course possible with verbs which are not used in the continuous forms (see **165–7** and **186**), i.e. the present perfect continuous could not replace the simple present perfect in the following examples:

He's been in hospital since his accident. How long have you known that?
They've always had a chauffeur.

Notice also that the present perfect continuous can be used with or without a time phrase. In this way it differs from the simple present perfect, which can only express this type of action by adding a time phrase such as 'for six days' 'since June', 'never'. When used without a time expression of this kind, the simple present perfect refers to a single completed action.

b A repeated action in the simple present perfect can sometimes be expressed as a continuous action by the present perfect continuous:

I've written six letters since breakfast.
I've been writing letters since breakfast.
I have knocked five times. I don't think anyone's in.
I've been knocking. I don't think anybody's in.

Note that the present perfect continuous expresses an action which is apparently uninterrupted; we do not use it when we mention the number of times a thing has been done or the number of things that have been done.

c There is, however, a great difference between a single action in the simple present perfect and an action in the present perfect continuous:

I've put coal on the fire (this job has been done).
I've been putting coal on the fire (this is how I've spent the last five minutes).

Tom: What have you done with my knife? (Where have you put it?)
Ann: I put it back in your drawer.
Tom (taking it out): But what have you been doing to it? The blade's all twisted. Have you been sawing wood with it?

Tom has dug the potato patch, so we can plant the potatoes tomorrow.
He has been digging; that's why he has got such a stiff back.

188 Some more examples of the present perfect and the present perfect continuous

A: I haven't seen your brother lately. Has he gone away?
B: Yes, he's been sent to America (= he has been sent).
A: When did he go?
B: He went last month.
A: Have you had any letters from him?
B: I haven't, but his wife has been hearing regularly.
A: Does she intend to go out and join him?
B: They've been thinking about it but haven't quite decided yet. I think it would be an excellent idea but they've had a lot of expense lately and perhaps haven't got the money.

A: Have you heard that Mr Pitt has been trying to train his Pekinese to obey him? He's (= he has) been at it all day and is completely exhausted.
B: Is the Pekinese exhausted too?

A: No, he thoroughly enjoyed it.
B: I've always heard that they are naturally disobedient dogs.
A: I think poor Mr Pitt has just discovered that for himself.

A: Mary has been seeing a lot of Mr Hook lately, hasn't she? Is there anything in it?
B: Yes. They've just announced their engagement.
A: Are you pleased about it?
B: Only moderately. She has been looking for a very rich man all her life and now she's (= she has) found one, and he's (= he has) been looking for a really competent secretary all his life and now he's found one, but apart from that they aren't really very well suited.
A: I've always heard that Mary has rather a bad temper.
B: So has he.

A: Do you see those people on that little sandy island? They've been waving handkerchiefs for the last half hour. Do you think they want anything?
B: Of course they do. The tide's coming in and very soon that little island will be under water. Have you been sitting here calmly and doing nothing to help them?
A: I've never been here before. I didn't know about the tides.

The Past Perfect Tense

189 a Form

This tense is formed with **had** and the past participle. It is therefore the same for all persons:

I had worked (I'd worked) he had not (hadn't) worked
had they worked? hadn't you worked?

b Use

i The past perfect is the past equivalent of the present perfect:

present: Ann has just left. If you hurry you'll catch her (see **180**).
past: When I arrived Ann had just left.

present: I've lost my case (see **181**).
past: He had lost his case and had to borrow Tom's pyjamas.

The past perfect, however, is not like the present perfect, restricted to actions whose time is not mentioned. We could therefore say:

He had left his case on the 4.40 train.

ii The present perfect can be used with **since/for/always/never** &c. for an action which began in the past and is still continuing or has only just finished (see **182**). The past perfect can be used similarly for an action which began before the time of speaking in the past and continued up to that time or stopped just before it:

present: He has been in the army for twenty years.
or since he was nineteen.

past: When I met him he was 39. He had been in the army for twenty years (*or* since he was nineteen) and couldn't imagine any other kind of life.

Compare this with 'He had been in the army', which only means that he was in it at one time but presumably was not in it at the time of speaking. Note however that the past perfect used with **for** could denote either an action which continues up to the time of speaking in the past or an action which was definitely completed before it:

He was in uniform. He had been a soldier for ten years and liked the life (he was still a soldier at the time of speaking).

but He had been a soldier for ten years. Then he had left the army and married. His sons were now six and five.

(See also **191** for the use of the past perfect in indirect speech.)

iii The past perfect is also the past equivalent of the simple past tense, and is used when from a certain point in the past the narrator or subject looks back on earlier action:

Tom was 23 when our story begins. His father had died five years before and since then Tom had lived alone. His father had advised him not to get married till he was 35, and Tom intended to follow this advice.

I had just poured myself out a glass of beer when the phone rang. When I came back from answering it the glass was empty: somebody had drunk the beer or thrown it away.

He met her in Paris in 1960. He had seen her last ten years before. Her hair had been grey then; now it was white.

or He met her in 1950 and again ten years later. Her hair, which had been grey at their first meeting, was now white.

But if we merely give the events in the order in which they occurred no past perfect tense is necessary:

Tom's father died when Tom was eighteen. Before he died he advised Tom not to marry till 35, and Tom at 23 still intended to follow this advice.

and He met her first in 1950 when her hair was grey. He met her again in 1960 (*or* didn't meet her again till 1960). Her hair was now white.

There is no looking back in the above two examples so no reason for a past perfect.
Note the difference of meaning in the following examples:

a She heard voices and realized that there *were* three people in the next room.
b She saw empty glasses and cups and realized that three people *had been* in the room (they were no longer there).

c He arrived at 2.30 and *was* told to wait in the V.I.P. lounge.
d He arrived at 2.30. He *had been* told to wait in the V.I.P. lounge.

In (c) he received his instructions *after* his arrival. In (d) he received them *before* arrival, possibly before the journey started.

190 Past and past perfect tenses in time clauses

a Clauses with **when**

When one past action follows another:

He called her a liar. She smacked his face.

we can combine them by using **when** and two *simple past* tenses:

When he called her a liar she smacked his face.

provided that it is clear from the sense that the second action followed the first and that they did not happen simultaneously. When two simple past tenses are used in this way there is usually the idea that the first action led to the second and that the second followed the first very closely:

When he opened the window the bird flew out.
The boys were throwing snowballs through the open window. When I shut the window they stopped throwing them.
When the play ended the audience went home.
When he died little children wept in the streets.

The *past perfect* is used after **when** when two simple past tenses might give the impression that the two actions happened simultaneously:

When she *had sung* her song she sat down. ('When she sang her song she sat down' might give the impression that she sang seated.)

or when we wish to emphasize that the first action was complete before the second one started:

When he had shut the window we opened the door of the cage (we waited for the window to be quite shut before opening the cage).

Similarly:

When he *had seen* all the pictures he said he was ready to leave (when he had finished looking at them).

Compare with:

When he *saw* all the pictures he expressed amazement that one man should have painted so many (immediately he saw them he said this).

b Two past actions can also be combined with **till/until, as soon as, before** (for as used as a time conjunction see 95). As above, *simple past* tenses are used except when it is necessary to emphasize that the first action was completely finished before the second one started:

I waited till it got dark. He refused to go till he *had seen* all the papers.
Before *I had known* him a week he tried to borrow money from me.
As soon as it began to rain we ran indoors.
As soon as his guests *had drunk* all his brandy they left his house.

c **after**, however, is normally followed by a perfect tense:

After the will had been read there were angry exclamations.

d We have already stated (**189**) that actions viewed in retrospect from a point in the past are expressed by the past perfect tense. If we have two such actions:

He *had been* to school but he *had learnt* nothing there, so was now illiterate.

and wish to combine them with a time conjunction, we can use **when** &c. with two past perfect tenses:

When he *had been* at school he *had learnt* nothing, so he was now illiterate.

But it is more usual to put the verb in the time clause into the simple past:

When he *was* at school he *had learnt* nothing, so he was now illiterate.

Similarly:

He *had stayed* in his father's firm till his father *died.* Then he had started his own business and was now a very successful man.

e Verbs of knowing, understanding &c., except when modified by a time expression, e.g. 'When she had known me *for a year* she invited me to tea', are not normally used in the past perfect tense in time clauses:

When I *knew* the work of one department thoroughly I was moved to the next department.

Compare with:

When I *had learnt* the work of one department I was moved.

f Time clauses containing past perfect tenses can be combined with a main verb in the conditional tense, but this is chiefly found in indirect speech and examples will be given in the next paragraph.

191 Use of the past perfect in indirect speech

a Present perfect tenses in direct speech become past perfect tenses in indirect speech provided the introductory verb is in the past tense:

He said, 'I've been in England for ten years.'
= He said that he had been in England for ten years.
He said, 'When you have worked for me for six months you'll get a rise.'
= He said that when I had worked for him for six months I would get a rise.
She said, 'I'll lend you the book as soon as I have read it myself.'
= She said that she would lend me the book as soon as she had read it herself.

b Simple past tenses in direct speech usually change similarly:

He said, 'I knew her well.'
= He said that he had known her well.

But there are a number of cases where past tenses remain unchanged (see **276**).

(For the past perfect after **wish** and after **as if/though**, see **271c**. For the past perfect after **if** and **if only**, see **222**.)

192 The past perfect continuous tense

a Form

This tense is formed with **had been** + the present participle. It is therefore the same for all persons:

I had been working they had not (hadn't) been working
had you been working? hadn't you been working?

It is not used with verbs which are not used in the continuous forms, except with **want** and sometimes **wish** (see **165–7**):

The boy was delighted with his new knife. He had been wanting one for a long time.

The present participle **being** is not, however, normally used in the present perfect continuous, so this tense has no passive form. The nearest passive equivalent of a sentence such as 'They had been picking apples' would be 'Apples had been picked', which is not the same thing (see (**b**)iii below, see also **186**).

b Use

The past perfect continuous bears the same relation to the past perfect that the present perfect continuous bears to the present perfect (see **187**).

i When the action began before the time of speaking in the past, and continued up to that time, or stopped just before it, we can often use either form (see **187a**):

It was now six and he was tired because he had worked since dawn.
= It was now six and he was tired because he had been working since dawn.

ii A repeated action in the past perfect can sometimes be expressed as a continuous action by the past perfect continuous (see **187b**):

He had tried five times to get her on the phone.
He had been trying to get her on the phone.

iii But there is a great difference between a single action in the simple past perfect and an action in the past perfect continuous (see **187c**):

By six o'clock I had mended the puncture and we were ready to start *i.e. this job had been done.*
but He had been mending the puncture *tells us how he had spent the previous* fifteen minutes.

Similarly:

He *had looked* through the keyhole and seen that there was nobody in the room (one single action).

and When I opened the door I found him on his knees outside. I knew that he *had been looking* through the keyhole (for the last half hour).

They *had sawn* up the fallen tree so we had a good store of firewood.

They *had been sawing*; that was why they were covered in sawdust.

18 The Future

193 Forms

The future tense in English is **shall/will** with the infinitive without **to**:

I shall (*or* will) go, he will go &c.

However, this tense is not used nearly so often as students naturally expect. Instead it is only one of a number of ways of expressing the future, and its place in the scheme will be more clearly seen if we deal first with some of the other methods.
The methods of expressing the future are as follows:

1 The simple present (not very important)
2 The present continuous
3 The **going to** form
4 The future tense
5 The future continuous
6 The future perfect tense

Each is used in a slightly different way. They will be taken in the above order.

194 The simple present (I go, he goes &c.)

As has already been mentioned, this tense can be used for a planned future action or series of actions, particularly when these concern a journey. It is often used by travel agencies:

We *leave* here at six, *arrive* in Dublin at midnight and *take* a plane on to Amsterdam.

However, this is not a very important use of the tense as any of the other future forms can be used here.

195 The present continuous (I am leaving, he is leaving &c.)

a This tense is used for a definite future arrangement. The time is nearly always given and is usually in the immediate future:

He is playing in the concert tonight.
We are meeting him after the performance.
She is leaving at the end of the week.

b The verbs **go** and **come** can be used in this tense without a time expression and may then imply a less definite arrangement:

Where are you going?
I am going for a walk. Are you coming with me?
Yes, I'm just coming. Wait for me.

c This method of expressing the future cannot be used with verbs which are not normally used in the continuous tenses (see **165**). These verbs should be put into the future tense **(shall/will)**:

I am meeting him tonight.
but I shall know tonight.
They will be there tomorrow.
You will feel better in the morning.

to see, however, can be used in this tense with a future meaning:

I am seeing him tomorrow (= I have an appointment with him).

to be can be used when it forms part of a passive verb:

He is being met at the station (= he will be met).
Our new piano is being delivered this afternoon.

This tense conveys little or no idea of intention (see **196**).

196 A note on the meaning of *future with intention*

Before dealing with the **going to** form, it is necessary to explain what we mean by *future with intention.*
When we say that a future form expresses *future with intention* we mean that it expresses a future action which is undertaken by the subject deliberately and in accordance with his own wishes.

1 **will** + infinitive *and*
2 the **going to** form can be used in this way.

When we say that a future form expresses *future without intention* we mean that it merely states that a certain action will occur in the future. We do not know whether it was arranged by the subject or by some other person and we do not know what the subject feels about it.

1 The present tense
2 The present continuous
3 The future tense (shall/will) *and*
4 The future continuous
are used in this way.

The **going to** Form

197 Form

The present continuous tense of the verb **to go** + infinitive with **to**. (We say, 'going *to*', for the same reason that we say, 'have *to*', 'used *to*' &c., i.e. to remind students of the **to** in the following infinitive):

I'm going to see him. She is not going to be there.
Is he going to lecture in English?

198 Use

a The **going to** form expresses the subject's intention to perform a certain future action. This intention is always premeditated and there is usually also the idea that some preparation for the action has already been made. Actions expressed by the **going to** form are therefore usually considered very likely to be performed, though there is not the same idea of definite future arrangement that we get from the present continuous.
The **going to** form can be used with or without a time expression.
The following points may be noted:

i The **going to** form can be used for the near future with a time expression as an alternative to the present continuous, because when the **going to** form is used with a definite time, the action which it expresses becomes very definite and there is then very little difference between these two future forms:

I am meeting Tom at the station at 6.0.
and I am going to meet Tom at the station at 6.0.

ii The **going to** form can be used with time clauses when we wish to emphasize the subject's intention:

He is going to be a dentist when he grows up.
What are you going to do when you get your degree?

Normally, however, the future tense (**shall/will**) is used with time clauses.

iii The **going to** form can be used without a time expression:

I am going to read you some of my own poems.
He is going to lend me his bicycle.

It then usually refers to the immediate or near future.

iv As seen in (ii) above, the **going to** form can be used with the verb **to be**. It is also sometimes found with other verbs not normally used in the continuous tenses:

I'm going to think about it. I'm sure I'm going to like it.

But on the whole it is safer to use the future tense here.

v Note that it is not very usual to put the verbs **go** and **come** into the **going to** form. Instead we generally use the present continuous tense: i.e. instead of 'I am going to go' we normally say 'I am going' and instead of 'I am going to come' we very often say 'I am coming'.

Note that we can also express intention by using **will** + infinitive. This form is compared with the **going to** form in **202**.

b The **going to** form is also used to express the speaker's feeling of certainty. It is used in this sense without a definite time, but usually refers to the near future:

That boy is going to be sick; he looks quite green.
It's going to rain; look at those clouds.
He is very ill; I'm afraid he is going to die.

The Future Tense

199 Form

a The future tense is formed with **shall/will** + infinitive (without **to**) for the 1st person singular and plural, and **will** + infinitive (without **to**) for the other persons. The negative is formed by putting **not** after the **shall** or **will**. The interrogative is formed by inverting the subject and the **shall** or **will** ('will' is not usual in the 1st person interrogative).

b

Affirmative	*Negative*	*Interrogative*
I shall/will work	I shall/will not work	shall I work?
you will work	you will not work	will you work?
he will work	he will not work	will he work?
we shall/will work	we shall/will not work	shall we work?
you will work	you will not work	will you work?
they will work	they will not work	will they work?

c Negative interrogative:

Shall I not work? Will he not work? &c.

d Contractions: **will** is contracted to **'ll**
will not to **won't**
shall not to **shan't**

The contraction **'ll** cannot be used when the infinitive is omitted:

Who will go? I **will.**

The second **will** could not be contracted.

200 **will** and **shall** in the 1st person singular and plural

I/we shall is the grammatically correct form:

I shall know tomorrow. I wonder if I shall see him.
We shall have to rebuild that wall.

I/we will is used for future for intention **(201f)**.

Compare I shall be there *which merely states the fact,*
with I will be there *which means* I intend to be there,
and I shan't see him again *which implies that there will be no opportunity for another meeting,*
with I won't see him again *which means* I refuse to see him again.

However, many people avoid **shall** except in the interrogative and use **will** all the time for affirmative and negative:

I will know tomorrow. I wonder if I will see him.
We will have to rebuild that wall.

adding **be** + the present participle when it is necessary to emphasize that the future is without intention:

I won't be seeing him again.
instead of I shan't see him. (See future continuous tense **207.**)

The student should therefore use **will** when in doubt.

201 Uses of the future tense

a To express the speaker's opinions, assumptions, speculations about the future. These may be introduced by verbs such as **think, know, believe, doubt, suppose, assume, expect, hope, be afraid, feels sure, wonder, I daresay,** etc. or accompanied by adverbs such as **probably, possibly, perhaps, surely** etc. but can be used without them:

(I'm sure) he'll come back. (I suppose) they'll sell the house.
(Perhaps) we'll find him at the hotel. They'll (probably) wait for us.

The future tense can be used with or without a time expression.
Going to is sometimes possible here also, but it makes the action appear more probable and (where there is no time expression) more immediate:

'He'll build a house' merely means 'this is my opinion', and gives no idea when the building will start,

but 'He's going to build a house' implies that he has already made this decision and that he will probably start quite soon.

b The future tense is used similarly for future habitual actions which we assume will take place:

Spring will come again. Birds will build nests. People will make plans. Other men will climb these stairs and sit at my desk. (*will be building/making/climbing/sitting* would also be possible.)

c The future tense is used with clauses of condition, time and sometimes purpose. (Remember that the future tense is not used **in** clauses of time and condition):

If I drop this glass it will break (see **216a**).
When it gets warmer the snow will start to melt (see **293**).
I'm putting this letter on top of the pile so that he'll read it first.

Note that if we replace the clauses by separate sentences we can still use the future tense for the following action:

Don't drop it. It will break.
It's getting warmer. Soon the show will start to melt (*or* will be starting).
I'm putting this letter on top. Then he'll open it first.

i.e. the future tense can be used for a future action which results from another action in the present or future.

d Verbs of the senses, of emotion, thinking, possessing etc. (see **165**) normally express the future by the future tense, though **going to** is sometimes possible. These verbs cannot, of course, express the future by the present continuous:

He'll be here at six. They'll know tonight. You'll have time for tea.

e The future tense is used, chiefly in newspapers and news broadcasts, for formal announcements of future plans. In conversations such statements would normally be expressed by the present continuous or **going to** form:

(newspaper extract): The President will open the new school tomorrow.

But Ann said: 'The President is opening the new school tomorrow.'

f The future tense with **will** for all persons (which can be more conveniently expressed by the phrase **will** + infinitive) can express intention. In the affirmative it is used chiefly with the first person:

'I will think about it' means 'I intend to think about it' but 'He/they/you will think about it' doesn't usually imply intention.

Won't however can be used for all persons to imply negative intention:

I won't do it = I refuse to do it. They won't do it = They refuse to do it.
(It needn't always have this meaning, but it often does.)

Future with Intention

202 will + infinitive and the going to form compared

Very often we can use either the **going to** form or **will** + infinitive, but there are differences between them, as a result of which there are occasions when only one of them is possible.
The chief difference is:

a The **going to** form always implies a *premeditated* intention, and often an intention + plan.

b **will** + infinitive implies intention alone, and this intention is usually, though not necessarily, *unpremeditated.*

If, therefore, the intention is accompanied by a plan, we must use **going to:**

I have bought some bricks and *I'm going to* build a garage.

If the intention is clearly unpremeditated, we must use **will:**

'There is somebody at the hall door.'
'*I'll go* and open it.'

When the intention is neither clearly premeditated nor clearly unpremeditated either **going to** or **will** may be used:

I will/am going to climb that mountain one day.
I won't/am not going to tell you my age.

Other differences:

c As already noted **will** + infinitive in the affirmative is used almost entirely for the first person. Second and third person intentions are therefore normally expressed by **going to:**

He is going to resign.

d **won't**, like **not going to**, can be used for all persons; but **won't** is the stronger form.

e **going to**, as already stated, usually refers to the fairly immediate future. **will** can refer either to the immediate or to the more remote future.

203 More examples of **going to** and **will**

a Examples of **going to** used to express intention:

Tom has just borrowed the axe; he is going to chop some wood.

'What are you doing with that spade?'
'I am going to plant some apple trees.'

She has bought some cloth; she is going to make herself a dress.

He is studying very hard; he is going to try for a scholarship.

'Why are you taking down all the pictures?'
'I am going to repaper the room.'

I have given up my flat in Paris because I'm going to live permanently in London.

Some workmen arrived today with a steamroller. I think they are going to repair the road in front of my house.

'Why is he carrying his guitar?'
'He is going to play it under Miss Pitt's window.'

Note that it would not be possible to substitute **will** for the **going to** in any of the above examples, as in each of them there is clear evidence of premeditation.

b Examples of **will** + infinitive

Ann: This is a terribly heavy box.
Tom: I'll help you to carry it.

Father: I've left my watch upstairs.
Son: I'll go and get it for you.

Mr X.: My car won't start.
Mr Y.: I'll come and give it a push.

Mother: Who will post this letter for me?
Son: I will.

Mr X.: Will you lend me £100?
Mr Y.: No, I won't.

c Some comparisons of **going to** and **will**

In answer to Mr Pitt's remark, 'There isn't any ink in the house', Mrs Pitt might reply:

either I'm going to get some today.
or I'll get some today.

The first would imply that some time before this conversation she realized that there was no ink and decided to buy some.
The second would imply that she had not previously decided to buy ink, but took the decision now, immediately after her husband's remark.

Similarly:

Ann: Where is the telephone book?
Tom: I'll get it for you (unpremeditated intention).

If, however, he had said, 'I'm just going to get it', it would mean that he had decided to do this before Ann spoke (presumably because he had anticipated that Ann would want it or needed it for himself).

Note that **will** does not have any meaning of intention when it is used as indicated in **201a**, **b**, **c**, **d**, and **e**, i.e. when it is used as part of the ordinary future tense (**shall/will**):

If he hurries he will find her. (Here the ordinary future tense must be used. 'Will' here carries no feeling of intention but is a mere statement of fact.)

204 Determination

The feeling of intention expressed by **will** can be strengthened into determination by stressing the **will** (or **won't** in the negative):

'I'll *come*' expresses intention (the stress normally falls on the infinitive), but 'I *will* come' (the **will** uncontracted and strongly stressed) expresses determination.
Similarly 'I won't come' normally expresses refusal, but 'I *won't* come' (with a strong stress on the **won't**) expresses absolute refusal, i.e. it means 'I am determined not to come'.

205 **will** must not be confused with **want** or **wish**

will + infinitive expresses intention, i.e. a wish + a decision to fulfil it. A wish alone must be expressed by **wish** or **want**: 'I'll go' expresses a wish to go + a decision to go. 'I wish (or want) to go' expresses wish only. It describes a state of mind, but gives no information about future intended actions.

The Future Continuous Tense

206 Form

This tense is formed with the future tense of the verb **to be** + the present participle:

I shall be working, you will be working
he will be working, we shall be working
you will be working, they will be working

(Contraction: I'll be working, he'll be working &c.)

Negative: I shall not (shan't) be working, he will not (won't) be working &c.
Interrogative: shall I be working? will you be working? &c.
Negative interrogative: shan't I be working? won't you be working? &c.

207 Use and comparison with the present continuous

The chief use of this tense is to express a future without intention. It is, therefore, very similar to the present continuous, but differs from it in the following points:

The present continuous tense implies a *deliberate* future action.
The future continuous tense usually implies an action which will occur in the normal course of events. It is therefore less definite and more casual than the present continuous:

I am seeing Tom tomorrow.
I'll be seeing Tom tomorrow.

The first implies that Tom or the speaker has deliberately arranged the meeting, but the second implies that Tom and the speaker will meet in the ordinary course of events (perhaps they work together).

This difference is not, however, very important and very often either tense can be used. We can say:

He'll be taking his exam next week.
or He is taking his exam next week.
He won't be coming to the party.
or He isn't coming to the party.

The present continuous can only be used with a definite time and for the near future, while the future continuous can be used with or without a definite time and for the near or distant future. We can say:

I am meeting him tomorrow.
but I'll be meeting him tomorrow/next year/some time (or without a time expression at all).

208 will + infinitive and the future continuous compared

a There is approximately the same difference between **will** + infinitive and the future continuous as between **will** + infinitive and the present continuous.
will + infinitive expresses future with intention.
The future continuous expresses future without intention:

I'*ll write* to Mr Pitt and tell him about Tom's new house.

Here the verb in italics expresses intention. The speaker announces a deliberate future action in accordance with his own wishes.
But in the sentence, 'I'*ll be writing* to Mr Pitt and I'll tell him about Tom's new house', the verb in italics expresses no intention. It is a mere statement of fact and implies that this letter to Mr Pitt will be written either as a matter of routine or for reasons unconnected with Tom's new house. Similarly:

'Tom won't cut the grass' = Tom refuses to cut it.
while 'Tom won't be cutting the grass' is a mere statement of fact, giving no information about Tom's feelings. Perhaps Tom is away, or ill, or will be doing some other job.

b **will** + infinitive can express invitation:

Will you have a cigarette? (see **224**)

or a polite request:

Will you help me to lift the piano? (see **225**)

or a command:

You will work in this room (see **226**).

The future continuous can have none of these meanings:

i Will you bring the piano in here? (polite request).
Yes, sir (possible answer).
but ii Will you be bringing the piano in here? (question about a future action).
Yes, I think I will *or* No, I think I'll put it upstairs (possible answers).

i You will work in this office under Mr Pitt (command).
but ii You will be working here (only a statement).

As before, the present continuous could be used here instead of the future continuous, provided that a time expression was added.

209 The future continuous can also be used, like other continuous tenses, to express an action which will continue for some time without definite limits. When used in this way with a time expression it implies that the action will start before the time mentioned and probably continue after it:

When I reach London it will probably be raining.
This time next year I shall be driving through Italy.

The Future Perfect

210 **a** Form

shall/will + perfect infinitive (without **to**):

I shall have worked, you will have worked &c.

b Use

It is used for an action which at a given future time will be in the past:

In two years' time (i.e. two years from now) I shall have taken my degree.
When we reach Valparaiso we shall have sailed all round the world.
By the end of the year your new maid will have broken all your cups.

It is always used with a time expression.

Remember that the usual rule prohibiting future tenses in time clauses applies here also, so that in a time clause the future perfect changes to the present perfect:

I shall have finished this by dinner time.

but When I *have finished* I'll tell you (present perfect used instead of the future perfect after **when**).

19 Sequence of Tenses

211 Subordinate clauses

A sentence can contain a main verb and one or more subordinate clauses. A subordinate clause is a group of words containing a subject and verb and forming part of a sentence:

We knew *that the bridge was unsafe.*
He gave it to me *because he trusted me.*
He ran faster *than we did.*
This is the picture *that I bought in Rome.*

(In each of the above examples the subordinate clause is in italics.)

For other examples see under conditional sentences, relative pronouns, and clauses of purpose, comparison, time, result, and concession. It is not necessary for the student to make a detailed study of clauses or even to be able to recognize the different kinds of clause, but it is necessary for him to learn to know which is the main verb of a sentence because of the important rule given below.

212 The sequence of tenses

When the main verb of a sentence is in a past tense, verbs in subordinate clauses must be in a past tense also:

Tense of verb in main clause		*Tense of verb in subordinate clause*
Present	He thinks that it will rain.	Future
Past	He thought that it would rain.	Conditional
Present	He sees that he has made a mistake	Present Perfect
Past	He saw that he had made a mistake	Past Perfect
Present	I work so hard that I am always tired.	Present
Past	I worked so hard that I was always tired.	Past
Present Perfect	He has done all that is necessary.	Present
Past Perfect	He had done all that was necessary.	Past
Present	He says that he is going to eat it.	Present Continuous
Past	He said that he was going to eat it.	Past Continuous

Note that a clause cannot be formed with an infinitive alone and that infinitives, therefore, are not affected by the above rule:

He wants to go to Lyons. He wanted to go to Lyons.

(i.e. the infinitive does not change).

The rule about sequence of tenses applies also to indirect speech when the introductory verb is in a past tense. (See under reported speech, chapter 28.)

20 The Conditional

The Conditional Tenses

213 The present conditional tense

This is formed with **should/would** + infinitive for the 1st person and **would** + infinitive for the other persons:

I should/would work, you would work (you'd work), he would work (he'd work) &c.

Negative: I should not (shouldn't) work, you would not (wouldn't work) &c.

Interrogative: should I work? would you work? &c.

Negative interrogative: should I not (shouldn't I) work? would you not (wouldn't you) work? &c.

This form is used:

1 As a past equivalent of the future tense.
2 In special idiomatic uses of **should** and **would** (see chapter 21).
3 In conditional sentences (see **216**).

214 As a past equivalent of the future tense

a **should/would** must be used instead of **shall/will** when the main verb of the sentence is in the past tense:

I hope that I shall succeed.
I hoped that I should succeed.
I know that he will be in time.
I knew that he would be in time (see also **212**).

b **shall/will**, therefore, in direct speech become **should/would** in indirect speech when the introductory verb is in the past tense:

I said, 'I shall be there.' = I said that I should be there.
He said, 'I shall be there.' = He said that he would be there. (**shall** becomes **would** when the subject changes from 1st to 2nd or 3rd person.)
He said, 'Tom will help me.' = He said that Tom would help him (see also chapter 28).

215 The perfect conditional tense

This is formed with **should/would** and the perfect infinitive:

I should have worked   you would have worked   &c.

Negative: I should not (shouldn't) have worked, you would not (wouldn't) have worked &c.

Interrogative: should I have worked? would you have worked? &c.

Negative interrogative: should I not (shouldn't I) have worked? would you not (wouldn't you) have worked? &c.

This form is used:

1 As a past equivalent of the future perfect tense:

I hope that he will have finished before we get back.
I hoped that he would have finished before we got back.

2 In conditional sentences.

(For special use of **should** + perfect infinitive see **233**.)

Conditional Sentences

Conditional sentences have two parts: the **if**-clause and the main clause:

In the sentence 'If it rains I shall stay at home', 'if it rains' *is the* **if**-*clause, and* 'I shall stay at home' *is the main clause.*

216 The three kinds of conditional sentence

There are three kinds of conditional sentence: each kind contains a different pair of tenses.

a Type 1. Probable condition

The verb in the **if**-clause is in the present tense; the verb in the main clause is in the future tense:

If he runs all the way he'll get there in time.
If you annoy the cat she will scratch you.

This type of sentence implies that it is quite probable that the action in the **if**-clause will be performed.

b Type 2. Improbable condition

The verb in the **if**-clause is in the simple past tense; the verb in the main clause is in the conditional tense:

If I dropped this it would explode.

There is no difference in time between the first and second type of conditional sentence. The second, like the first, refers to the present or future, and the past tense in its **if**-clause is not a true past tense but a subjunctive, which indicates improbability or unreality.

Type 2 is used:

i when we don't expect the action in the **if**-clause to take place:

If he ran all the way he would get there in time (but I don't suppose he will run all the way).
If a burglar came into my room I should throw something at him (but I don't expect a burglar to come in).
If I dyed my hair blue my skin would look whiter (but I have no serious intention of dyeing my hair).

ii when the supposition is contrary to known facts:

If I were you I should plant potatoes there.
If we had a helicopter we could get there quite quickly (but we haven't a helicopter).
If I knew his address I'd give it to you (but I don't know it).

Sometimes the same **if**-clause could have two possible meanings:

If he ran all the way *could imply* but I don't think he will *or* but he doesn't.

The meaning, however, is normally clear from the context. At one time ambiguity of this type was avoided by using **were** + infinitive instead of the past tense in type 2(i):

If he were to run/if a burglar were to come/if I were to dye my hair (see also **219**).

Nowadays this use of **were** is considered rather formal but it is sometimes found in written English.

c Type 3. Impossible condition

The verb in the **if**-clause is in the past perfect tense; the verb in the main clause is in the perfect conditional:

If I had known of your arrival I should have met you (but I didn't know so I didn't meet you).
If he had fallen through the ice he would have drowned (but he didn't fall, so he didn't drown).

Here we know that the condition cannot be fulfilled because the sentence refers only to past events.

217 Special use of will/would and should in if-clauses

Normally **will/would** and **should** cannot be used after **if** in conditional sentences. There are, however, certain exceptions:

a **will/would** used, not in a future sense, but to mean **am/was willing, don't/didn't mind** can be placed after **if**:

i **if you will/would** is particularly useful in polite requests:

If you will/would kindly wait a moment I'll ask the manager to speak to you.
= If you are willing to wait/don't mind waiting.
or Please wait and I'll ask the manager &c.

If you would let me have an answer by return I should be very grateful.
= Please let me have an answer by return, and I shall be grateful.

ii Similarly with other persons:

If he'll listen to me I'll give him some advice (= if he is willing to listen).
He said he'd give me £5 if I would keep my mouth shut (= if I was willing to do this).
If he would leave his gun outside we'd all feel a lot safer (= if he wouldn't mind leaving it).

These three sentences could, of course, be written 'If he listens/If I kept/ If he left' but the exact shade of meaning would then be lost.

iii **won't** can be used when it means **refuses**:

If he won't come we'll ask someone else.

b **will** can also be used to express obstinate insistence **(227b)** (the **will** is strongly stressed in speech):

If you will put handfuls of salt into everything you cook no wonder you are always thirsty (if you insist on putting).

c **would like** and **would care**, which are equivalents of **want** and **wish** can be used in type 1:

i If you would like to come I'll get a ticket for you.
ii You can leave your case here if you'd like to.

But if the **if**-clause consists only of **if you would like**, i.e. if there is no object of any kind after **like**, we usually omit the **would**, leaving **if you like**:

i If you like, I'll get a ticket for you.
ii You can leave your case here if you like.

Similarly Come with us if you like.
but Come with us if you'*d* like *to*.
and I'll get you a copy if you like.
but I'll get you a copy if you'*d* like *one*.

d **should** + infinitive can be used in type 1 instead of a simple present when we wish to imply that the action in the **if**-clause, though possible, is unlikely. It is often combined with an imperative:

If anyone should ring up say that I'll be back at eight.
If this machine should fail to give satisfaction we guarantee to refund the purchase money.

should is often placed first and the **if** omitted:

Should this machine fail &c.

Occasionally **should** + infinitive is used similarly in type 2:

Of course if the police should find out we'd all be in the most terrible trouble.

218 Possible variations of the tense rules

a Two present tenses instead of present and future

Two present tenses are used to express natural laws and habitual reactions:

If you heat ice it turns to water.
If I say, 'Yes,' he says, 'No.'

b Two present tenses or two past tenses can be used as in:

If you don't like your job why don't you change it?
If you knew he needed money why didn't you lend him some?
He says that the neighbours are always complaining, but if he insists on burning old rubber tyres in his garden what can he expect?

These of course are not true conditional sentences for the **if** is replaceable by **since** or **seeing that**.

c **if** + present tense can be followed by an imperative or **must** or **should** &c. or any expression of advice:

If you see him tell him to write to me.
If you suffer from vertigo you shouldn't look over the edges of cliffs.
If he turns round you must pretend to be looking in a shop window.
If he is sick he ought to be in bed/he had better go to bed.

d The present tense with **may** or **can**

The future tense when used in a conditional sentence expresses a certain result. If instead of certainty we wish to express possibility we use **may**:

If he starts now he will be in time (certain result).
If he starts now he may be in time (possible result).

may or **can** can also express permission:

If you are in a hurry you can take my car.

e Similarly the past tense can be used with **might** or **could**:

If you tried again you would succeed (certain result).
If you tried again you might succeed (possible result).
If it stopped snowing you could go out (ability or permission).

and the past perfect with **might** or **could** and the perfect infinitive:

If he had seen you he would have helped you (certainty).
If he had seen you he might have helped you (possibility).
If I had had a rope I could have climbed it (ability).

f In type 3 the past perfect may be combined with a present conditional in sentences such as 'If he had taken my advice he would be a rich man now', where the action in the **if** clause is a *past* action but the action in the main clause is in the *present*.

g The present perfect or present continuous may replace the present tense in type 1:

If you have finished that exercise I'll show you how to do the next one.
If you are staying for another night I'll ask the manager to give you a better room.

219 The subjunctive **were**

a In type 2 **were** can be used instead of **was**. We can say:

If I/he were *instead of* if I/he was.

were is more usual than **was** in type 2(ii):

If Tom were here (but he is not here).

In type 2(i) either can be used but it is always safer to use **were**:

If I was/were offered a ticket I'd take it.

Note that 'If I were you, I should . . . ' is a very good way of expressing advice:

If I were you I should tell him the truth.

The **if**-clause is often omitted:

I should tell him the truth.

b **were** + infinitive can replace a simple past tense in type 2(i):

If she offered him £500 *could be replaced by* If she were to offer him £500.

(See **216b**.) Here **were** must be used for all persons.

220 Inversion of subject and auxiliary, with **if** omitted

Where **if** is followed by an auxiliary verb, e.g. by **were, had,** or **should,** it is possible to invert auxiliary and subject and omit the **if**:

If I were rich = were I rich (**were** must be used with this construction, never **was**).

If he had known = had he known.
If war should break out = should war break out.

221 if replaced by **unless, but for, provided (that)** and **supposing**

a **unless** + affirmative verb = **if** + negative verb:

Unless you go = if you don't go.
Unless the floods go down we shan't be able to use the ford.

b **but for** = if it were not for/if it had not been for:

But for the storm we should have arrived earlier = if it hadn't been for the storm.

c **provided (that)** can replace **if** when there is a rather stronger idea of limitation or restriction. It is chiefly used with permission:

You can camp in my field provided you promise to leave no mess.

d **supposing/suppose** can be used to express 'what will/would happen if?' or 'what would have happened if?':

Supposing the plane is late? = what will happen if it is late?
Supposing no one had been there? = what would have happened if no one had been there?

suppose/supposing can also introduce suggestions:

Suppose *you* try now? = why don't you try? what about you trying?

There is of course no idea of condition here.

222 if only

only can be placed after **if** and indicates hope, a wish or regret according to the tense used with it.

if only + present tense/**will** expresses hope:

If only he comes in time = we hope he will come.
If only he will listen to her = we hope he will be willing to listen.

if only + past/past perfect expresses regret (it has the same meaning as **wish** + past or past perfect):

If only he didn't drive so fast = { we wish he didn't drive so fast. / we are sorry he drives so fast. }
If only you hadn't said, 'Liar'. = { we wish you hadn't said 'Liar'. / we are sorry you said, 'Liar'. }

if only + **would** can express regret about a present action as an alternative to **if only** + past tense (it has the same meaning as **wish** + **would**):

If only he would drive more slowly = we are sorry that he isn't willing to drive more slowly.

or a not very hopeful wish concerning the future:

If only the rain would stop = we wish it would stop *but implies that we think it will go on.* (See also **wish 271c**.)

if only clauses can stand alone as above or form part of a full conditional sentence.

223 Some more examples

a Type 1

If you have really mislaid the documents you had better inform the police.
The dog won't attack you if you sit quite still.
If you aren't going to eat any more I'll ask the waiter to bring the coffee.
Unless you wear boots you may get bitten by snakes.
If she doesn't want the raspberries you can have them.
If he won't (= refuses to) mow the grass I'll have to do it myself.
If they can't buy a house why don't they build one?
If you *will* (obstinate insistence) make tactless remarks like that it is hardly surprising that people avoid you.
He can stay with me provided he agrees to help with the housework.
If you'll move up a little, Mr X, there'll be room beside you for Miss Y.
Supposing your car breaks down in the middle of the desert?
Should you require anything else please ring the bell for the attendant.

b Type 2

Why did he ask if he knew already?
What would you do if you saw a ghost?
If you wouldn't mind letting me stand on your shoulders I think I could fix it.
I wouldn't sell it even if he were to offer me all the gold in China.
Supposing he tried to blackmail you?

If she would only tell me what is on her mind I might be able to help her.
He said that he'd smuggle me out in his yacht provided I didn't ask any questions.
If they would only take their boots off before coming in, it would be easier to keep the floor clean.
If I were you I should say nothing about it.

c Type 3

If he had taken his grandmother's advice he would be a rich man now.
If our transmitter had been working we could have sent out an S.O.S.
If you had left that wasp alone it wouldn't have stung you.
We might have had lobster for lunch if the cat hadn't stolen it.
If only the tape-recorder hadn't made such a noise!
If you had known he was a murderer would you have gone to the police?
Had you obeyed orders none of this would have happened.
But for my lifebelt I should have been drowned.
If the first clock had been invented by someone south of the Equator, clock hands would go round the other way.

21 Other uses of 'Will', 'Would', 'Shall', and 'Should'

(In all these uses **will, would, shall,** and **should** must be understood to be followed directly by an infinitive.)

Will

224 **will you?** can express an invitation:

Will you have some more wine?
Will you come to tea tomorrow?

When speaking informally we often omit **will you?** and say:

Have some more wine. Come to tea tomorrow.

Note the difference between:

Will you come with me? (an invitation)
and Are you coming with me? } (requests for information).
or Will you be coming? }

The first expects the answer 'I'd like to very much, thank you' or 'I'm sorry but I'll be busy on that day'.
The second and third merely expect 'Yes', or 'No', without thanks or apology.
In the past, i.e. in indirect speech, it is possible to use **would**:

He asked if I would have some more wine.

But it is more usual to avoid the verb:

He offered me some more wine.
He invited (asked) me to tea/dinner &c.

or to use the object + infinitive construction:

He asked me to dine with him.
He invited me to accompany him.

225 **will you?** can express a request:

Will you type this, please? Will you give him this letter?
Will anyone who saw this accident please telephone the nearest police station? (wireless announcement)

would you? can also be used for a request in the present:

Would you show me the way to the station?
Would you give him this letter?

would you? is less authoritative than **will you?**
In the past, i.e. in indirect speech, it is possible to use **would**:

He asked if I would show him the way.

But it is more common to use the object + infinitive construction:

He asked me to show him the way.

Note that **will you?** and **would you?** without infinitives are sometimes placed after an imperative:

Come here, will you? Shut the door, would you?

But this is not very polite except when used between people who know each other very well.

226 will in the affirmative can express a command:

'You will stay here till you are relieved', said the officer.
All boys will attend roll-call at 9 o'clock (school notice).

This is a formal, impersonal type of command, similar to **must** or **is/are to** but more peremptory. It implies the speaker's confidence that the order will be obeyed and is therefore much used in schools and in military &c., establishments.

Note that if we change **will** + infinitive into the future continuous we remove all idea of command:

You will work here under Mr Pitt *is a command, but* You will be working here under Mr Pitt *is only a statement.*

In the past, i.e. in indirect speech, we use the **be** + infinitive construction i.e. **was/were** + infinitive, or **tell** or **order** &c., with object + infinitive (see **280, 281**):

He said that she was to work under Mr Pitt.
or He told her to work under Mr Pitt.

It is not possible to use **would** here.

227 will can express a habit

a Habits are normally expressed by the simple present tense, but **will** + infinitive can be used instead when we wish to emphasize the characteristics of the performer rather than the action performed:

A dog usually obeys his master *expresses a habit, but* A dog will usually obey his master *emphasizes that this is one of the characteristics of a dog.*

This is not a very important use of **will**, but the past form **would** has a much wider use and often replaces **used to** when there is a series of actions:

They would come for us at dawn and we would mount our horses and go back with them to their camp where we would spend the day hunting and feasting (= they used to come and we used to mount &c.).

will and **would** can be contracted here.

b **will** can also express obstinate insistence, usually habitual:

If you *will* keep your watch half an hour slow it is hardly surprising that you are late for your appointments.

would is used in the past:

We all tried to stop him smoking in bed but he *would* do it.

will and **would** are not contracted here and are strongly stressed.

228 **will** can introduce an assumption:

He'll be there by now = I'm sure he is there.

It can be followed by the perfect infinitive:

He'll have reached Paris by now = I'm sure he has reached Paris.
You'll have heard about this = I'm sure you have heard about this.

Would

229 With the verbs **like** and **care** and the adverbs **rather** and **sooner**

a **would like** can be used instead of the present tense of the verb **want** and is a more polite form. Either **would** or **should** can be used for the 1st person:

instead of I want to see Mr Pitt *we can say* I would like to see Mr Pitt.
and instead of I want some pears *we can say* I would like some pears.

Similarly in the interrogative:

Mr Pitt is busy now. Would you like to see Mr Jones?

In the negative, however, we must use **do not want,** as **would not like** means 'would dislike':

No, I don't want to see Mr Jones, thank you.

Used with a noun 'Would you like?' may express an invitation:

Would you like another glass of wine? = Will you have another glass?

b **would care** can be used in the same way with a present meaning but only in the interrogative and negative:

Would you care to see my etchings? = would you like to see my etchings?
Would you care *for* some more wine? = would you like some more wine?

Note that the preposition **for** must be placed between **care** and a noun.

c **rather/sooner** can be placed after **would** to express preference:

I would rather go = I would prefer to go.

Similarly in comparisons:

He would rather listen to others than **talk** himself.

(With this construction the infinitive without **to** is used after **than.** See also **272.**)

230 Other uses of **would**

a As has already been noted **would** is the past equivalent of **will** when **will** is used for the ordinary future:

He knows he will be late. He knew he would be late.

b **would** similarly is the past equivalent of **will** used to express intention:

I said, 'I will help him.' He said, 'I won't lend you a penny.'
I said that I would help him. He said that he wouldn't lend me a penny.

But notice that whereas **would** used for future or intention is restricted to subordinate clauses as in the above examples, **wouldn't** used for negative intention can stand alone:

He won't help me today (he refuses to help).
He wouldn't help me yesterday (he refused to help).

would cannot be used in this way. So to put a sentence such as 'I will help him today' into the past, we have to replace **will** by another verb:

I wanted to help him yesterday *or* intended to help/offered to help.

c **would** as already noted is also the past equivalent of **will** as used for habits and obstinate insistence:

They *would wait* for us at the bridge (= used to wait).
She *would come* though we warned her that it would be rough (= insisted on coming).

d **would** can express a polite request:

Would you please let me know about this as soon as possible.
Would you mind waiting a moment, please.

e **would** is used after **wish**:

i to express a not very hopeful wish concerning the future:

I wish it would stop raining.

will is never used after **wish**.

ii to express regret that another person is unwilling to do something that the speaker approves of, or persists in doing something that the speaker disapproves of:

I wish he would go to dances = I'm sorry he doesn't go to dances (I wish he went *would also be possible here*).
I wish he wouldn't keep talking about his illnesses = I'm sorry he does keep talking about them (I wish he didn't *would also be possible*).

(For other constructions with **wish** see **271**.)

f **would** can be used similarly after **if only** (see **222**).

Shall

Apart from its use in the future tense **shall** can be used as follows:

231 **shall I? shall we?** in requests for orders or advice, offers, suggestions:

a How shall I cook it? Where shall we put this?

b When the request is for advice only either **shall** or **should** may be used:

Which one shall I buy? *or* Which one should I buy?

c offers:

Shall I wait for you? Shall I help you to pack?

d suggestions:

Shall we meet at the theatre? (See **279** for **shall I/we?** in reported speech.)

232 **shall** in the 2nd and 3rd persons is used:

a To express the subject's intention to perform a certain action or to cause it to be performed.

b To express a command.

Both these uses are old-fashioned and formal and normally avoided in modern English.

a Examples of **shall** used to express the speaker's intention:

You shall have a sweet (I'll give you a sweet
or I'll see that you get a sweet).
He shan't come here (I won't let him come).
They shall not pass (We won't let them pass).

In the past, i.e. in indirect speech, it is usually necessary to change the wording:

He said, 'You shall have a sweet.' = He promised me a sweet.

b Examples of **shall** used to express a command:

Yachts shall go round the course, passing the marks in the correct order (yacht-racing rules).
Members shall enter the names of their guests in the book provided (club rules).

This construction is chiefly used in regulations or legal documents. In less formal English **must** or **are to** would be used instead of **shall** in the above sentences.
When sentences of this type are reported in indirect speech, **shall** is usually replaced by **must, have/had to, is/was to**:

Regulations: Each competitor shall wear a number.
The regulations say that each competitor must/has to/is to/wear a number.
The regulations said that each competitor must/had to/was to/wear a number.

should would be grammatically possible here but would weaken the idea of command.

c **shall you?** is sometimes used in written English as an alternative to the future continuous tense:

Shall you go? *can replace* Will you be going?

shall you? is an old-fashioned form which is coming back into use, possibly because it is shorter and neater than the future continuous tense.

Should

233 **should** is used to express duty and to indicate a correct or sensible action

It is therefore a usual way of expressing advice:

You should pay your debts (duty).
You shouldn't tell lies (duty).
You should eat more fruit (advice).
You've spelt it wrong. There should be another 's' (correct action).
Shops should remain open till later in the evening (sensible action).
They shouldn't allow parking in this street; it's too narrow.

should here has the same meaning as **ought** (see **155**). It is less forceful than **must** or **have to** because no authority is involved.
should + present infinitive has a present or future meaning:

You should go today/tomorrow.

It need not change in indirect speech:

He said I should go that day/the next day.

should + perfect infinitive (you should have gone) expresses a past unfulfilled duty or sensible action which was not performed:

You should have stopped at the red lights (but you didn't).

Similarly in the negative:

You shouldn't have been rude to him (but you were rude).

234 **that . . . should** can be used after certain verbs as an alternative to a gerund or infinitive construction

a **suggest, propose insist (on)** take either gerund or **that . . . should**:

Tom suggested selling the house.
Tom suggested *my selling* the house (possessive adjective + gerund).
Tom suggested *that I should sell* the house (pronoun + **should**).
Tom suggested that *Ann should sell* the house (noun + **should**).

Tom suggested that the house should be sold (passive construction with **should**).

i.e. **should** is usual when the subject of the suggested action is expressed by a noun. (A noun in the possessive case + gerund: *He suggested Ann's selling the house*, is possible but less usual.) **should** is also the usual way of expressing a suggestion in the passive voice. This rule applies also to **b, c,** below.

Similarly:

He insisted on being present when work started.
He insisted that nothing should start till he arrived.

He proposed (our) postponing the trip.
He proposed that we/Ann and I should postpone the trip.
He proposed that the trip should be postponed.

b **recommend, advise** can take either gerund or infinitive or **should**:

He recommended (my) buying new tyres.
He recommended me/Tom and me to buy new tyres.
He recommended that I/that Tom and I should buy new tyres.
He recommended that new tyres should be bought.

c **determined, was determined, agreed,** and **demanded** take either infinitive or **should**:

He determined/was determined to get there first.
He determined/was determined that nobody should get there before him.
He agreed to divide the prize between Tom and Ann.
He agreed that Tom and Ann should share the prize.
He agreed that the prize should be shared between Tom and Ann.

With the present tenses of these verbs **that . . . shall** is possible, but the infinitive construction is generally preferred.

d **arrange, stipulate** and **be anxious** can be followed by **for** + object + infinitive or a **should** construction:

I am anxious for nobody to know where I am going.
I am anxious that nobody should know where I am going.

He was anxious for everyone to have a chance to vote.
He was anxious that everyone should have a chance to vote.

He arranged for me to study with his own children.
He arranged that I should study with his own children.

He stipulated for the best materials to be used.
He stipulated that the best materials should be used.

e **order, command, urge** normally take an object + infinitive construction:

He urged the committee to buy the site.

But **that . . . should** is sometimes used, particularly in the passive:

He urged that the site should be bought.
He ordered Tom to go (he spoke directly to Tom).
He ordered that Tom should go (he probably told someone else to tell Tom).

He commanded the men to shut the gates.
He commanded that the men should shut the gates.
He commanded that the gates should be shut.

In the above constructions the **should** is sometimes omitted, particularly before the verb **be**:

He proposed that Sir Francis (should) be made a freeman of the city.

235 **that . . . should** after **it is/was** + certain adjectives

a **that . . . should** can be used after **it is/was necessary, advisable, essential, better, vital, important**, after **right, fair, natural, just** (these are often preceded by **only**) and after **reasonable**, as an alternative to a **for** + infinitive construction:

It is better for him to hear it from you.
that he should hear it from you.
It is essential for him to be prepared for this.
that he should be prepared for this.

should is sometimes omitted as shown in **234**:

It is essential that he be prepared.

Other examples:

We felt that it was only right that she should have a share.
It is advisable that everyone should have a map.

b **that . . . should** can be used after **it is/was strange, odd, surprising, amazing, annoying, ridiculous, ludicrous, absurd** and similar adjectives as an alternative to **that** + present/past tense:

It is ridiculous that we should be short of water in a country where it is always raining.
It is strange that the car should break down today in exactly the same place where it broke down yesterday.

The perfect infinitive is sometimes used when referring to past events:

It is amazing that she should have said nothing about the murder (amazing that she said).

236 Other uses of **should**

a After **don't know why/see no reason why/can't think why** &c. when the speaker queries the reasonableness or justice of an assumption:

I don't know why you should think that I did it.

The perfect infinitive is usual when the assumption was in the past:

I can't think why he should have said that it was my fault.

b Idiomatically with **who, where, what** in dramatic expressions of surprise:

What should I find but an enormous spider!

Quite often the surprise is embarrassing:

Who should come in but his first wife!

Note that both these types of expression are rather similar to those in **235b** and could be rewritten:

It is extraordinary that you should think that.
It was surprising/embarrassing that his first wife should come in.

c After **lest** and sometimes after **in case**:

i **lest** is sometimes placed after expressions of fear or anxiety:

He was terrified lest he should slip on the icy rocks.

The perfect infinitive is used when the anxiety concerns a past action:

She began to be worried lest he should have met with some accident.

ii **lest** can also be used in purpose clauses to mean 'for fear that':

He dared not spend the money lest someone should ask where he had got it.

in case, which is more usual than **lest** here, can be followed by **should** or by an ordinary tense:

in case someone should ask/someone asked

d **should** is sometimes used in purpose clauses as an alternative to **would/could**:

He wore a mask so that no one should recognize him.

e To express an assumption:

He should be there by now = it is reasonable to assume this.
He should have finished by now (**should** + perfect infinitive).

These assumptions are slightly less confident than assumptions with **will**:

He will be there = I am quite certain of this.

Note however that **should** is not used when the action assumed is displeasing or inconvenient to the speaker:

Let's not go shopping today. The shops **will** be crowded (**should** could not replace **will**).

but Let's go early tomorrow when they **will/should** be fairly empty.

f In conditional sentences instead of the present tense:

If you should decide to go on horseback remember to bring food for the horses.

g In indirect commands when the recipient of the command is not necessarily addressed directly:

He ordered that Tom should leave the house (see **281b** and **c**).

22 The Infinitive

237 Verbs followed by the infinitive

The most useful of these are: learn, remember, forget, promise, swear, consent, agree, neglect, refuse, propose, regret, try, endeavour, attempt, fail, care, hope, hesitate, prepare, decide, determine, undertake, manage, arrange, cease, seem:

He promised to obey me. We hope to start tomorrow.

There are also the auxiliaries: be, have, will, shall, can, ought, need, dare, do, used, and must (of these **will, shall, can, do,** and **must** are followed by the infinitive without **to**):

We'll have to hurry. You should try again.

and the following verbs when used with **how**: discover, wonder, find out, understand, know and explain:

I discovered how to start the engine.
He explained how to use the parachute.

Note that remember, propose, regret, attempt and try can also be followed by a gerund (see **256**).

238 Verbs followed by the infinitive or by object + infinitive

The most important of these are: want, wish, love, hate, like, prefer, ask, help, expect, beg, mean, intend:

I want to go.	I want you to go.
I asked to speak to the manager.	I asked her to speak to the manager.
They helped to push the car.	They helped us to push the car.
I expect to be there.	I expect him to be there.

Note that **expect** + infinitive merely expresses a thought about the future, so that 'I expect to be there' means 'I think that I shall be there'. **expect** + personal object + infinitive may have this meaning; so that 'I expect him to be there' can mean 'I think that he will be there', but it very often means, 'I think it is his duty to be there/I shall be annoyed if he is not there.' **expect** + non-personal object + infinitive can sometimes have this second meaning:

He expects supper to be ready when he comes home from work = He expects his wife to have it ready &c.

love and **hate** are used with object + infinitive only in colloquial English:

I'd hate my husband to know about this.

Note that when a verb + object + infinitive construction is put into the passive it becomes subject + passive verb + infinitive:

Active: He asked me to help.
Passive: I was asked to help ('by him' should not be added).
Active: They expect her to be ready.
Passive: She is expected to be ready.

love, like, hate, mean, intend, and **it wants** (= **requires**) can also be followed by a gerund, see **256**.
wish can be followed by **that** + a past, past perfect or conditional tense (see **271**. **want,** however, can never be followed by **that**).

239 Verbs followed by object + infinitive

a The most important of these are: tell, order, invite, oblige, compel, allow, permit, teach, instruct, warn, urge, advise, tempt, encourage, request, forbid, show how, remind:

He told us to meet him here. She showed them how to open the safe.

Passive equivalents:

We were told to meet him here. They were shown how to open the safe.

b There are also the verbs of sensation **see, feel, hear** &c., the verbs **watch,** and **make, let** and **bid,** all of which take the infinitive without **to:**

I heard her leave the house. I saw him pick it up.
They made us work all night. He let them go.

In the passive the **to** is normally retained except after **let:**

She was heard to leave the house. He was seen to pick it up.
We were made to work all night.
but They were let go.

Note that verbs of sensation can be followed also by an **-ing** form (the present participle), so that we can say:

I heard her coming in *or* I heard her come in.

The infinitive implies that the action is complete. The present participle can be used for both complete and incomplete actions. Therefore: 'I heard him tell his class what to do in case of fire' would imply that I heard all the instructions, whereas if I say, 'I heard him telling his class what to do in case of fire', it is not clear whether I heard all the instructions or only part of them.
The participle is therefore the more usual form but the infinitive is necessary if we wish to emphasize that the action has been performed. Infinitives are also preferred when there is a series of actions:

I saw him enter the room, open a drawer and take out a revolver.

advise, allow, permit can be followed also by the gerund (see **256**).

240 Verbs and expressions followed by the infinitive without to

a **will, shall, can, do, must, may, let**

b the expressions **would rather** (see **272**), **would sooner, rather than, sooner than, had better**:

Tom: You had better tell him that you have lost it.
Ann: I would rather/sooner wait a few days; it may turn up.

Rather/sooner than see it wasted, his mother ate it herself (= she didn't want to see it wasted so she ate it herself).

c **need** and **dare** except when they are conjugated with **do** or **will/would**:

You need not say anything.
but You won't need to say anything.
You don't need to say anything.
I dare not wake him.
but I don't/didn't dare (to) wake him (with **dare** the **to** can be omitted).
I wouldn't dare to interrupt them.

d Verbs of sensation, **make** and **bid** except in the passive, and **watch**:

I saw him hide the box *but* He was seen to hide it.
He made them hurry *but* They were made to hurry.
He bade me hold my tongue. She watched me pack.

e **help** may be followed by an infinitive with or without **to**:

He helped me (to) push the car.

f The prepositions **but** and **except** are followed by the infinitive without **to**:

There was nothing to do but wait till he came back.
He will do anything except lend you money.

241 Verbs of knowing and thinking &c.

a **be sure** can be followed by an infinitive or by a construction with **that**, but there is an important difference in meaning:

He is sure to succeed = the speaker believes this.
but He is sure that he will succeed = he believes this himself.

b **think, believe, consider, know, feel, understand, suppose** &c. can be followed by object + **to be**:

I consider him to be the best candidate.

But it is much more common to use **that** + an ordinary tense:

I consider that he is the best candidate.

When however these verbs are used in the passive they are more often followed by an infinitive than by the **that** construction:

He is known to be honest = It is known that he is honest.
He is thought to be the best player = It is thought that he is the best player.

Note, however, that **suppose** when used in the passive often conveys an idea of duty:

You are supposed to know the laws of your own country = it is your duty to know.

The continuous infinitive can also be used:

He is thought to be hiding in the woods = people think that he is hiding.
He is supposed to be washing the car = he should be washing it.

When the thought concerns a previous action we use the perfect infinitive:

They are believed to have landed in America = It is believed that they landed.

suppose + perfect infinitive need not necessarily convey an idea of duty:

They are supposed to have discovered America = It is thought that they did.
but You are supposed to have finished by now *would normally mean* You should have finished (see also **275**.)

c **seem** and **appear** can also be followed by present, continuous or perfect infinitive:

He seems to know us = I think he knows us.
He seems to be waiting for us = I think he is waiting.
There appears to have been a misunderstanding.

Other Uses of the Infinitive

For the **be** + infinitive construction and for **to be about** + infinitive, see **111**.

242 The infinitive is used to express purpose (see also **288**):

He went to London to learn English.
They came in quietly so as not to wake the children.

Note that it is not usual to put an infinitive of purpose after the imperative of **go** and **come**. Instead we usually change the infinitive into another imperative joining the two by **and**, so that we say:

Go and help him *not* Go to help him.
Come and wash up *not* Come to wash up.

see however seems to be an exception to this rule for we can say either:

Come to see me *or* Come and see me.
and Go to see him *or* Go and see him.

for + gerund is used to express the general purpose of things:

A knife is a tool for cutting with.
A chair is a piece of furniture for sitting on.

But when we are considering a particular purpose we use the infinitive:

I want a knife to cut the bread with (to cut this particular loaf).
He hasn't got a chair to sit on (for him to sit on).

243 a The infinitive is used after **only** to express a disappointing sequel

He hurried to the house only to find that it was empty.
= He hurried to the house and was disappointed when he found &c.
He survived the crash only to die in the desert.
= He survived the crash but died.

b The infinitive can be used as a connective link without **only**, and without any idea of misfortune:

He returned home to learn that his daughter had just become engaged.

But this use is mainly confined to such verbs as **learn, find, see, hear, be told** &c., as otherwise there might be confusion between an infinitive used connectively and an infinitive of purpose.

244 The infinitive can be used after **the first, the second** &c., **the last, the only** and sometimes after superlatives to replace a relative clause (see also **54a**)

He loves parties; he is always the first to come and the last to leave (= the first who comes and the last who leaves).
He is the second man to be killed in this way (= the second man who was killed).
She was the only one to survive the crash (the only one who survived).

the first, last &c., can be used here either by themselves, as in the first example, or followed by a noun or pronoun, as in the other examples.
Note the infinitive here has an *active* meaning. When a passive sense is required a passive infinitive is used:

the best play to be performed that year (= the best play that was performed)

Compare this with:

the best play to perform (= the best play for you to perform/the play you should perform, see **245**)

245 The infinitive can be placed after nouns and pronouns to show how they can be used or what is to be done with them (see also **54b**)

I have letters to write (= that I must write).
Would you like something to drink?
She said, 'I can't go to the party; I haven't anything to wear' (that I can wear).
A house to let = a house that the owner wants to let.

Note that the (active) infinitive here has a *passive* meaning (compare with **244** above). The passive infinitive is possible after **there is/are** + noun/pronoun: i.e. we can say:

There are sheets to be mended *or* sheets to mend.

But the active infinitive is more usual. Note that the passive infinitive conveys only the idea of duty:

sheets to be mended *could mean only* sheets that must be mended,
but books to read *could mean* books that I must read
or books that I can read

The infinitive can be used in the same way with prepositions:

someone *to talk to* a tool *to open* it *with* a case *to keep* my records *in*
something *to talk about* a cup *to drink out of*
a pen *to write with* a table *to write on*

(See **77** for the position of prepositions and **242** for the difference between the infinitive and **for** + gerund.)

246 Infinitive after adjective + noun/pronoun

a after **it is/was** + adjective + **of you/him** &c.:

It is good of you to help me.
It was clever of him to find his way here.
It was brave of the policemen to tackle the armed man.

wise, kind, good, nice, honest, generous, cowardly, selfish, silly, stupid, wicked, careless &c., can also be used in this way.

b after **it/that** + **is/was/would be** + adjective + noun:

That's a stupid place to park a car.
That would be a very rude thing to say.
It was a queer time to choose.

Adjectives in (**a**) above can be used here, and also strange, crazy, mad, odd, funny (= odd), extraordinary, astonishing, amazing, pointless, ridiculous &c. Comments of this type can also be expressed as exclamations:

What a terrible night to be out in!
What a funny name to give a dog!
What an odd place for a picnic!

The adjective is often omitted in expressions of criticism or disapproval:

What a (silly) way to bring up a child!

247 The infinitive used after adjectives

a after adjectives expressing emotion:

I was delighted to see him.
He'll be angry to find that nothing has been done.
I'm sorry to say I can't find your key anywhere.

Other adjectives of this type are: happy, glad, relieved, astonished, amazed, surprised, horrified, disgusted, disappointed, sad.

it is/was + adjective can also be followed by an infinitive in such sentences as:

It is lovely to see miles and miles of open country.
It was dreadful to find oneself alone in such a place.
It was dreadful for him to find himself alone in such a place.
It is easy to talk; you haven't got to make the decision.
It is easy for you to talk; you haven't got to make the decision.

for + noun/pronoun can usually be added, as shown. This construction is really a rearrangement of a sentence whose subject is an infinitive or an infinitive phrase. It would be possible in each case to begin with the infinitive:

To see miles and miles of open country is lovely.
To find oneself alone in such a place was dreadful.

But the **it is/was** construction is much the more usual (see **249**).

c Sentences of the above type can also follow a verb such as **find, think**:

It was easy for him to leave the house unobserved.
He found that it was easy to leave the house unobserved.
or He found it easy to leave &c.

He thought that it was amusing to have two different identities.
or He thought it amusing to have &c.

d An infinitive is often placed after the adjectives **easy, hard, difficult, awkward, impossible** &c.:

The book is easy to read.
This car is hard to park.
His actions are impossible to justify.

248 The infinitive after too, enough and so . . . as

a too + adjective/adverb + infinitive

i Infinitives used in this way can have an *active* meaning:

You are too young to understand (= you don't understand because you are too young).
It's too soon to say if the scheme will work (= we cannot say yet).
It was too late to do anything (= he couldn't do anything; it was too late).

for + noun/pronoun could be added to the last two examples:

It is too soon for us to say. It was too late for him to do anything.

Example of **too** + adverb:

He works too slowly to be much use to me (= so slowly that he isn't much use).

ii Infinitives can also be used in this way a *passive* meaning:

The coffee is too hot; we cannot drink *it* *could be expressed*
The coffee is too hot to drink (too hot to be drunk).

Notice that **it**, the object of **drink**, disappears in the **too** + infinitive con-truction, because the infinitive though active in form is passive in meaning. Similarly:

The case is too heavy to carry (too heavy to be carried).

For + noun/pronoun can be added as above:

The case is too heavy for her to carry.

Note that the infinitive can be followed by a preposition:

The ice is too thin to walk on (too thin to be walked on).
The windows were too dirty to see through.

b adjective/adverb + **enough** + infinitive

Here again the infinitive can have either an active or a passive meaning, and can be preceded when necessary by **for** + noun/pronoun:

You are old enough to know better (= you should know better at your age).
She didn't hit him hard enough to knock him down.
He was intelligent enough to turn off the gas.

In the three examples above the infinitive is used in an active sense. In the following example it is used in a passive sense and with a preposition:

The light wasn't strong enough (for us) to read by (= we couldn't read by the light; it wasn't strong enough).

enough may be followed by a noun:

He doesn't earn enough money to live on.
We hadn't enough time to do it properly.

have + **enough** + noun here is often replaceable by **have** + **the** + **noun**:

We hadn't the time to do it properly.
He had the sense to keep his mouth shut.

c **so** + adjective/adverb + **as** + infinitive:

He was so foolish as to leave his car unlocked.
He spoke so intolerantly as to annoy everybody.

This is an alternative to the **enough** construction shown in (b) above; but note that 'He was foolish enough to leave his car unlocked' can mean either that he did it or merely that he was capable of doing it, while the **so . . . as** construction implies that he actually did it. The **so . . . as** construction is not however very often used except as a form of request:

Would you be so kind *as* to forward my letters.

It is important not to forget the **as**.

249 The infinitive as subject

An infinitive or an infinitive phrase can be the subject of a verb, and can be placed first in the usual way:

To hesitate would have been fatal.
To obey the laws is everyone's duty.
To save money now is practically impossible.
To lean out of the window is dangerous.

But it is more usual to place the pronoun **it** first, and move the infinitive or infinitive phrase to the end of the sentence:

It would have been fatal to hesitate.
It is everyone's duty to obey the laws.
It is practically impossible to save money now.
It is dangerous to lean out of the window.

The gerund can be used instead of the infinitive when the action is being considered in a general sense, but it is always safe to use an infinitive. When we wish to refer to one particular action we must use the infinitive:

He said, 'Do come with me.' It was impossible *to refuse.*

(Here we are referring to one particular action, so the gerund is not possible.)

but It is not always easy *to refuse* invitations *can be replaced by*
Refusing invitations is not always easy.

(Here the action is considered in a general sense, and either gerund or infinitive is possible.) (See also 253.)

Infinitives are used in some well-known sayings:

To know all is to forgive all. To err is human, to forgive divine.
To work is to pray.

The perfect infinitive can also be used as subject of a sentence:

To have made the same mistake twice was unforgivable.

Similarly with **it** first:

It is better to have loved and lost than never to have loved at all.

250 The infinitive represented by its to

An infinitive can be represented by **to** alone to avoid repetition. This is chiefly done after such verbs as: **want, wish, like, hate, hope, try**, after the auxiliaries: **have, ought, need**, and with **used, be able**, and the **going to** form:

Did you see the Pyramids?
No, I wanted to (see them) but there wasn't time.

I didn't mean to take a taxi but I had to (take one) as I was late.

Would you like to come with me? Yes, I'd love to.

He wanted to go but he wasn't able to.

Did you get a ticket?
No, I tried to, but there weren't any left.

Do you do your own housework?
I used to, but now I've got a maid.

Have you fed the dog?
No, but I'm just going to.

The Perfect Infinitive

This is formed with the infinitive of **have** and the past participle:

to have worked to have spoken

251 Use with auxiliary verbs

a With **should**, **would**, **might**, and **could** to form the perfect conditional, which is used in the third type of conditional sentence (see **216c**):

If I had seen her I should have invited her.

b With **should** or **ought** to express unfulfilled obligation:

He should have helped her (but he didn't).
I shouldn't have gone out (but I did).
He oughtn't to have gone near that bull (but he did). (See **156**, **233**.)

c With **was**, **were** to express an unfulfilled plan or arrangement (see **111b**):

The house was to have been ready today but as there has been a builders' strike it is still only half finished.

d With **should/would like** to express an unfulfilled wish:

I should like to have seen it (but it wasn't possible).

This could also be expressed:

I should have liked to see it *or* I should have liked to have seen it.

i.e. we can put either or both verbs into the perfect infinitive without changing the meaning.

would is used in the second and third person:

He would like to have emigrated (but his wife successfully opposed the idea).

e With **could** to express past unused ability:

I could have climbed that mountain (but I didn't).
He could have helped me (but he didn't). (See also **132**.)

f With **needn't** to express an unnecessary past action (see also **149**):

We needn't have hurried. Now we are too early.
You needn't have cooked it. We could have eaten it raw.

g With **may/might** in speculations about past actions:

He may have come = It is possible that he came.
He might have come = It is possible that he came (the use of **might** increases the doubt).
He may not/might not have come = It is possible that he didn't come.

might must be used when the main verb is in the past:

She said that he mightn't have come (see also **126b**).

h With **can't, couldn't,** and **must** to express deductions

can't or **couldn't** + perfect infinitive expresses negative deduction (see **153**).

There is no difference in meaning between **can't** and **couldn't** used in this way, but **couldn't** must, of course, be used when the main verb is in a past tense:

He can't/couldn't have moved the piano himself. It takes two men to lift it.
but We knew he couldn't have crossed the river, because the bridge was broken and there was no boat.

i **must** + perfect infinitive expresses an affirmative deduction (see **152**):

Someone must have been here recently; these ashes are still warm.
He must have come this way; here are his footprints.

23 The Gerund

252 Form and use

The gerund has exactly the same form as the present participle:

running, working, speaking &c.

It can be used in the following ways:

1 as subject of a sentence
2 after prepositions
3 after certain verbs
4 in noun compounds (**11c**) e.g. a diving board (a board for diving off).

253 The gerund as subject

As already seen (**249**), either infinitive or gerund can be the subject of a sentence when an action is being considered in a general sense. We can say:

It is easier to read French than to speak it.
or Reading French is easier than speaking it.

(For gerund or infinitive after **than** see **291b**.)

There is no difference between these forms, but the gerund usually implies that the speaker or person addressed has had personal experience of the action, having performed it himself probably more than once, i.e. in the second of the above examples we get the impression that the speaker can, or has tried to, read and speak French while the speaker in the first example *may* only be expressing an opinion or theory.
Similarly in the sentences:

It requires patience to look after children *and* Looking after children requires patience

the second implies that the speaker has looked after children.

The gerund can also imply that the action is being considered as a habit:
Eating between meals is bad for the figure *and* It is bad for the figure to eat between meals

are both correct but the first emphasizes the idea of habit.

The gerund is used in short prohibitions:
No smoking. No loitering. No spitting.

But these cannot be followed by an object, so prohibitions involving an object are usually expressed by an imperative:
Do not touch these wires. Do not feed the lions.

Gerunds are used in the saying 'Seeing is believing'.

254 Gerunds after prepositions

a When a verb is placed immediately after a preposition the gerund form must be used:

He insisted on seeing her. I have no objection to hearing your story again.
Can you touch your toes without bending your knees?
He is good at telling lies. She is fond of climbing.
He was accused of smuggling.
They were charged with driving to the public danger.
He was fined for being drunk in charge of a car.
I am quite used to waiting in queues.
He prefers being neutral to taking sides.
A corkscrew is a tool for taking corks out of bottles.
Do you feel like going for a swim?
What about leaving it here and collecting it on the way back?
He is thinking of emigrating. I'm sorry for keeping you waiting.
His wife raised the money by selling her jewellery.
After pocketing everything of value the thieves set fire to the place.

b A number of verb + preposition/adverb combinations take the gerund. The most common of these are: **be for/against, care for, give up, keep on, leave off, look forward to, put off, see about, take to** (for **go on** see **258g**):

I don't care for standing in queues.
He took to ringing us up in the middle of the night.
Eventually the dogs left off barking.
I have seen the film; now I am looking forward to reading the book.

255 The word **to**

This word often causes confusion as it can be either (**a**) a part of an infinitive, or (**b**), a preposition:

a **to** placed after the auxiliary verbs **be, have, ought, used** and after **going** (in expressions such as the **going to** form) is part of the infinitive of the following verb and is only added to remind students that the preceding verb takes the full infinitive, i.e. the infinitive with **to.**

to is often also placed after **love, like, hate, want, try, hope, mean** and some others (see **250**) to avoid repetition of an infinitive already mentioned:

Did you buy cheese?
No. I meant *to*, but the shop was shut (I meant to buy some).

b Otherwise **to** placed after a verb will probably be a preposition and will be followed by noun/pronoun or gerund. Note particularly the following expressions: **look forward to, take to, be accustomed to, be used to:**

I am looking forward to my holidays/to next weekend/to it.
I am looking forward to *seeing* you.
I am used to heat/hard work/bad food/noise/dust/it.
I am used to *standing* in queues.

Be careful not to confuse **I used to/he used to** &c., which expresses a past habit or routine (e.g. They used to burn coal; now they burn oil fuel only) with **I am used to/he is used to** &c., which means **I am accustomed to/familiar with:**

I am used to the cold (it doesn't worry me).
He is used to working at night (he doesn't mind it).

A good way of finding out whether a **to** is a preposition or a part of an infinitive is to see if it is possible to put a noun/pronoun after it. For example a noun/pronoun could be placed after **I am accustomed to:**

I am accustomed to it/accustomed to the dark.

This **to** therefore is a preposition, and verbs used after it must be gerunds. If, however, we put a noun/pronoun after **have to**, it would not make sense. This **to** therefore is part of an infinitive.

256 The gerund must be used after the following verbs

Stop, finish, dread, detest, prevent, avoid, risk, admit, deny, recollect, resent, delay, postpone, defer, enjoy, fancy, imagine, forgive, pardon, excuse, suggest, keep (= continue), understand, mind (= object), consider, miss, involve, resist, save (= save oneself the trouble of), anticipate.
The gerund is used also after the expressions: **can't stand** (= endure), **can't help** (= prevent/avoid), **it's no use/no good**, and after the adjective **worth:**

He didn't want to risk getting wet as he had only one suit.
Try to avoid travelling in the rush hour.
He denied having been there (perfect gerund, see **261**).
He resented being punished (passive gerund, see **262**).
They tried to prevent the river (from) flooding the town.
Forgive my interrupting you/Forgive me for interrupting you.
She suggested waiting till dawn. I couldn't help laughing.
It's no use looking through the keyhole. I couldn't resist buying one.
Fancy having to get up at five a.m. every day!
Putting in a new window will involve (mean) cutting away part of the roof.
She dreads getting old.
If we buy plenty of food now it will save shopping again this week.
Most women enjoy shopping. He detests writing letters.
Would you mind waiting a few minutes? Would you consider emigrating?
I can't understand his resigning his job (= I can't understand why he resigned).
I don't anticipate meeting any opposition.
I came late and missed seeing Tom winning the high jump.
There's nothing here worth buying.
He postponed making a decision till he had been given more information.
Stop talking.

'Stop' meaning 'cease', as above, must be followed by the gerund. But 'stop' meaning 'halt' can be followed by an infinitive of purpose:

I stopped (halted) to speak to her.

Note also the expression 'I dread to think':

I dread to think what will happen if we don't get there in time.

This is much the same as, 'I am afraid to think (so I don't think)' (see **258g**).

257 The verb **mind**

a This verb is used chiefly in the interrogative and negative:

Would you mind waiting a moment? I don't mind walking.

b It can be followed directly by a gerund, in which case the gerund refers to the subject; or by a noun or possessive adjective + gerund, in which case the gerund refers to the person represented by the noun or the possessive adjective:

I don't mind living here (I live here and don't object to it).
I don't mind *his* living here (he lives here and I don't object to this).
He didn't mind leaving home (he left home quite happily).
He didn't mind Ann leaving home (Ann left and he was quite happy about it; see **260b** for case of noun).

c **Would you mind?** is one of the most usual ways of making a request:

Would you mind not smoking? (Please don't smoke.)
Would you mind moving your car? (Please move it.)

Note change of meaning when a possessive adjective precedes the gerund:

Would you mind *my* moving your car? = Would you object if I moved it? (This is not a request but a polite query.)
Do you mind *if I move it*? *is a possible alternative to* Would you mind my moving it?
but Do you mind *my moving it*? *may mean that the action has already started.*

As seen above, **mind** can be followed by an **if**-clause. It can never be followed by an infinitive.
Section **b** above applies also to the majority of verbs listed in **256**, but not to verbs meaning 'forgive'.
The accusative personal pronoun can be used with gerunds instead of a possessive adjective (see **260a**).

258 Either gerund or infinitive can be used after the following verbs:

a begin, start, continue
b attempt, intend, can't bear
c love, like, hate, prefer,
d remember, regret
e permit, allow, advise, recommend
f it needs/requires/wants
g try, propose, mean, go on, used to, be afraid (of)

a After **begin, start** and **continue** either infinitive or gerund may be used without any difference, but if the verb following **begin/start** is a verb of **knowing** or **understanding** it is usually put into the infinitive:

I began working *or* I began to work *but* I began to understand (no alternative).

b After **attempt, intend, can't bear** gerunds are possible but infinitives are more usual:

Don't attempt to do it by yourself *is more usual than* Don't attempt doing it by yourself.

c **love, like (= enjoy), hate, prefer** when used in the conditional are followed by the infinitive:

Would you like to come with me or would you prefer to stay here?
I'd love to come with you. I'd hate to spend all my life here.

When used in the present or past they are usually followed by the gerund:

I like riding. I liked riding.
He hates waiting for buses. He hated waiting.
He prefers walking to bicycling.

But the infinitive is not impossible and is particularly common in the USA:

They love/loved to run on the sands.

Note however that **like** can also mean 'think wise or right,' and is then always followed by the infinitive:

She likes them to play in the garden (she thinks they are safe there).
I like to go to the dentist twice a year (I think this wise).

Compare this with 'I like going to the dentist', which implies that I enjoy my visits.

Similarly:

I don't like to go = I don't think it right to go.
while I don't like going = I don't enjoy going.

Notice also another difference between these two negative forms:

I don't like to go *usually means* I don't go (because I don't think it right).
while I don't like going *usually means* I go, although I don't enjoy it.

d **remember/regret** are used with the gerund when the verb expressed by the gerund precedes the **remember/regret**:

I remember seeing my grandmother wearing a hat just like that (**seeing** is the first action; **remembering** the second).
I regret going there (I went there; now I am sorry I went).

The infinitive is used for an action which follows the **remember/regret**:

I'll remember to post your letter. He remembered to shut the door.
I regret to say that we have no news for you.

e After **permit, allow, advise, recommend** the infinitive is used if the person concerned is mentioned. If the person is not mentioned the gerund is used:

I don't allow him to smoke a pipe *but* I don't allow smoking.

The gerund after **allow** and **permit** cannot have an object.

f **it needs/wants/requires** can be followed either by the gerund or by the passive infinitive, the gerund being the more usual:

The grass wants cutting *or* wants to be cut.
These machines need regulating *or* need to be regulated.

g **try, propose, mean, go on, be afraid (of), used to** have different meanings according to whether they are used with gerund or infinitive.
try usually means **attempt** and is followed by the infinitive:

They tried to put wire netting all round the garden = they made this attempt.

The sentence doesn't tell us whether they succeeded or not.
try can also mean **make the experiment** and is then followed by the gerund:

They tried putting wire netting all round the garden.

This means that they put wire netting round the garden to see if it would solve their problem (presumably they were trying to keep out rabbits and foxes). We know that they succeeded in performing the main action; what we don't know is whether this action had the desired effect, i.e. kept the foxes out.

propose meaning **intend** usually takes the infinitive:

I propose to start tomorrow.

propose meaning **suggest** takes the gerund:

I propose waiting till the police get here.

mean meaning **intend** takes the infinitive:

I mean to get to the top by sunrise.

mean meaning **involve** (used only with an impersonal subject) takes the gerund:

He is determined to get a seat for the ballet even if it means standing in a queue all night.

go on = **continue** and is normally followed by the gerund. But it is used with an infinitive, usually of a verb like **tell, talk, explain** &c. when the speaker continues talking about the same topic but introduces a new aspect of it:

He began by showing us where the island was and went on to tell us about its climate.

Compare 'He went on talking about his accident', which implies that he had been talking about it before with: 'He went on to talk about his accident', which implies that he had been speaking about himself or his journey but that the accident was being introduced for the first time.

used to + infinitive expresses a past habit:

I used to smoke (implies that I don't smoke now).

to be used to = **to be accustomed to** and takes the gerund/noun/pronoun:

I am used to standing in queues (so I don't mind it).

be afraid of + gerund merely expresses a fear. It is normally used with involuntary actions:

He was afraid of falling/being caught/missing his train.

be afraid + infinitive 'I was afraid to move', means that the subject is too frightened to perform the action in the infinitive. Note that these will normally be deliberate actions:

He was afraid to jump so he stayed where he was.
He was afraid to say anything so he kept quiet.

Remember also **stop (257)**.

259 Some other uses of **ing** forms

a Verbs of sensation take the **ing** form, or the infinitive without **to**:

I heard the bombs dropping (*or* drop).
He felt the house shaking (*or* shake).

b After **go** and **come** verbs denoting physical activity and the verb **to shop** are often put into the **ing** form:

They are going swimming. We went shopping yesterday.
I am going riding this afternoon. I wanted him to come sailing with me.

c Notice also the expressions: keep someone waiting/working/standing &c., catch someone doing something (usually something wrong):

I caught him stealing my apples.

The **ing** form in the above cases is not the gerund but the present participle. This, however, is a mere technical difference, which may be ignored for practical purposes.

d Note also the construction spend/waste time/hours/minutes/days/ + **ing**:

We wasted hours looking for the house.
They spent three years working on the dictionary.

260 **a** Pronouns and possessive adjectives with gerunds

In formal English the possessive adjective is used with the gerund, but in spoken and less formal English, it is very common to use the accusative personal pronoun instead:

She doesn't mind my (*or* me) coming in late.
It's no use their (*or* them) complaining.
He left the house without our (*or* us) knowing anything about it.

When the **ing** form is a present participle, as in **259**, we have to use the pronoun:

I saw him coming in (no alternative).
He heard me opening the door.
She kept us waiting.

b Nouns with gerunds

Similarly in formal English, nouns denoting persons are put into the possessive case when used with gerunds:

I disliked my mother's interfering in the affair.

But in informal English the genitive is usually dropped:

I disliked my mother interfering.

261 The perfect gerund (having worked, having spoken &c.)

This can be used instead of the present form of the gerund (working, speaking &c.) when we are referring to a past action:

He was accused of deserting his ship *or* He was accused of having deserted his ship.

The perfect gerund is fairly usual after **deny**:

He denied having been there.

Otherwise the present form is much the more usual.

262 The passive gerund

form:

present: being written
past: having been written

He was punished by being sent to bed without any supper.
I remember being taken to Paris as a small child.
The safe showed no signs of having been touched.

24 The Participles

263 The present (or active) participle

Form: the infinitive + **ing**, e.g. working, loving, sitting (see **162**)

Use:

a as an adjective:

running water   floating wreckage   dripping taps   growing crops

b to form the continuous tenses:

he is working   you have been dreaming   we are being followed.

c after verbs of sensation (see **239b**, **259a**):

I saw flames rising and heard people shouting.

d after **go** and **come** (see **259b**):

They are going ski-ing this winter.

and in certain expressions:

keep someone waiting   catch someone doing something

e When two actions by the same subject occur simultaneously it is usually possible to express one of them by a present participle. The participle can be before or after the finite verb:

He rode away. He whistled as he went. = He rode away whistling.
He holds the rope with one hand and stretches out the other to the boy in the water = Holding the rope with one hand, he stretches &c.

f When one action is immediately followed by another by the same subject the first action can often be expressed by a present participle. The participle must be placed first:

He opened the drawer and took out a revolver.
= Opening the drawer he took out a revolver.

She raised the trapdoor and pointed to a flight of steps.
= Raising the trapdoor she pointed to a flight of steps.

We take off our shoes and creep cautiously along the passage.
= Taking off our shoes we creep cautiously along the passage.

It would seem more logical here to use the perfect participle and say 'having opened, having lifted, having taken off', but this is not necessary except when the use of the present participle might lead to ambiguity. 'Eating his dinner he rushed out of the house' would give the impression that he left the house with his plate in his hand. Here therefore it would be better to say 'having eaten his dinner'.

g When the second action forms part of the first, or is a result of it we can express the second action by a present participle:

She went out, slamming the door.
He fired, wounding one of the bandits.
I fell, striking my head against the door and cutting it (here we have three actions, the last two expressed by participles).

The participle need not necessarily have the same subject as the first verb:

The plane crashed, its bombs exploding as it hit the ground.

h The present participle can also replace **as/since/because** + subject + verb, i.e. it can help to explain the action which follows:

Knowing that he wouldn't be able to buy food on his journey he took large supplies with him = As he knew &c.
Fearing that the police would recognize him he never went out in daylight = As he feared &c.

Note that **being** at the beginning of a sentence will normally mean 'as he is/as he was':

Being a student he was naturally interested in museums = *Because/as* he was a student. *It could not mean* *while* he was a student.

The subject of the participle need not be the same as the subject of the following verb:

The *day* being fine, *we* decided to go swimming

but in cases like this the participle must follow its noun/pronoun. 'Being fine the day, we decided' is incorrect, but, 'Being athletic, Tom found the climb quite easy' is all right, as Tom is the subject of both the participle and the following verb.

It is possible to use two or more participles, one after the other:

Realizing that he hadn't enough money and *not wanting* to borrow from his father, he decided to pawn his watch.

Not knowing the language and *having* no friends in the country, he found it impossible to get a job.

264 The perfect participle active

Form: **having** + past participle e.g. having done, having seen

Use: The perfect participle can be used instead of the present participle in sentences of the type shown in **263f** (i.e. where one action is immediately followed by another with the same subject):

Tying one end of the rope to his bed he threw the other end out of the window.
Having tied one end of the rope to his bed he threw the other &c.

The perfect participle emphasizes that the first action is complete before the second one starts but is not normally necessary in combinations of this kind, except when the use of the present participle might lead to confusion:

Reading the instructions, he snatched up the fire extinguisher *might give the impression that the two actions were simultaneous.*

Here, therefore, the perfect participle would be better:

Having read the instructions, he snatched up the fire extinguisher.

The perfect participle is however necessary when there is an interval of time between the two actions:

Having failed twice he didn't want to try again.

It is also used when the first action covered a period of time:

Having been his own boss for such a long time he found it hard to accept orders from another.

265 The past participle (passive) and the perfect participle passive

a Form: the past participle of regular verbs is formed by adding **ed** or **d** to the infinitive e.g. worked, loved.
For the past participle of irregular verbs see **296**.

Use:

i as an adjective:

stolen money   a written report   fallen trees   broken glass

ii to form the perfect tenses/infinitives and participles and the passive voice:

he has seen   to have loved   it was broken

iii the past participle can replace a subject + passive verb just as the present participle can replace a subject + active verb:

She enters. She is accompanied by her mother.
= She enters, accompanied by her mother.

He was aroused by the crash and leapt to his feet.
= Aroused by the crash, he leapt to his feet.

The bridge had been weakened by successive storms and was no longer safe.
= Weakened by successive storms, the bridge &c.
or Having been weakened (see below).

(As) he was convinced that they were trying to poison him he refused to eat anything.
= Convinced that they were trying to poison him, he refused &c.

b The perfect participle passive (**having been** + past participle) is used when it is necessary to emphasize that the action expressed by the participle happened before the action expressed by the next verb:

Having been warned about the bandits, he left his valuables at home. (He had been warned &c.).
Having been bitten twice, the postman refused to deliver our letters unless we chained our dog up. (He had been bitten &c.).

266 Misrelated participles

A participle is considered to belong to the noun/pronoun which precedes it:

Tom, horrified at what he had done, could at first say nothing.
Romeo, believing that Juliet was dead, decided to kill himself.
A man carrying a large parcel got out of the bus.

Note that the participle may be separated from its noun/pronoun by a main verb:

Jones and Smith came in *followed* by their wives.
She rushed past the policeman, *hoping* he wouldn't ask what she had in her suit-case.

If there is no noun/pronoun in this position the participle is considered to belong to the subject of the following main verb:

Stunned by the blow, *Peter* fell heavily (Peter had been stunned).
Believing that he is alone, *Arcite* expresses his thoughts aloud.

If this principle is disregarded confusion results. 'Waiting for a bus a brick fell on my head' makes it appear that the brick was waiting for a bus, which is nonsense. A participle linked in this way to the wrong noun/pronoun is said to be 'misrelated'. The above sentence should be rewritten: 'As I was waiting for a bus a brick fell on my head.'

Other examples of misrelated participles:

When using this machine it must be remembered . . .
Correct form When using this machine you must remember . . .

Believing that I was the only person who knew about this beach, the sight of someone else on it annoyed me very much.
Correct form As I believed I was the only person &c.

267 Present participle adjectives and past participle adjectives

Care must be taken not to confuse these. Present participle adjectives e.g. *amusing*, *tiring*, *horrifying* are active and mean 'having this effect'.
Past participle adjectives e.g. *amused*, *tired*, *bored* are passive, and mean 'affected in this way'.

The play was boring. The audience was bored.

The work was tiring. The workers soon became tired.

The scene was horrifying. The spectators were horrified.

An infuriating woman (she made us furious).
An infuriated woman (something had made her furious).

25 The Imperative

268 The second person imperative

The second person imperative has the same form as the infinitive without **to**:

Work! Come! Go! Write!

The negative is formed by putting **do not (don't)** before the imperative:

Don't work! Don't come!

The pronoun **you** is understood but not normally expressed.
The affirmative imperative can be made more persuasive by putting **do** first:

Do come.

(For indirect commands see **280, 281.**)

269 First and third person imperative

Form: **let** + noun/pronoun + infinitive without **to**:

Let us go/let's go (**let us** is usually contracted).
Let him come. Let them do it.

The negative is formed by putting **not** before the infinitive:

Let's not go.

Third person negatives are very rarely used:

Let them not go *would normally be expressed by* They must not go/I don't want them to go.

(For **let, let's** in indirect speech see **282**).

26 The Subjunctive

270 Present subjunctive

Form: The present subjunctive has exactly the same form as the infinitive: therefore the present subjunctive of **to be** is **be** for all persons, and the present subjunctive of all other verbs is the same as their present tense except that **s** is not added for the third person singular:

The king lives here (simple present tense).
Long live the king! (subjunctive).

Use:

a The present subjunctive is used in certain exclamations to express a wish or hope, very often involving supernatural powers:

God bless you!	God forgive you!	Goodbye! (God be with you)
Heaven help us!	Heaven be praised!	
Damn you!	Curse this fog!	

b It is sometimes used in poetry, either to express a wish or in clauses of condition or concession:

Stevenson: Fair the day *shine* as it shone in my childhood (= may the day shine/I hope it will shine).
Shakespeare: If this *be* error, and upon me proved (if this *is* error).
Byron: Though the heart *be* still as loving (though the heart *is*).

Notice also the phrase **if need be**, which means 'if it is necessary':

If need be we can always bring another car.

c As seen in **234** certain verbs are followed by **should** + infinitive constructions. When the infinitive is **be**, the **should** is sometimes omitted:

He suggested that a petition (should) be drawn up.

The infinitive thus left alone becomes a subjunctive. Sometimes the **should** is omitted before other verbs:

I recommended that each competitor (should) receive £1.

271 Past subjunctives used after **if/if only, as if/though** and after **wish**

Form: The past subjunctive has the same form as the simple past tense in all verbs except **to be**, whose past subjunctive is **were** for all persons (see **219** for use of **were** in conditional sentences). The past perfect subjunctive is the same as the past perfect indicative.

a As shown in **216** the *past* subjunctive can be used after **if** and **if only** to express improbability or unreality *in the present*:

If it rained for six months (improbable)
If we all lived underground (unreal)
If only we had a rope! (unreal)

Past perfect subjunctives are used when the supposition refers to the past:

If it had rained last month (but it didn't rain)
If we had had a rope we could have saved him (but we had no rope)

(For **if only** + **would** see **221**.)

b The past subjunctive can be used similarly after **as if/as though** to indicate unreality or improbability or doubt in the present (there is no difference between **as if** and **as though**):

He behaves as if he owned the place (but he doesn't own it *or* probably doesn't own it *or* we don't know whether he owns it or not).
He talks as though he knew where she was (but he doesn't know *or* he probably doesn't know *or* we don't know whether he knows or not).
He orders me about as if I were his wife (but I am not).

The verb preceding **as if/though** can be put into a past tense without changing the tense of the subjunctive:

He talks/talked as though he knew where she was.

After **as if/though** we use a past perfect when referring to a real or imaginary action in the past:

He talks about Rome as though he had been there himself (but he hasn't *or* probably hasn't *or* we don't know).

Again the verb preceding **as if/though** can be put into a past tense without changing the tense of the subjunctive.

He looks/looked as though he hadn't had a decent meal for a month.

c The past subjunctive is used after **wish** to indicate an unreal situation in the present, so that 'I wish I knew' implies that I don't know.

wish + past subjunctive is really an expression of regret:

I wish I knew = I'm sorry I don't know.
I wish you had time = I'm sorry you haven't time.

wish can be put into the past tense without changing the subjunctive:

He wished he knew = he was sorry he didn't know.

When the action regretted occurred in the past, we use the past perfect:

I wish he hadn't gone = I'm sorry he went.
I wish you hadn't told him = I'm sorry you told him.

As before, **wished** can be used in the same way:

He wished he had taken her advice = he was sorry he hadn't taken it.

Note that this is only one of the uses of **wish**. Normally **wish** is followed by an infinitive and has the same meaning as **want** + infinitive or **would like** + infinitive:

I wish to see the manager = I want to see the manager *or* I would like to see the manager.

But **wish** is slightly more authoritative than **want** or **would like.**

Compare I wish to know (= I want someone to tell me).
with I wish I knew (= I'm sorry I don't know).

(For **wish** + **would** see 230e.)

272 Past subjunctive used after **it is time** + subject and **would rather/sooner** + subject

a After **it is time** we can either use a past subjunctive or a **for** + object + infinitive construction:

It is time we went *or* It is time for us to go.

There is a slight difference in meaning: the **for** + infinitive construction implies that the correct time has arrived; the subjunctive implies that it is already a little late:

Compare It is time for you to start earning your own living (i.e. the proper time has arrived; you have finished your education &c.).
with It is time you started earning your own living (which implies that you have passed the usual age for starting work).

high is sometimes added to make the expression more emphatic:

You are eight years old; it's high time you learnt to tie your own shoes.

b **would sooner/would rather** are followed by the infinitive (without to) when there is no change of subject, i.e. when the subject of **would rather/sooner** is the subject of the action which follows:

Tom would rather go = Tom would prefer to go.
Ann would rather stay = Ann would prefer to stay.

But when the person who expresses the preference is *not* the subject of the action which follows we use **would prefer** + object + infinitive or **would rather/sooner** + subject + past subjunctive:

She wants to fly but I'd rather she went by train (*or* I'd prefer her to go by train).

Similarly:

Child: Can I have my tea on the floor with the cat?
Mother: I'd rather you sat at the table.

27 The Passive Voice

273 a Form

i The passive of an active tense is formed by putting the verb **to be** into the same tense as the active verb and adding the past participle of the active verb:

Active: We *keep* the butter here.
Passive: The butter *is kept* here.

Active: They *broke* the window.
Passive: The window *was broken.*

Active: People *have seen* wolves in the streets.
Passive: Wolves *have been seen* in the streets.

Note the passive of continuous tenses. This sometimes seems difficult because it requires the present continuous form of **to be**, which is not otherwise much used:

Active: They *are repairing* the bridge
Passive: The bridge *is being repaired*

Active: They *were carrying* the injured player to the ambulance.
Passive: The injured player *was being carried* to the ambulance.

Other continuous tenses are exceedingly rarely used in the passive, so that sentences such as:

They have/had been repairing the road
and They will/would be repairing the road

are not normally put into the passive.

ii Auxiliary + infinitive combinations are made passive by using a passive infinitive:

Active: You *must shut* these doors.
Passive: These doors *must be shut.*

Active: You *ought to open* the windows.
Passive: The windows *ought to be opened.*

Active: They *should have told* him (perfect infinitive active).
Passive: He *should have been told* (perfect infinitive passive).

iii The passive gerund is **being** + past participle:

Active: I remember my father *taking* me to the Zoo.
Passive: I remember *being taken* to the Zoo by my father.

iv Students may like to see a table of active tenses and their passive equivalents.

Tense/verb form	*active voice*	*passive voice*
simple present	keeps	is kept
present continuous	is keeping	is being kept
simple past	kept	was kept
past continuous	was keeping	was being kept
present perfect	has kept	has been kept
past perfect	had kept	had been kept
future	will keep	will be kept
conditional	would keep	would be kept
present infinitive	to keep	to be kept
perfect infinitive	to have kept	to have been kept
present participle/gerund	keeping	being kept
perfect participle	having kept	having been kept

b Use

The passive voice is used in English when it is more convenient or interesting to stress the thing done than the doer of it, or when the doer is unknown:

My watch was stolen *is much more usual than* Thieves stole my watch.

Note that in theory a sentence containing a direct and an indirect object, such as 'Someone gave her a bulldog' could have two passive forms:

She was given a bulldog.
A bulldog was given to her.

The first of these is much the more usual, i.e. the *indirect* object becomes the subject of the passive verb.

274 Prepositions with passive verbs

a In a passive sentence the agent, or doer of the action, is very often not mentioned (see **273**). When the agent is mentioned it is preceded by **by**:

Active: Dufy painted this picture.
Passive: This picture was painted by Dufy.

Active: Who wrote it? What caused this crack?
Passive: Who was it written *by*? What was it caused *by*?

Note, however, that the passive form of such sentences as:

Smoke filled the room/Paint covered the lock
will be The room was filled with smoke/The lock was covered with paint.

We are dealing here with the materials used, not with the agents.

b When a verb + preposition + object combination is put into the passive, the preposition will remain immediately after the verb:

Active: We must *write to* him.
Passive: He must be *written to.*

Active: You can *play with* these cubs quite safely.
Passive: These cubs can be *played with* quite safely.

Similarly with verb + preposition/adverb combinations:

Active: They threw away the old newspapers.
Passive: The old newspapers were thrown away.

Active: He looked after the children well.
Passive: The children were well looked after.

275 Infinitive constructions after passive verbs

a after **think, consider, know, acknowledge, believe, understand, find, claim, report, say**

sentences of the type 'People think/consider/know &c. that he is . . .' have two possible passive forms:

i It is thought/considered/known &c. *that he is . . .*
ii He is thought/considered/known &c. *to be . . .*

Similarly:

People said that he was jealous of her.
i = It was said that he was jealous of her.
ii *or* He was said to be jealous of her.

The infinitive construction is the neater of the two. It is chiefly used with **to be** though other infinitives can sometimes be used:

He is thought to have information which will be useful to the police.

When the thought concerns a *previous* action we use the perfect infinitive so that:

People know that he *was* . . .
i = It is known that he was . . .
ii *or* He is known *to have been* . . .

People believed that he was . . .
i = It was believed that he was . . .
ii *or* He was believed *to have been* . . .

This construction can be used with the perfect infinitive of any verb.

b after **suppose**

i **suppose** in the passive can be followed by the present infinitive of any verb but this construction usually conveys an idea of duty and is not therefore normally the equivalent of **suppose** in the active:

You are supposed to know how to drive = it is your duty to know/you should know.
though He is supposed to be in Paris *could mean either* He ought to be there *or* People suppose he is there.

ii **suppose** in the passive can similarly be followed by the perfect infinitive of any verb. This construction may convey an idea of duty but very often does not:

You are supposed to have finished = you should have finished.
but He is supposed to have escaped disguised as a woman = people suppose that he escaped &c.

c Note that an infinitive placed after a passive verb is normally a full infinitive, i.e. an infinitive with **to**:

Active:	We saw them *go* out.	He made us *work*.
Passive:	They were seen *to go* out.	We were made *to work*.

let, however, is used without **to**:

Active:	They let us go.
Passive:	We were let go.

28 Reported Speech

276 Direct and indirect (or reported) speech

There are two ways of relating what a person has said: direct and indirect.

In *direct speech* we repeat the original speaker's exact words:

He said, 'I have lost my umbrella.'

Remarks thus repeated are placed between inverted commas, and a comma or colon is placed immediately before the remark.
Direct speech is found in conversations in books, in plays, and quotations.

In *indirect speech* we give the exact meaning of a remark or speech, without necessarily using the speaker's exact words:

He said that he had lost his umbrella.

Indirect speech is normally used in conversation, though direct speech is sometimes employed here to give a more dramatic effect. When we turn direct speech into indirect, some changes are usually necessary. These are most easily studied by considering statements, questions, and commands separately.

Statements in indirect speech: tense changes necessary.

When the introductory verb (**say, tell, remark** &c.), is in the present, present perfect or future, direct statements can be reported without any changes of tense:

He *says*, 'The train *will* be late.' = He *says* the train *will* be late.

But when the introductory verb is in the past tense, which it usually is, the following tense changes are necessary:

a The future, future continuous, simple present, present continuous, present perfect and present perfect continuous tenses change as follows:

Direct speech		*Indirect speech*
future	*to*	conditional
future continuous	*to*	conditional continuous
simple present	*to*	simple past
present continuous	*to*	past continuous
present perfect	*to*	past perfect
present perfect continuous	*to*	past perfect continuous

He said, 'Ann will be in Paris on Monday.'
= He said that Ann would be in Paris on Monday.

He said, 'I'll be using the car myself on the 24th.'
= He said that he would be using the car himself on the 24th.

'I never eat meat', he explained.
= He explained that he never ate meat.

b In theory the past tense changes to the past perfect, but in spoken English it is often left unchanged, provided this can be done without causing confusion about the relative times of the actions:

He said, 'I loved her' *must become* He said he had loved her *as otherwise there would be a change of meaning.*
but He said, 'Ann arrived on Monday' *could be reported*
He said Ann arrived (*or* had arrived) on Monday.

In written English past tenses usually do change to past perfect but there are the following exceptions:

i Past/past continuous tenses used in time clauses do not normally change:

He said, 'When we were living/lived in Paris . . . '
= He said that when they were living/lived in Paris . . .

The main verb of such sentences can either remain unchanged or become the past perfect:

He said, 'When we were living/lived in Paris we often saw Paul.'
He said that when they were living/lived in Paris they {often saw Paul. / had often seen Paul.}

ii A past tense used to describe a state of affairs which still exists when the speech is reported remains unchanged:

She said, 'I decided not to buy the house because it *was* on a main road.'
= She said that she had decided not to buy the house because it *was* on a main road.

iii **would, should, ought, had better, might, used to, could** and **must** do not normally change:

He said, 'I might be there.'
= He said that he might be there.
She said, 'I would help him if I could.'
= She said that she would help him if she could.

For **must** see also **286**, for **could** see **287**.

iv Conditional sentences type 2 remain entirely unchanged, and past tenses (subjunctives) used after **wish, would, rather, it is time**:

He said, 'If my children were older I would emigrate.'
= He said that if his children were older he would emigrate.
He said, 'I wish I knew.'
= He said that he wished he knew.
She said, 'I'd rather Tom went.'
= She said that she'd rather Tom went.

c the past continuous tense in theory changes to the past perfect continuous but in practice usually remains unchanged except when it refers to a completed action:

She said, 'We were thinking of selling the house but we have decided not to.'
= She said that they had been thinking of selling the house but had decided not to.

but He said, 'When I saw them last they were playing tennis'

would normally be reported

He said that when he saw them last they were playing tennis

though it would also be possible to say:

He said that when he had seen them last they had been playing tennis.

277 Other changes necessary when turning direct speech into indirect speech

a In indirect speech the conjunction **that** can be placed immediately after the introductory verb, but it is not essential and is often omitted:

He said, 'I have seen a ghost.'
= He said (that) he had seen a ghost.

b Pronouns and possessive adjectives normally change from first or second person to third person except when the speaker is reporting his own words:

I said, 'I like my new house.'
= I said that I liked my new house (speaker reporting his own words).
He said, 'I've forgotten the combination of my safe.'
= He said that he had forgotten the combination of his safe.
'You've overcooked the steak again, Mary,' he said.
= He told Mary that she had overcooked the steak again.

But notice that sometimes a noun must be inserted to avoid ambiguity:

Tom said, 'He came in through the window' *would not normally be reported*
Tom said he had come in through the window.

This might give the impression that Tom himself had come in this way; but if we use a noun there can be no confusion:

Tom said that the man/the burglar/the cat &c. had come in . . .

Pronoun changes may affect the verb when it is in the future or conditional:

He says, 'I shall be there.'
= He says that he will be there.
He said, 'I shall be there.'
= He said that he would be there.

c this and these

this used in time expressions usually becomes **that**:

He said, 'She is coming this week.'
= He said that she was coming that week.

Otherwise **this** and **that** used as adjectives usually change to **the**:

He said, 'I bought this pearl/these pearls for my mother.'
= He said that he had bought the pearl(s) for his mother.

this, these used as pronouns can become **it, they/them**:

He came back with two blood-stained knives and said, 'I found *these* beside the king's bed.'

= He said that he had found *them* beside the king's bed.

He said, 'We will discuss this tomorrow.'

= He said that they would discuss it (the matter) the next day.

this, these used as either adjectives or pronouns to indicate choice or to distinguish some things from others usually become **the one near him/the one(s) that he had chosen** or some such phrase:

'Which will you have?' I asked. 'This (one)', he said.

= I asked which one he would have and he said he would have the one near him.

d Adverbs and adverbial phrases of time change as follows:

Direct	*Indirect*
today	that day
yesterday	the day before
the day before yesterday	two days before
tomorrow	the next day/the following day
the day after tomorrow	in two days' time
next week/year &c.	the following week/year &c.
last week/year &c.	the previous week/year &c.
a year &c. ago	a year before/the previous year

'I saw her the day before yesterday,' he said.

= He said he'd seen her two days before.

'I'll do it tomorrow,' he promised.

= He promised that he would do it the next day.

'I'm starting the day after tomorrow, mother,' he said.

= He told his mother that he was starting in two days' time.

She said, 'My father died a year ago.'

= She said that her father had died a year before/the previous year.

But if the speech is made and reported on the same day these time changes are not necessary:

At breakfast this morning he said, 'I'll be very busy today.'

= At breakfast this morning he said that he would be very busy today.

Logical adjustments are of course necessary if a speech is reported one/two days after it is made. On Monday Jack said to Tom:

I'm leaving the day after tomorrow.

If Tom reports this speech on the next day (Tuesday) he will probably say:

Jack said he was leaving tomorrow.

If he reports it on Wednesday, he will probably say:

Jack said he was leaving today.

e **here** can become **there** but only when it is clear what place is meant:

We met at the bridge and he said, 'I'll be here again tomorrow.'

= We met at the bridge and he said that he'd be there again the next day.

Usually **here** has to be replaced by some phrase:

She said, 'You can sit here, Tom.'
= She told Tom that he could sit beside her/on the rug &c.
but He said, 'Come here, boys' *would normally be reported as*
He called the boys.

278 Questions in indirect speech

Example of a direct question: He said, 'Where is she going?'
Example of an indirect question: He asked where she was going.

When we turn direct questions into indirect speech, the following changes are necessary:

Tenses, pronouns and possessive adjectives, and adverbs of time and place change as in statements.
The interrogative form of the verb changes to the affirmative form. The question mark (?) is therefore omitted in indirect questions:

He said, 'Where *does she live*?'
= He asked where *she lived*.

If the introductory verb is **say**, it must be changed to a verb of inquiry, e.g. **ask, inquire, wonder, want to know** &c.:

He said, 'Where is the station?'
= He asked where the station was.

ask, inquire, can also be used in direct speech. They are then usually placed at the end of the sentence:

'Where is the station?' he inquired.

ask can be used with an indirect object:

He said, 'What have you got in your bag?'
= He asked (me) what I had got in my bag.

But **inquire, wonder, want to know** cannot take an indirect object, so if we wish to report a question where the person addressed is mentioned, we must use **ask**:

He said, 'Mary, when is the next train?'
= He asked Mary when the next train was (if we use **inquire, wonder** or **want to know** we must omit 'Mary').

If the direct question begins with a question word (**when, where, who, how, why** &c., the question word is repeated in the indirect question:

He said, 'Why didn't you put on the brake?'
= He asked (her) why she hadn't put on the brake.
She said, 'What do you want?'
= She asked (them) what they wanted.

If there is no question word **if** or **whether** is placed after the introductory verb:

'Is anyone there?' he asked.
= He asked if anyone was there.

279 Questions beginning **shall I/we** and **will you/would you/could you**

a Questions beginning **shall I/we** can be of four kinds:

i speculations, or requests for information about a future event:

'Where shall I be this time next year?'
'When shall I know the result of the test?'

These follow the ordinary rule about **shall/will**. Speculations are usually introduced by **wonder**:

He wondered where he would be in a year's time/at that time in the following year.
She asked when she would know the result of her test.

ii requests for instructions or advice:

'What shall I do with it?' (= tell me what to do with it).

These are expressed in indirect speech by **ask**, **inquire** &c., with **should** or the **be** + infinitive construction; requests for advice are normally reported by **should**:

'Shall we send it to your flat, sir?' he said.
= He asked the customer { if they were to send it to his flat. / if they should send it to his flat. }

'What shall I say, mother?' she said.
= She asked her mother what she should say (request for advice).

iii offers:

'Shall I bring you some tea?' *could be reported*
He offered to bring me some tea.

iv Suggestions:

'Shall we meet at the theatre?' *could be reported*
He suggested meeting at the theatre.

b Questions beginning **will you/would you/could you** may be ordinary questions but may also be requests, commands or invitations:

He said, 'Will you be there tomorrow?' (ordinary question)
He asked if she would be there the next day.

but He said, 'Will you help me, please?' (request)
= He asked me to help him (see **280e**).

He said, 'Will you have a drink/Would you like a drink?' (invitation)
= He offered me a drink *or* asked if I would have/would like a drink.

He said, 'Will you have lunch with me tomorrow?' (invitation)
= He invited me/asked me to lunch with him the following day.

'Will you post this for me?' he said.
= He asked if I would post it for him.
or He asked/told me to post it for him.

'Could/would you wait a moment?' he said.
= He asked me to wait a moment.

280 Indirect commands

direct command: He said, 'Lie down, Tom.'
indirect command: He told Tom to lie down.

Changes necessary when we turn direct commands into indirect commands:

a The introductory verb, **say**, &c., changes to a verb of command or request, such as **tell, order, command, ask** &c. (see example above).

b The introductory verb of the indirect command must be followed immediately by the person addressed and the infinitive (i.e. the accusative + infinitive construction):

He said, 'Get your coat, Tom.'
= He told Tom to get his coat.

In direct commands the person addressed is often not mentioned:

He said, 'Go away.'

But in indirect commands the person addressed must be included, so that in cases such as the above it is necessary to add a noun or pronoun:

He told *me* (*him*, *her*, *the children* &c.) to go away.

Similarly:

He said, 'Please say nothing about this.'
= He asked her (us/them) to say nothing about it.

c Negative commands are expressed by **not** + infinitive:

He said, 'Don't move, boys.'
= He told the boys *not to move.*

d **beg, urge, remind, warn, advise, recommend** and **invite** are often useful in indirect commands/requests:

He said, 'Please, please give me another chance.'
= He begged them to give him another chance.

She said, 'Remember to thank Mrs Pitt when you are saying good-bye.'
= She reminded them to thank Mrs Pitt when they were saying good-bye.

'Don't go near the water, children,' she said.
= She warned the children not to go near the water.

'Stop taking tranquillizers,' I said/advised.
= I advised him to stop taking tranquillizers.

'Go on, John, hit him,' she said.
= She urged John to hit the other boy.

Notice that advice can also be expressed by the conditional construction **if I were you I should** + infinitive:

'If I were you I should leave the town at once,' he said.

This would normally be expressed by **advise** in indirect speech:

He advised me to leave the town at once.

e Commands/requests introduced by **will you/would you/could you**:
We have already seen (**279b**) that **will you/would you/could you** can introduce either questions or requests. When used for requests they are expressed in indirect speech by **ask** + object + infinitive.

He said, 'Will you/would you/could you sign my autograph book, please?'
= He asked the champion to sign his autograph book.

will you either at the beginning or end of a sentence can express a command. This is more authoritative than polite and often indicates impatience. It is expressed in indirect speech by **tell**:

'Shut the door, will you,' he shouted.
= He told us to shut the door.
'Will you stop talking,' he said.
= He told them to stop talking.

281 Other ways of expressing indirect commands

a The **be** + infinitive construction with **say** or **tell**:

He said (told me) that I was to wait.

This is a possible alternative to the **tell** + object + infinitive construction (**280**), so that:

He said, 'Don't open the door' *could be reported*
He told me not to open the door.
or He said that I wasn't to open the door.

The **be** + infinitive construction is particularly useful in the following cases:

i When the command is introduced by a verb in the present tense:

He *says*, 'Meet me at the station' *would normally be reported* He says that we are to meet him at the station. (He tells us to meet him *would be possible but much less likely*.)

ii When the command is preceded by a clause (usually of time or condition):

He said, 'If she leaves the house follow her' *could be reported*
He said that if she left the house I was to follow her.
or He told me to follow her if she left the house.

(If we use the **tell** + infinitive construction we must change the order of the sentence so as to put the command first.)

Similarly:

He said, 'When you go out lock both doors' *could be reported*
He said that when I went out I was to lock both doors.
or He told me to lock both doors when I went out.

b **say** or **tell** with a **should** construction can be used similarly, but normally indicates advice rather than command:

He said, 'If your brakes are bad don't drive so fast.'
= He said (told me) that if my brakes were bad I shouldn't drive so fast.
or He advised me not to drive so fast if my brakes were bad (note change of order here, as with **tell** = infinitive above).

c **urge, order, command, advise** and **recommend** can also be used with **should**, but express *command*, not advice as in **b** above. So we can say:

i He ordered troops to guard the gate (active).
ii *or* He ordered the gate to be guarded (passive).
iii *or* He ordered that troops should guard the gate (active).
iv *or* He ordered that the gate should be guarded (passive).

d Note that when an indirect command is expressed by an object + infinitive construction, as in **c**(i) above, there is normally the idea that the person who is to obey the command is addressed directly. But when the command is expressed by the **be** + infinitive construction (**a** above) or by **say** + **should** (**b** above) the recipient of the command need not necessarily be addressed directly. The command may be conveyed to him by a third person.

282 **let's, let him/them** and second person suggestions

a **let's**

i **let's** usually expresses a suggestion and becomes **suggest** in indirect speech, so that:

He said, 'Let's leave the case at the station.' *would be reported*
He suggested leaving the case at the station.
or He suggested that they/we should leave the case at the station. (See **234a** for constructions with **suggest**.)
and He said, 'Let's stop now and finish it later' *would be reported*
He suggested stopping then and finishing it later.
or He suggested that they/we should stop then and finish it later.

Similarly in the negative:

He said, 'Let's not say anything about it till we hear more facts.'
= He suggested not saying anything/saying nothing about it till they/we heard more facts.
or He suggested that they/we shouldn't say anything till they/we heard &c.

But **let's not** used alone in answer to an affirmative suggestion is often reported by some phrase such as: opposed the idea/was against it/objected. So that:

'Let's sell the house', said Tom.
'Let's not,' said Ann *could be reported*
Tom suggested selling the house but Ann was against it.

ii **let's/let us** sometimes expresses a call to action. It is then usually reported by **urge/advise** + object + infinitive (see also **281c**):

The strike leader said, 'Let's show the bosses that we are united.'
The strike leader urged the workers to show the bosses that they were united.

The headmaster said, 'Let us not miss this splendid opportunity.'
= The headmaster urged his staff not to miss the splendid opportunity.

b let him/them

i In theory **let him/them** expresses a command. But very often the speaker has no authority over the person who is to obey the command:

'It's not my business,' said the postman. 'Let the government do something about it.'

Here, the speaker is not issuing a command but expressing an obligation. Sentences of this type are therefore normally reported by **ought/should**:

He said that it wasn't his business and that the government should/ought to do something about it.

ii Sometimes, however, **let/him them** does express a real command. It is then usually reported by **say** + **be** + infinitive, or **command/order** with **should** (**281a, c**):

'Let no one speak to this girl,' said the headmaster.
= The headmaster said that no one was to speak to the girl.
or The headmaster ordered that no one should speak to her.

'Let the gates be left open,' said the commander.
= The commander said that the gates were to be left open.
or The commander ordered that the gates should be left open.

iii Sometimes **let him/them** is more a suggestion than a command. In such cases it is usually reported by **suggest**, or **say** + **should** (see **281b**):

She said, 'Let them go to their consul. Perhaps he'll be able to help them.'
= She suggested their going to their consul.
or She suggested that they should go to their consul.
or She said that they should to go their consul.

iv Remember that **let** is also an ordinary verb meaning **allow/permit** and followed by the infinitive without **to**:

'Let him come with us, mother, I'll take care of him,' I said.
= I asked my mother to let him come with us and promised to take care of him.

c Second person suggestions are normally expressed by:

I suggest (your) + gerund *or* **what about (your)** + gerund *or* **suppose you** + infinitive. (These constructions can, of course, be used with other persons also.) All would normally be reported by **suggest** with a gerund or **should** construction. So that:

He said, 'I suggest (your) waiting till dark.'
and He said, 'What about waiting till dark?'
and He said, 'Suppose you wait till dark?' *would all be reported*
He suggested my waiting till dark/that I (should) wait.

why don't you + infinitive is also a very useful way of expressing a suggestion. It is reported by **suggest** or **advise**:

He said, 'The job would suit you. Why don't you apply for it?'
= He said that the job would suit me and suggested my applying for it.
or and advised me to apply for it.

But **why don't you** can, of course, be an ordinary question:

'Why don't you play the oboe any more?' I asked.
= I asked him why he didn't play the oboe any more.

283 Exclamations and yes and no

a Exclamations must become statements in indirect speech. Various constructions are possible:

Exclamations with **what a . . . , how . . . ,** such as: 'He said, 'What a dreadful thing!' *or* 'How dreadful!' are expressed in indirect speech by: 'He said that it was . . . ':
He said that it was a dreadful thing/dreadful.

Exclamations such as 'ugh!' 'oh!' 'heavens!' are usually expressed by 'He gave an exclamation of disgust/surprise &c.' *or* 'He exclaimed with disgust/surprise'.

Note also:

He said, 'Thank you.'	He thanked me.
He said, 'Curse this wind.'	He cursed the wind.
He said, 'Good morning!'	He greeted me/wished me a good morning.
He said, 'Happy Christmas!'	He wished me a happy Christmas.
He said, 'Congratulations!'	He congratulated me.
He said, 'Liar!'	He called me a liar.
He said, 'Damn!'	He swore.

b **yes** and **no** are expressed in indirect speech by subject + appropriate auxiliary verb:

He said, 'Can you swim?' and I said, 'No.'
= He asked (me) if I *could* swim and I said *that I couldn't.*

He said, 'Will you have time to do it?' and I said, 'Yes.'
= He asked if I *would* have time to do it and I said *that I would.*

284 Mixed types

'I don't know the way. Do you?' he asked.
= He said that he didn't know the way and asked her if she did.

He said, 'Someone's coming. Get behind the screen.'
= He said that someone was coming and told me to get behind the screen.

She said, 'Ugh! It's a snake. Don't go near it, children.'
= She exclaimed with disgust that it was a snake and told the children not to go near it.

285 say, ask and tell

a **say** can be used with direct or indirect speech, and with or without the person addressed (preceded by **to**):

He said, 'The roof is leaking.'
'The roof is leaking,' he said.
'The roof is leaking,' he said to me (**say to** is not normally placed *before* a passage of indirect speech).

When used with indirect speech **say (to)** is normally placed first, but **say to** is not much used with indirect speech, **tell** being normally preferred:

He said that the roof was leaking.
He said to me (*or* told me) that the roof was leaking.

b **tell** must be followed by the person addressed except as shown in (v) and (vi) below.

i It is sometimes used with direct speech, being then always placed at the end of a sentence:

'He hasn't come,' she told me.

ii but its chief use is with indirect speech:

She told me that he hadn't come.

iii or with indirect commands:

She told us to sit down and keep quiet.

iv Notice also **tell . . . how** + infinitive:

She told us how to open the safe.
He told us how to find the house.

v **tell** can also mean **narrate/relate**, being often combined with **about** or **how**:

He told us about/of his adventures in the desert.
He told (us) how he had crossed the desert on foot (**tell . . . how** followed by a *clause* can be used without the person addressed).

vi Note also **tell** stories/tales/lies/the truth (here the person addressed need not be mentioned):

He told (me) lies. He always tells (his mother) the truth.

c **ask**

We can ask questions or ask **for** something with or without the person addressed:

'Can I have 6d?' he said. He asked (her) for 6d.
'Why is it so dark?' he asked (me). He asked (me) why it was so dark.

Requests expressed by **ask** + infinitive normally require the person addressed.

He said, 'Please don't tell anyone.'
= He asked *her* not to tell anyone.

ask can be followed directly by the infinitive, but the meaning is different:

He asked to see the drawings = he said that he wished to see them/he asked us to show them to him.

286 must and needn't

a **must** used for deductions, permanent commands/prohibitions and to express intention or advice remains unchanged:

i deductions:

She said, 'I'm always running into him; he must live quite near here.'
= She said that she was always running into him and that he must live quite near.

ii permanent command:

He said, 'People must obey their country's laws.'
= He said that people must obey their country's laws.

iii **must** used casually to express intention:

She said, 'I must tell you about a dream I had last night.'
= She said that she must tell me about a dream she had had the previous night.

He said, 'We must have a party to celebrate this.'
= He said that they must have a party to celebrate it.

iv advice:

She said, 'You must see *Othello*; it's marvellous.'
= She said that I must see *Othello* &c.

Alternatively **advise/recommend** &c. could be used:

She strongly advised me to see *Othello*.

b **must** used for obligation can remain unchanged. Alternatively it can change as follows:

I/we must can become **would have to** or **had to**

would have to is used when the obligation depends on some future action, or when the fulfilment of the obligation appears remote or uncertain, i.e. when **must** is clearly replaceable by **will have to**:

i when **must** is combined with a time clause or an expression of doubt or condition:

'But perhaps he hasn't got a snorkel,' said Tom.
'In that case, we must (will have to) lend him one,' said Ann.
= Ann said that in that case they would have to lend him one.

'If the floods get any worse we must (= will have to) leave the house,' he said.
= He said that if the floods got any worse they would have to leave.

'When it stops snowing we must start digging ourselves out,' I said.
= I said that when it stopped snowing we would have to start &c.

ii when the time for fulfilment of the obligation is fairly remote:

'We must mend the roof properly next year,' he said.
= He said that they would have to mend the roof properly the following year.

iii When no plans have yet been made for fulfilling the obligation. This occurs chiefly with obligations which have only just arisen:

'I have just received a telegram,' he said; 'I must go home at once.'
= He said that he had just received a telegram and would have to go &c.

But **had to** would be more usual here if in fact he did go at once, i.e. **had to** would imply that he went at once.

had to is the usual form for obligations where times for fulfilment have been fixed, or plans made, or when the obligation is fulfilled fairly promptly, or at least by the time the speech is reported:

He said, 'I must wash my hands' (and presumably went off to do this).
= He said that he had to wash his hands.

Tom said, 'I must be there by nine tomorrow.'
= Tom said that he had to be there by nine the next day.

would have to would be possible here also but would imply that the obligation was self-imposed and that no outside authority was involved. **had to** could express either an outside authority (i.e. that someone had told him to be there) or a self-imposed obligation.
All difficulties about **had to/would have to** can of course be avoided by keeping **must** unchanged. In all the above examples **must** could have been used instead of **had to/would have to.**

c **you/he/they must** can always remain unchanged, and usually do. Alternatively **must** here can become **had to/would have to** just as **I/we must** changes:

He said, 'You must start at once.'
= He said that she must/had to start at once.

But **would have to** is less usual here because it removes the idea of the speaker's authority:

Tom said, 'If you want to stay on here you must work harder.'
= Tom said that if she wanted to stay on she must/would have to work harder.

must implies that Tom himself insists on her working harder: **would have to** merely implies that this will be necessary.

d **must I/you/he?** can change similarly but as **must** in the interrogative usually concerns the present or immediate future it usually becomes **had to:**

'Must you go so soon?' I said.
= I asked him if he had to go so soon.

e **must not**

I must not usually remains unchanged.
you/he must not remains unchanged or is expressed as a negative command (see **280** and **281**):

He said, 'You mustn't tell anyone.'
= He said { that she mustn't tell. / that she wasn't to tell.
He told her not to tell.

f needn't

needn't can remain unchanged and usually does. Alternatively it can change to **didn't have to/wouldn't have to** just as **must** changes to **had to/would have to**:

I said, 'If you can lend me the money I needn't go to the bank.'
= I said that if he could lend me the money I needn't/wouldn't have to go to the bank.

He said, 'I needn't be in the office till ten tomorrow morning.'
= He said that he needn't/didn't have to be in the office till ten the next morning.

He said, 'You needn't wait.'
= He said that I needn't wait.

need I/you/he? behaves exactly in the same way as **must I/you/he?** i.e. it normally becomes **had to**:

'Need I finish my pudding?' asked the small boy.
= The small boy asked if he had to finish his pudding.

287 could

a could reported by **ask** or **invite**

could you (invitation) is reported by **ask/invite**:

He said, 'Could you come to dinner tomorrow?'
= He asked her to dinner the next day.

could you (request) is reported by **ask** + infinitive:

'Could you get the tickets?' he said
= He asked me to get the tickets.

could I have can often be reported by **ask for**:

'Could I have a drink?' he said = He asked for a drink.

could I see/could I speak to can usually be reported by **ask for/ask to see/ask to speak to**:

He said, 'Could I see Mr Smith?'
= He asked for Mr Smith/asked to see Mr Smith.

He said, 'Could I speak to Tom, please?'
= He asked for Tom/asked to speak to Tom.

b could for permission

could for present permission does not change:

'Could I use your phone?' he said.
= He asked if he could use my phone.

could for past permission can remain the same or change to **was/were allowed to** or **had been allowed to**:

He said, 'When I was a child I couldn't interrupt my parents'
= He said that when he was a child he couldn't/wasn't allowed to interrupt his parents.

c **could** for ability:

could for present ability does not change:

I said, 'Could you stand on your head?'
= I asked him if he could stand on his head.

could for past ability can remain unchanged or become **had been able:**

He said, 'I could read when I was three'
= He said that he could read/had been able to read when he was three.

d **could** in conditional sentences type 2

could in **if**-clauses remains unchanged:

She said, 'If I could drive I'd take you there myself.'
= She said that if she could drive she'd take me there herself.

could in the main clauses remains unchanged when the supposition is contrary to fact:

She said, 'If I had some flour I could make a cake' (but she hasn't any flour).
= She said that if she had some flour she could make a cake.

but can change to **would be able to** in sentences where the supposition could be fulfilled:

She said, 'If you got out of my light I could see what I was doing.'
= She said that if I got out of her light she would be able to see what she was doing.

29 Clauses of Purpose, Comparison, Reason, Time, Result, and Concession

Purpose

288 Purpose is normally expressed by an infinitive

a By a simple infinitive:

He went to France *to learn* French.
They went into the fields *to pick* mushrooms.

When there is a personal object of the main verb, the infinitive will refer to this and not to the subject:

He sent his *son* to the town *to buy wine* (i.e. the son was to buy the wine).

b By **so as** or **in order** with the infinitive:

He is studying higher mathematics *in order to qualify* for a better salary.

This construction can be used

i With a negative purpose:

He left his gun outside *so as not to frighten* his wife.
He came in quietly *so as not to wake* the child.

ii When there is a personal object of the main verb, but the purpose refers to the subject:

Peter sent his son into the garden *so as to have* some peace (Peter was to have the peace). *Compare with* Peter sent his son into the garden *to play* (the son was to play).

iii When the purpose is less immediate:

We joined the library *so as to have* plenty to read.
She learnt French *in order to help* her husband with his work.

A simple infinitive could be used in (iii) above but the **so as/in order** form is slightly more usual.

289 Purpose expressed by clauses of purpose

Clauses are necessary when the person to whom the purpose refers is mentioned, instead of being merely understood as in **288**:

Ships carry lifeboats so that the crew can escape if the ship goes on fire.

a Purpose clauses are usually expressed by

so that + **will/would** or **can/could** + infinitive.

can/could is used here to mean **will/would be able to**:

They make £10 notes a different size from £5 notes so that blind people can tell the difference between them (can tell = will be able to tell).
They wrote the notices in several languages so that foreign tourists could (= would be able to) understand them.

can and **will** are used when the main verb is in a present, present perfect or future tense; **could** and **would** are used when the main verb is in a past tense. See the examples above and also:

I {am lighting / light / have lit / will light} the fire so that the house will be warm when they return.

I {have given / will give} him a key so that he can get into the house whenever he likes.

I pinned the note to his pillow so that he would be sure to see it.
There were telephone points every half-mile so that drivers whose cars had broken down {would be able to / could} summon help.

Note that if the **that** is omitted from purpose clauses with **can/could**, the idea of purpose may disappear. A sentence such as:

He took my shoes so (that) I couldn't leave the house
would normally mean He took my shoes to prevent me leaving the house
but He took my shoes so I couldn't leave the house
would normally mean He took my shoes; therefore I wasn't able to leave.

b Purpose clauses can also be formed by:

{**so that** / **in order that** / **that**} + {**may/might** / **shall/should**} + infinitive.

These are merely more formal constructions than those shown in a above. There is no difference in meaning.

Note that

so that can be followed by **will/can/may/shall** or their past forms, while

{**in order that** / or **that**} are limited to **may/shall** or their past forms.

that used alone is rarely found except in very dramatic speech or writing, or in poetry:

And wretches hang that jurymen may dine (18th century poem).

The rules about sequence of tenses are the same as those shown above:

We carved their names on the stone so that/in order that future generations should/might know what they had done.
These men risk their lives so that/in order that we may live more safely.

may in the present tense is much more common than **shall**, which is comparatively rarely used. In the past tense either **might** or **should** can be used. In theory **might** expresses ability (replacing **could** above) and **should** is used in other cases (replacing **would** above). In practice, however, this distinction is usually disregarded.
The student should know the above forms but should not normally need to use them very much, as for all ordinary purposes **so that** + **can/will** should be quite sufficient.

c Negative purpose clauses are made by putting the auxiliary verb (usually **will/would** or **should**) into the negative:

He wrote his diary in cipher so that his wife wouldn't be able to read it.
He changed his name so that his new friends shouldn't know that he had once been accused of murder.
Criminals usually telephone from public telephone boxes so that the police won't be able to trace the call.

Negative purpose clauses can, however, usually be replaced by **to prevent** + noun/pronoun + gerund, or **to avoid** + gerund:

She always shopped in another village so that she wouldn't meet her own neighbours *or* *to avoid meeting* her own neighbours.

He dyed his beard { so that we shouldn't recognize him. / *to prevent us recognizing* him. / *to avoid being* recognized (passive gerund).

These infinitive phrases are preferred to negative purpose clauses.

290 in case and lest

Clauses introduced by **in case** and **lest** are rather similar to purpose clauses. **lest** means **for fear that** and is followed by **should** + infinitive. **in case** means **for fear that** or **on the chance that**. **in case** can be followed by **should** + infinitive but is usually followed by the simple present or simple past tense. Note the sequence of tenses with **in case**:

He doesn't dare (to) leave the house { lest he should be recognized. / in case he should be recognized. / in case he is recognized.

He didn't dare (to) leave the house { lest he should be recognized. / in case he should be recognized. / in case he was recognized.

in case and **lest** can be used with two types of action:

a with an action which the speaker or subject of the main verb wishes to prevent:

She never took him near the river { lest he should fall in. / in case he should fall in/in case he fell in. }

b With actions which the speaker or subject of the main verb is taking precautions against or preparing for:

Put the cork back in the bottle in case the cat knocks it over.
He carries a spare wheel in case he has a puncture.
She didn't dare open the door { in case it was the escaped murderer. / lest it should be the escaped murderer. }

lest is less common than **in case** and is rarely used in modern spoken English.

291 Comparisons

a Comparisons with **like**

like can be followed by noun/pronoun or gerund. It should not be followed by subject + verb:

There was a terrible storm; it was like the end of the world.
Getting money from him is like getting blood from a stone.

b Comparisons with **as . . . as** and **than.**

as . . . as and **not so/as . . . as** are used with the positive form of an adverb or adjective. **than** is used with the comparative form:

I can't run *as* (*or* so) fast *as* he can.
He runs faster *than* me/*than* I do.

i **as/than** can be followed by a noun/pronoun only, the verb being understood but not mentioned:

She is taller than her brother (is).
Tom drives more carefully than Ann (does).
Small cars are easier to park than big ones (are).

When pronouns are used in this way (without the verb) they are usually put into the accusative form. (This is accepted in colloquial English but is not grammatical. In written English it is better to use the nominative pronoun and the verb):

She doesn't work as hard as me (as hard as I do).
He is older than you (are).
I can swim better than him (better than he does).
We pay more rent than them (than they do).

ii Very often, however, the verb is necessary, and cannot be omitted:

This is not as easy as I thought it would be.
It is later than you think.
I am not so stupid as I look.
It is even darker today than it was yesterday.
She had no sooner left the house than it began to rain.

iii **as/than** can also be followed by an infinitive or a gerund:

It is better to say too little than (to) say too much.
He found riding as tiring as walking.

The infinitive is used if the verb before **than/as** is, or contains, an infinitive:

He finds it easier to do the cooking himself than (to) teach his wife to cook.
It is as easy to do it right as (to) do it wrong.
Even lazy people would rather work than starve.

When **than/as** is preceded by an infinitive without **to** it is followed by an infinitive without **to**. Otherwise the **to** is optional.
The gerund is used in other cases, i.e. when the verb preceding **than/as** is a gerund or when the action is represented by a pronoun:

This is more amusing than sitting in an office.
Skiing is more exciting than skating.
It is as easy as falling off a log.
He cleaned his shoes, which was better than doing nothing.

c Comparisons with superlatives present no difficulty:

He is the youngest of the family.
This was the strangest part of the whole story.
Is this the highest building in New York?
It was the most beautiful that I had ever seen.

292 Clauses of reason

These are introduced by **because**, **as** and **since** and sometimes **if**, (for **because** and **for** see **93**):

We camped there because it was too dark to go on.
As we hadn't any money we couldn't buy anything to eat. (See also **95**.)
Since you won't take advice there is no point in asking for it.
If (= since) you wanted to go to sea, why didn't you?

293 Time clauses

These are introduced by conjunctions of time such as **when**, **as**, **while**, (see **95**, **190**), **until/till** (see **83**), **after**, **as soon as**, **whenever**, **since** &c.:

I'll stay here *till/until you get back.*
I can't give an opinion *till I have heard all the details.*
After the customers had gone the cleaners started work.
As soon as we lit the fire clouds of smoke filled the room.
Whenever he saw a bookmaker he shook his fist at him.
They have moved house three times *since they got married.*
I haven't seen him *since he left school.*
The sooner we start, the sooner we'll be finished.

Remember that verbs *in* time clauses cannot be in a future or conditional tense. Therefore:

i when a future perfect tense becomes part of a time clause it changes to the present perfect:

They *will have finished* by two o'clock.
but *As soon as they have finished* we can use the court.

ii Similarly a future tense changes to a present tense:

He *will arrive* at six.
but *When he arrives* he will tell us all about it.

iii A conditional tense changes to a past tense:

We knew that he *would arrive* at six.
but We knew that till he *arrived* nothing could be done.

A future or conditional tense can be used after **when** provided **when** does not introduce a time clause:

He asked when the train *would get in* (this is not a time clause but a noun clause, object of **asked**).

294 Clauses of result

These are expressed by **so . . . that** or **such . . . that** and follow the usual rules about sequence of tenses (see **212**).

such is an adjective and is used before an adjective + noun:

They had *such* a *fierce dog* that no one dared to go near their house.
He spoke for *such* a *long time* that people began to think he would never stop.

so is an adverb and is used before adverbs and with adjectives which are not followed by their nouns:

The snow fell *so fast* that our footsteps were covered up in a few minutes.
Their dog was *so fierce* that no one dared come near it.
His speech went on for *so long* that people began to fall asleep.

Note however that **such** is never used before **much** and **many**. **so** is used even when **much** and **many** are followed by nouns:

There was so much dust that we couldn't see what was happening.
So many people complained that in the end they took the programme off.

Note that **such** + **a** + adjective + noun is replaceable by **so** + adjective + **a** + noun, so that 'such a good man' is replaceable by 'so good a man'. This is only possible when a noun is preceded by **a/an**. It is not a very usual form but may be met in literature.
Sometimes for emphasis **so** is placed at the beginning of the sentence. It is then followed by the inverted form of the verb (see **72**):

So terrible was the storm that whole roofs were ripped off.

295 Clauses of concession

These are introduced by **though, although** (see **91**), **even if, however** + adjective/adverb and sometimes by **whatever. as** is also possible, but only in the adjective + **as** + **be** construction:

However rich people are they always seem anxious to make more money.
However carefully you drive you will probably have an accident eventually.
Whatever you do, don't tell him that I told you this.
No matter what you do don't touch this switch.
Even if/though you don't like him you can still be polite.
Patient as he was, he had no intention of waiting for three hours (though he was patient).

may + infinitive can be used in hypothetical cases:

However frightened you may be yourself, you must remain outwardly calm.

should + infinitive can be used after **even if** just as it can after **if** in conditional sentences, to express the idea that the action expressed by the infinitive is not very likely to take place:

Even if he should find out he won't do anything about it.

30 List of Irregular Verbs

296 The verbs in italics are verbs which are not very common in modern English but may be found in literature.

When a verb has two possible forms and one is less usual than the other, the less usual one will be printed in italics.

Compounds of irregular verbs form their past tenses and past participles in the same way as the original verb:

come	came	come
overcome	overcame	overcome
set	set	set
upset	upset	upset

present and infinitive	*simple past*	*past participle*
abide	*abode*	*abode*
arise	arose	arisen
awake	awoke	awaked†
be	was	been
bear	bore	borne/born*
beat	beat	beaten
become	become	became
befall	*befell*	*befallen*
beget	*begot*	*begotten*
begin	began	begun
behold	*beheld*	*beheld*
bend	bent	bent
bereave	bereaved	bereaved/bereft*
beseech	*besought*	*besought*
bid (command)	*bade*	*bidden*
bid (offer)	bid	bid
bind	bound	bound
bite	bit	bitten
bleed	bled	bled
blow	blew	blown
break	broke	broken
breed	bred	bred
bring	brought	brought
broadcast	broadcast	broadcast
build	built	built
burn	burnt/burned	burnt/burned
burst	burst	burst
buy	bought	bought

† This past participle, however, is not very much used. Instead we normally use **awakened**, the past participle of the regular verb **awaken**.

* These past participles are not optional but carry different meanings and should be checked by the student in a reliable dictionary.

present and infinitive	*simple past*	*past participle*
can (present only)	could	been able
cast	cast	cast
catch	caught	caught
chide	*chid*	*chidden*
choose	chose	chosen
cleave	*clove/cleft*	*cloven/cleft**
cling	clung	clung
clothe	clothed/clad	clothed/clad
come	came	come
cost	cost	cost
creep	crept	crept
crow	crowed/*crew*	crowed
cut	cut	cut
dare	dared/*durst*	dared/*durst*
deal	dealt	dealt
dig	dug	dug
do	did	done
draw	drew	drawn
dream	dreamt/dreamed	dreamt/dreamed
drink	drank	drunk
drive	drove	driven
dwell	*dwelled*/dwelt	*dwelled*/dwelt
eat	ate	eaten
fall	fell	fallen
feed	fed	fed
feel	felt	felt
fight	fought	fought
find	found	found
flee	fled	fled
fling	flung	flung
fly	flew	flown
forbear	forbore	forborne
forbid	forbade	forbidden
forgive	forgave	forgiven
forsake	forsook	forsaken
freeze	froze	frozen
get	got	got
gild	gilded/gilt	gilded/gilt
gird	*girded/girt*	*girded/girt*
give	gave	given
go	went	gone
grind	ground	ground
grow	grew	grown
hang	hung/hanged	hung/hanged*
have	had	had
hear	heard	heard
hew	hewed	hewed/hewn

* See footnote * on page 201.

present and infinitive	*simple past*	*past participle*
hide	hid	hidden
hit	hit	hit
hold	held	held
hurt	hurt	hurt
keep	kept	kept
kneel	knelt	knelt
knit (= unite/draw together)	knit	knit
(**knit** [= make garments from wool] is a regular verb)		
know	knew	known
lay	laid	laid
lead	led	led
lean	leant/leaned	leant/leaned
leap	leapt/leaped	leapt/leaped
learn	learnt/learned	learn/learned
leave	left	left
lend	lent	lent
let	let	let
lie	lay	lain
light	lit/lighted	lit/lighted
lose	lost	lost
make	made	made
may (present only)	might	—
mean	meant	meant
meet	met	met
mow	mowed	mowed/mown
must (present only)	had to	—
ought (present only)	—	—
pay	paid	paid
put	put	put
read	read	read
rend	*rent*	*rent*
rid	rid	rid
ride	rode	ridden
ring	rang	rung
rise	rose	risen
run	ran	run
saw	sawed	sawed/sawn
said	said	said
see	saw	seen
seek	sought	sought
sell	sold	sold
send	sent	sent
set	set	set
sew	sewed	sewed/sewn
shake	shook	shaken
shall (present only)	should	—
shear	sheared/*shore*	sheared/shorn
shed	shed	shed

present and infinitive	*simple past*	*past participle*
shine	shone	shone
shoe	shoed/*shod*	shoed/*shod*
shoot	shot	shot
show	showed	showed/shown
shrink	shrank	shrunk
shut	shut	shut
sing	sang	sung
sink	sank	sunk
sit	sat	sat
slay	*slew*	*slain*
sleep	slept	slept
slide	slid	slid
sling	slung	slung
slink	slunk	slunk
slit	slit	slit
smell	smelled/smelt	smelled/smelt
smite	*smote*	*smitten*
sow	sowed	sowed/sown
speak	spoke	spoken
speed	speeded/sped	speeded/sped
spell	spelt/spelled	spelt/spelled
spend	spent	spent
spill	spilt/spilled	spilt/spilled
spin	spun	spun
spit	spat	spat
split	split	split
spread	spread	spread
spring	sprang	sprung
stand	stood	stood
steal	stole	stolen
stick	stuck	stuck
sting	stung	stung
stink	stank/stunk	stunk
strew	strewed	strewed/strewn
stride	strode	stridden
strike	struck	struck
string	strung	strung
strive	strove	striven
swear	swore	sworn
sweep	swept	swept
swell	swelled	swelled/swollen
swim	swam	swum
swing	swung	swung
take	took	taken
teach	taught	taught
tear	tore	torn
tell	told	told
think	thought	thought
thrive	thrived/throve	thrived/thriven
throw	threw	thrown
thrust	thrust	thrust
tread	trod	trodden/trod

present and infinitive	*simple past*	*past participle*
understand	understood	understood
undertake	undertook	undertaken
wake	woke/waked	woken/waked
wear	wore	worn
weave	wove	woven
weep	*wept*	*wept*
wet	wetted/wet	wetted/wet
will (present only)	would	—
win	won	won
wind	wound	wound
wring	wrung	wrung
write	wrote	written

31 Verbs + Prepositions/Adverbs

297 In modern English it is very usual to place prepositions or adverbs after certain verbs so as to obtain a variety of meanings:

look for = search for, seek
look out = beware
look after = take care of
give up = abandon (a habit or attempt)
give away = give to someone/anyone

The student need not try to decide whether the combination is verb + preposition or verb + adverb, but should consider the expression as a whole. It is also important to learn whether the combination is transitive (i.e. requires an object) or intransitive (i.e. cannot have an object):

look for is transitive: I am looking for my passport.
look out is intransitive: Look out! This ice isn't safe!

Each of the combinations given in the following pages will be marked 'tr' (= transitive) or 'intr' (= intransitive), and the examples given of the use of each will help to emphasize this distinction.
Note that it is possible for a combination to have two or more different meanings, and to be transitive in one/some of these and intransitive in others:

e.g. 'take off' can mean 'remove'. It is then a transitive expression:

He took off his hat.

'Take off' can also mean 'rise from the ground' (used of aircraft). Here it is intransitive:

The plane took off at ten o'clock.

Transitive expressions

a The position of the object: noun objects are usually placed at the end of these expressions:

I am looking for *my glasses.*

With some expressions, however, they can be placed either at the end or immediately after the verb, i.e. before the short word. We can say:

He took off *his coat* *or* He took *his coat* off.

Pronoun objects are sometimes placed at the end of the expression:

I am looking for *them.*

But they are more often placed immediately after the verb:

He took *it* off.

This position is usual before the following short words: up, down, in, out, away, off, and on (except when used in the expression 'call on' = visit). Examples given of the use of each expression will show all possible positions of noun or pronoun objects.

I'll give *this old coat* away. (I'll give away *this old coat*/I'll give *it* away.)

i.e. with this expression the noun object can come before or after the **away**; the pronoun object must come before the **away**. When only one example is given the student may assume that the pronoun object has the same position as the noun object.

b When these expressions are followed by a verb object the gerund form of the verb is used:

He kept on blowing his horn.

Where gerunds are usual this will be shown by examples.

Note that some expressions can be followed by an infinitive:

It is up to you to decide this for yourself.
Some of the younger members *called on the minister to resign.*
The lecturer *set out to show* that most illnesses were avoidable.

go on can be followed by either infinitive or gerund but there is a considerable difference in meaning.

298 Verb + preposition/adverb combinations

account

account for (tr) = give a good reason for, explain satisfactorily (some action or expenditure):

A treasurer must account for the money he spends.
He has behaved in the most extraordinary way; I can't account for his actions at all/I can't account for his behaving like that.

allow

allow for (tr) = make provision in advance for, take into account (usually some additional requirement, expenditure, delay etc.):

Tom: It is 400 miles and I drive at 50 m.p.h., so I'll be there in eight hours.
Ann: But you'll have to allow for delays going through towns and for stops for refuelling.
Allowing for depreciation your car should be worth £500 this time next year.

answer

answer back (intr), *answer somebody back* = answer a reproof impudently:

Father: Why were you so late last night? You weren't in till 2 a.m.
Son: You should have been asleep.
Father: Don't answer me back. Answer my question.

ask

ask for (tr) = request, demand:

The men asked for more pay and shorter hours.

ask for somebody

a = ask for news of:

I met Tom at the party; he asked for you (asked how you were/how you were getting on).

b = ask to speak to:

Go to the office and ask for the Secretary.

ask someone in (object before **in**) = invite him to enter the house:

He didn't ask me in; he kept me standing at the door while he read the message.

ask someone out (object before **out**) = invite him to an entertainment or to a meal (usually in a public place):

She had a lot of friends and was usually asked out in the evenings, so she very seldom spent an evening at home.

back

back away (intr) = step or move back slowly (because confronted by some danger or unpleasantness):

When he took a snake out of his pocket everyone backed away and stood watching it from a safe distance.

back out (intr) = withdraw (from some joint action previously agreed on), discontinue or refuse to provide previously promised help or support:

He agreed to help us but backed out when he found how difficult it was.

back somebody up = support morally or verbally:

The headmaster never backed up *his staff* (backed *them* up). If a parent complained about a master he assumed that the master was in the wrong.

be

be in (intr) = be at home/in this building.
be out (intr) = be away from home/from this building for a short time – not overnight.
be away (intr) = be away from home/from this place for at least a night.
be back (intr) = have returned after a long or short absence:

I want to see Mrs Pitt. Is she in?
No, I'm afraid she's out at the moment
or No, I'm afraid she's away for the weekend.
When will she be back?
She'll be back in half an hour/next week.

be for (tr) = be in favour of (often used with gerund).
be against (tr) = be opposed to (often used with gerund):

I'm for doing nothing till the police arrive/I'm against doing anything till the police arrive.

be in for (tr) = be about to encounter (usually something unpleasant):

Look at the wind-sock! I'm afraid we're in for a rough flight.
If you think that the work is going to be easy you're in for a shock.

be over/past (intr) = be finished:

The storm is over now; we can go on.

be up (intr) = be out of bed:

Don't expect her to answer the door bell at nine o'clock on Sunday morning. She won't be up.

be up to (tr) = be physically or intellectually strong enough (to perform a certain action). The object is usually **it**, though a gerund is possible:

After his illness he continued in office though he was no longer up to the work/ up to doing the work.

be up to something/some mischief/some trick/no good = be occupied or busy with some mischievous act:

Don't trust him; he is up to something/some trick.
The boys are very quiet. I wonder what they are up to.

Note that the object of **up to** here is always some very indefinite expression such as these given above. It is never used with a particular action.

it is up to someone (often followed by an infinitive) = it is his responsibility or duty:

It is up to parents to teach their children manners.
I have helped you as much as I can. Now it is up to you (you must continue by your own efforts).

bear

bear out (tr) = confirm:

This report bears out *my theory* (bears *my theory* out/bears *it* out).

bear up (intr) = support bad news bravely, hide feelings of grief:

The news of her death was a great shock to him but he bore up bravely and none of us realized how much he felt it.

blow

blow out (tr) = extinguish (a flame) by blowing:

The wind blew out *the candle* (blew *the candle* out/blew *it* out).

blow up (tr or intr)

a = destroy by explosion, explode, be destroyed:

They blew up *the bridges* so that the enemy couldn't follow them (blew *the bridges* up/blew *them* up).
Just as we got to the bridge it blew up.

b = fill with air, inflate:

The children blew up *their balloons* and threw them into the air (blew *the balloons* up/blew *them* up).

boil

boil away (intr) = be boiled until all (the liquid) has evaporated:

I put the kettle on the gas ring and then went away and forgot about it. When I returned, the water had all boiled away and the flame had burnt a hole in the kettle.

boil over (intr) = to rise and flow over the sides of the container (used only of hot liquids):

The milk boiled over and there was a horrible smell of burning.

break

break down figures = take a total and sub-divide it under various headings so as to give additional information:

You say that 10,000 people use this library. Could you break that down into age-groups? (i.e. say how many of these are under 25, over 50 &c.).

break down a door &c. = cause to collapse by using force:

'If you don't let us in we'll break down *the door*,' said the bandits (break *the door* down/break *it* down).

break down (intr) = collapse, cease to function properly, owing to some fault or weakness:

a used of people, it normally implies a temporary emotional collapse:

He broke down twice when giving evidence on his son's death (i.e. he was overcome by his sorrow, he wept).

b it can express collapse of mental resistance:

At first he refused to admit his guilt but when he was shown the evidence he broke down and confessed.

c when used of health it implies a serious physical collapse:

After years of overwork his health broke down and he had to retire from business.

d it is very often used of machines:

The car broke down when we were driving through the desert and it took us two days to repair it.

e it can be used of negotiations:

The negotiations broke down (i.e. were discontinued) because neither side would compromise.

break in (intr), *break into* (tr)

a = enter by force:

Thieves broke in and stole the silver.
Thieves broke into the house &c.

break in (intr), *break into* (a conversation &c.) (tr)

b = interrupt someone by some sudden remark:

I was telling them about my travels when he broke in with a story of his own.

break in (a young horse/pony &c.) (tr) = train him for use:

You cannot ride or drive a young horse safely before he has been broken in.

break off (tr or intr) = detach or become detached:

He took a bar of chocolate and broke off a bit/broke a bit off/broke it off.
A piece of rock broke off and fell into the pool at the foot of the cliff.

break off (tr) = terminate (used of agreements or negotiations):

Ann has broken off *her engagement* to Tom (broken *her engagement* off/broken. *it* off).

break off (intr) = stop talking suddenly, interrupt oneself:

They were arguing but broke off when someone came into the room.

break out (intr)

a = begin (used of evils such as wars, epidemics, fires, &c.):

War broke out on August 4th.
A bad fire broke out in the cellars of the market.

b = escape by using force from a prison &c.:

They locked him up in a room but he broke out (= smashed the door and escaped).
The police are looking for two men who broke out of prison last night.

break up (tr or intr) = disintegrate, cause to disentegrate:

If that ship stays there she will break up/be broken up by the waves.
The old ship was towed away to be broken up and sold as scrap.
Divorce breaks up a lot of families (breaks *families* up/breaks *them* up).

break up (intr) = terminate (used of school terms, meeting, parties &c.):

The school broke up on July 30 and all the boys went home for the holidays.
The meeting broke up in confusion.

bring

bring (someone) round (tr; object usually before **round**)

a = persuade someone to accept a previously opposed suggestion:

After a lot of argument I brought him round to my point of view.

b = restore to consciousness:

She fainted when she heard the news but a little brandy soon brought her round.

bring (a person or thing) round (tr; object usually before **round**) = bring him/it to my (your/his) house:

I have finished that book you lent me; I'll bring it round (i.e. to your house) tonight.

bring up (tr)

a = educate and train children:

She brought up *her children* to be truthful (brought *her children* up/brought *them* up).

b = mention:

At the last committee meeting, the treasurer brought up *the question* of raising the annual subscription (brought *the question* up/brought *it* up).

burn

burn down (tr) = destroy completely by fire (used of buildings):

The mob burnt down *the embassy* (burnt *the embassy* down/burnt *it* down).

call

1. *call* meaning *visit* (for a short time)

call at a place

I called at the bank and arranged to transfer some money.
This ship calls at Genoa.

call for = visit a place to collect a person or thing:

I am going to a dance with Tom. He is calling for me at eight so I must be ready then.
Let's leave our suitcases in the left luggage office and call for them later on when we have the car.

call in is intransitive, and has the same meaning as **look in** and the colloquial **drop in**:

Call in/look in on your way home and tell me how the interview went.

call on a person:

He called on all the housewives in the area and asked them to sign the petition.

2. Other meanings of *call on, in, for*

call for (tr) = require, demand (the subject here is often an impersonal word or phrase such as: the situation/this sort of work/this &c.; the object is then usually some quality e.g. courage/patience/a steady hand &c.):

The situation calls for tact.
You've got the job! This calls for a celebration.

But it can also be used with a personal subject:

The workers are calling for strike action.
The relations of the dead men are calling for an inquiry.

call in a person/call him in = send for him/ask him to come to the house to perform some service. **send for** is more authoritative than **call in**, which is therefore a more polite form:

It was too late to call in *an electrician* (call *an electrician* in/call *him* in).
There is some mystery about his death; the police have been called in.

call on somebody (usually + infinitive) = ask him to do something/ask him to help. This is a rather formal way of making a request and is chiefly used on formal occasions or in speeches &c. There is usually the idea that the person called on will consider it his duty to comply with the request:

The President called on his people to make sacrifices for the good of their country.
The chairman called on the secretary to read the minutes of the last meeting.

3. Other combinations with *call*

call off (tr) = cancel something not yet started, or abandon something already in progress:

They had to call off *the match* (call *the match* off/call *it* off) as the ground was too wet to play on (cancel).
When the fog got thicker the search was called off (abandoned).

call out (tr) = summon someone to leave his house to deal with a situation outside. It is often used of troops when they are required to leave their barracks to deal with civil disturbances:

The police couldn't control the mob so troops were called out.
The Fire Brigade was called out several times on the night of November 5 to put out fires started by fireworks.
Doctors don't much like being called out at night.

call up (tr)

a = summon for military service:

In most countries men are called up at the age of eighteen (call up *men*/call *men* up/call *them* up).

b = telephone:

I called Tom up and told him the news (call up *Tom*/call *him* up).

care

not to care about (tr) = to be indifferent to:

The professor said that he was interested only in research; he didn't care about his students.

care for (tr)

a = like (seldom used in the affirmative):

He doesn't care for films about war.

b = look after (not much used except in the passive):

The house looked well cared for (= had been well looked after/was in good condition)

carry

carry on (intr) = continue (usually work or duty):

I can't carry on alone any longer; I'll have to get help.

carry on with (tr) is used similarly:

The doctor told her to carry on with the treatment.

carry out (tr) = perform (duties), obey (orders, instructions), fulfil (threats):

You are not meant to think for yourself; you are here to carry out my orders.
He carried out his threat to cut our water supply (= he threatened to do it and he did it).
He read the instructions but he didn't carry them out.

catch

catch up with (tr), *catch up* (tr or intr) = overtake, but not pass:

I started last in the race but I soon caught up with *the others* (caught *them* up/caught up).

You've missed a whole term; you'll have to work hard to catch up with *the class* (catch *them* up/catch up).

clean

clean out a room/cupboard/drawer &c. = clean and tidy it thoroughly:

I must clean out *the spare room* (clean the *spare room* out/clean *it* out).

clean up a mess e.g. anything spilt:

Clean up *any spilt paint* (clean *the spilt paint* up/clean *it* up).

clean up (intr) is used similarly:

These painters always clean up when they've finished (= leave the place clean).

clear

clear away (tr) = remove articles, usually in order to make space:

Could you clear away *these papers* (clear *these papers* away/clear *them* away)?

clear away (intr) = disperse:

The clouds soon cleared away and it became quite warm.

clear off/out (intr) = go away (colloquial; as a command it is definitely rude):

'You clear off,' said the farmer angrily. 'You've no right to put your caravans in my field without even asking permission.'

clear out (tr) a room/cupboard/drawer &c. = empty it, usually to make room for something else:

I'll clear out *this drawer* and you can put your things in it (clear *this drawer* out/clear *it* out).

clear up (intr) = become fine after clouds or rain:

The sky looks a bit cloudy now but I think it will clear up.

clear up (tr or intr) = make tidy and clean:

When you are cooking it's best to clear up as you go, instead of leaving everything to the end and having a terrible pile of things to deal with.
Clear up *this mess* (clear *this mess* up/clear *it* up).

clear up (tr)

a = finish (some work which still remains to be done):

I have some letters which I must clear up before I leave tonight.

b = solve (a mystery):

In a great many detective stories the police are baffled but an amateur detective comes along and clears up *the mystery* (clears *it* up).

close

close down (tr or intr) = shut permanently (of a shop or business):

Trade was so bad that many small shops closed down and big shops closed some of *their branches* down (closed down *some branches*/closed *them* down).

close in (intr) = come nearer, approach from all sides (used of mist, darkness, enemies &c.):

As the mist was closing in we decided to stay where we were.

close up (intr) = come nearer together (of people in a line):

If you children closed up a bit there'd be room for another one on this seat.

come

come across/upon (tr) = find by chance:

When I was looking for my passport I came across these old photographs.

come along/on (intr) = come with me, accompany me. 'Come on' is often said to someone who is hesitating or delaying:

Come on, or we'll be late.

come away (intr) = leave (with me):

Come away now. It's time to go home.

come away/off (intr) = detach itself:

When I picked up the teapot the handle came away in my hand.

come in (intr), *come into* (tr) = enter:

Someone knocked at my door and I said, 'Come in.'
Come into the garden and I'll show you my roses.

come off (intr)

a = succeed, of a plan or scheme (used in negative):

She told her husband that she was going to spend the week with her mother in York whereas in fact she was going to Paris. She tried to cover her tracks by writing postcards to her husband and asking a friend in York to post them. But the scheme didn't come off because the friend forgot to post them till the following week.

b = take place; happen as arranged:

'When is the wedding coming off?' 'Next June.'

If we say 'The duchess was to have opened the bazaar' we imply that this plan was made but didn't come off (she arranged to open it but later had to cancel this arrangement).

c = end its run (of a play, exhibition &c.):

Waiting for Godot is coming off next week. You'd better hurry if you want to see it.

come out (intr)

a = be revealed, exposed (the subject here is normally *the truth/the facts/the whole story* &c. and usually refers to facts which the people concerned were trying to keep hidden, i.e. scandals &c.):

They deceived everybody till they quarrelled among themselves; then one publicly denounced the other and the whole truth came out.

b = be published (of books):

Her new novel will be coming out in time for the Christmas sales.

c = disappear (of stains):

Ink stains don't usually come out.

come round (intr)

a = finally accept a previously opposed suggestion:

Her father at first refused to let her study abroad but he came round (to it) in the end (i.e. said she could go).

b = come to my (your/his &c.) house:

I can't come to dinner but I could come round after dinner and tell you the plan.

come round/to (intr; stress on **to**) = recover consciousness:

When we found him he was unconscious but he came round/to in half an hour and explained that he had been attacked and robbed.

come up (intr)

a = rise to the surface:

A diver with an aqualung doesn't have to keep coming up for air; he can stay underwater for quite a long time.
Weeds are coming up everywhere.

b = be mentioned:

The question of the caretaker's wages came up at the last meeting.

come up (intr), *come up to* (tr) = approach, come close enough to talk:

A policeman was standing a few yards away. He came up to me and said, 'You can't park here.'

crop

crop up (intr) = appear, arrive unexpectedly or by accident (the subject is normally an abstract noun such as *difficulties/the subject* &c. or a pronoun):

At first all sorts of difficulties cropped up and delayed us. Later we learnt how to anticipate these.

cut

cut down a tree = fell it:

If you cut down *all the trees* you will ruin the land (cut *the trees* down/cut *them* down).

cut down (tr) = reduce in size or amount:

We must cut down expenses or we'll be getting into debt.
'This article is too long,' said the editor. 'Could you cut it down to 2000 words?'

cut in (intr) = pass one car when there isn't room to do this safely, as another car is coming from the opposite direction:

Accidents are often caused by drivers cutting in.

cut off (tr) = disconnect, discontinue supply (usually of gas, water, electricity &c.). The object can either be the commodity or the person who suffers:

The Company has cut off *our electricity supply* (cut *our supply* off/cut *it* off) because we haven't paid our bill.
They've cut off the water (= our water supply) temporarily because they are repairing one of the main pipes.
We were cut off in the middle of our (telephone) conversation (this might be accidental or a deliberate action by the switchboard operator).

cut someone off = form a barrier between him and safety (often used in connexion with the tide, especially in the passive):

We were cut off by the tide and had to be rescued by boat.

be cut off (intr) = be inconveniently isolated (the subject is usually a place or residents in a certain place):

You will be completely cut off if you go to live in that village because there is a bus only once a week.

cut out (tr)

a = cut from a piece of cloth/paper &c. a smaller piece of a desired shape:

When I am making a dress I mark the cloth with chalk and then cut *it* out (cut out *the dress*/cut *the dress* out).
Young people often cut out photographs of their favourite film stars and pin them to the walls.

b = omit, leave out:

If you want to get thin you must cut out *starch* (cut *it* out).

be cut out for (tr) = be fitted or suited for (used of people, usually in the negative):

His father got him a job in a bank but it became clear that he was not cut out for that kind of work (= he wasn't happy and not good at the work).

cut up (tr) = cut into small pieces:

They cut down the tree and cut it up for firewood (cut the tree up/cut up the tree).

die

die away (intr) = become gradually fainter till inaudible:

The prisoners waited till the sound of the warder's footsteps died away.

die down (intr) = become gradually calmer and finally disappear (of riots, fires, excitement, &c.):

When the excitement had died down the shopkeepers took down their shutters and reopened their shops.

die out (intr) = become extinct (of customs, races, species of animals &c.):

Elephants would die out if men were allowed to shoot as many as they wished.

do

do away with (tr) = abolish:

The government should do away with the regulations restricting drinking hours.

do up (tr) = redecorate:

When I do *this room* up I'll paint the walls in stripes (do up *this room*/do *it* up).

do without (tr) = manage in the absence of a person or thing:

We had to do without petrol during the war.

The object is sometimes understood but not mentioned:

If there isn't any milk we'll have to do without (it).

draw

draw back (intr) = retire, recoil:

It's too late to draw back now; the plans are all made.

draw up (tr) = make a written plan or agreement:

My solicitor drew up *the lease* and we both signed it (drew *it* up).

draw up (intr) = stop (of vehicles):

The car drew up at the kerb and the driver got out.

drop

drop in (intr) = pay a short unannounced visit:

He dropped in for a few minutes to ask if he could borrow your car ('drop in is more colloquial than 'call in').

drop out (intr) = withdraw, retire from a scheme or plan:

We planned to hire a bus for the excursion but now so many people have dropped out that it will not be needed.

enter

enter for (tr) = become a candidate (for a contest, exam, &c.):

Two hundred competitors have entered for the motor-scooter race.

fade

fade away (intr) = disappear, become gradually fainter (usually of sounds):

The band moved on and the music faded away.

fall

fall back (intr) = withdraw, retreat (this is a deliberate action, quite different from **fall behind**, which is involuntary):

As the enemy advanced we fell back.

fall back on (tr) = use in the absence of something better:

We had to fall back on dried milk as fresh milk wasn't available.
He fell back on the old argument that if you educate women they won't be such good wives and mothers.

fall behind (intr) = slip into the rear through inability to keep up with the others, fail to keep up an agreed rate of payments:

At the beginning the whole party kept together but by the end of the day the women and weaker men had fallen behind.
He fell behind with his rent and the landlord began to become impatient.

fall in with someone's plans = accept them and agree to co-operate:

Tom to Harry (with whom he is arranging to share a flat): I'll fall in with whatever you suggest as regards sharing expenses.

fall in (intr) of troops &c. = get into line

fall out (intr) of troops &c. = leave the lines:

The troops fell in and were inspected. After the parade they fell out and went back to their barracks.

fall off (intr) = decrease (of numbers, attendance &c.):

Orders have been falling off lately; we must advertise more.
Cinema attendances usually fall off in summer.

fall on (tr) = attack violently (the victim has normally no chance to defend himself as the attackers are too strong. It is also sometimes used of hungry men who attack their food when they get it):

The wolves fell on the flock of sheep and killed them all.
The starving men fell on the food (= devoured it).

fall out (intr) = quarrel:

When thieves fall out honest men get their own (proverb).

fall through (intr) = fail to materialize (of plans):

My plans to go to Greece fell through because the journey turned out to be much more expensive than I had expected.

feed

be fed up (intr), *be fed up with* (tr) = be completely bored (slang):

I'm fed up with this wet weather. I'm fed up with waiting; I'm going home.

feel

feel up to (tr) = feel strong enough (to do something):

I don't feel up to dealing with the matter now. I'll do it in the morning.
I don't feel up to it.

fill

fill in/up forms &c. = complete them:

I had to fill in *three forms* to get my new passport (fill *three forms* in/fill *them* in).

find

find out (tr) = discover as a result of conscious effort:

In the end I found out what was wrong with my wireless.
The dog found out the way to open the door/found it out.

find someone out = discover that he has been doing something wrong (this discovery is usually a surprise because the person has been trusted):

The cashier had been robbing the till for months before he was found out.

fix

fix up (tr) = arrange:

The club has already fixed up *several matches* for next season (fixed *several matches* up/fixed *them* up).

get

get about (intr) = circulate; move or travel in a general sense:

The news got about that he had won the Irish Sweep and everybody began asking him for money.
He is a semi-invalid now and can't get about as well as he used to.

get away (intr) = escape:

Don't ask him how he is because if he starts talking about his health you'll never get away from him.
I hooked an enormous fish but it got away.

get away with (tr) = perform some illegal or wrong act without being punished; usually without even being caught:

He began forging cheques and at first he got away with it but in the end he was caught and sent to prison.

get back (tr) = recover possession of:

If you lend him a book he'll lend it to someone else and you'll never get *it* back (get back *your book*/get *your book* back).

get back = reach home again:

We spent the whole day in the mountains and didn't get back till dark.

get off (intr)

a = be free to leave, be allowed to leave (usually work or duty):

I had a lot to do in the office and didn't get off till eight.

b = be acquitted or receive no punishment (compare with **get away with it**, which implies that the offender is not even caught):

He was tried for theft but got off because there wasn't sufficient evidence against him (was acquitted).
The boy had to appear before a magistrate but he got off (received no punishment) as it was his first offence.

get on (intr), *get on with* (tr)

a = make progress, be successful:

How is he getting on at school?
He is getting on very well with his English.

b = live, work &c., amicably with someone:

He is a pleasant friendly man who gets on well with nearly everybody.
How are you and Mr Pitt getting on?

get out (intr) = escape from, leave (an enclosed place):

Don't worry about the snake. I've put it in a cardboard box. It can't get out.
News of the Budget got out before it was officially announced.
I don't very often get out (= out of the house) because I have too much to do.

Note that the imperative 'Get out', except when it means 'descend' (from a vehicle), is very rude.

get out of (tr) = free oneself from an obligation or habit:

I said that I'd help him. Now I don't want to but I can't get out of it (= free myself from my promise).
He knows that he smokes too much but says that he can't get out of the habit.
Some people live abroad to get out of paying heavy taxes.

get over (tr) = recover from (illness, distress, or mental or physical weakness):

He is just getting over a bad heart attack.
I can't get over her leaving her husband like that (= I haven't recovered from the surprise; I am astonished).
He used to be afraid of heights but he has got over that now.

get it over (the object is usually **it**, which normally represents something unpleasant) = deal with it and be finished with it:

If you have to go to the dentist why not go at once and get it over?

(Be careful not to confuse this with **get over it**, which is quite different.)

get round a person = coax him into letting you do what you want:

Girls can usually get round their fathers.

get round a difficulty/a regulation = find some solution to it/evade it:

If we charge people for admission we will have to pay tax on our receipts; but we can get round this regulation by saying that we are charging not for admission but for refreshments. Money paid for refreshments is not taxed.

get through (tr or intr) = finish a piece of work, finish successfully:

He got through his exam all right (= passed it).

get through (intr) = get into telephone communication:

I am trying to call London but I can't get through; I think all the lines are engaged.

get up (tr) = organize, arrange (usually an amateur entertainment or a charitable enterprise):

We got up a *subscription* for his widow (got *a subscription* up).
They got up *a concert* in aid of the Life Boat Association (they got *it* up).

get up (intr) = rise from bed, rise to one's feet, mount:

I get up at seven o'clock every morning.

(For get used to mean enter/leave vehicles, see 79.)

give

give something away = give it to someone (who need not be mentioned):

I'll give *this old coat* away (give away *this old coat*/give *it* away).

give someone away (object before away) = betray him:

He said that he was not an American but his accent gave him away (i.e. told us that he was an American).

give back (tr) = restore (a thing) to its owner:

I must call at the library to give back *this book* (to give *this book* back/to give *it* back).

give in (intr) = yield, cease to resist:

At first he wouldn't let her drive the car but she was so persuasive that he eventually gave in.

give out (intr) = become exhausted (of supplies &c.):

The champagne gave out long before the end of the reception.
His patience gave out and he slapped the child hard.

give out (tr)

a = announce verbally:

They gave out *the names of the winners* (gave *the names* out/gave *them* out).

b = distribute, issue:

The teacher gave out *the books* (i.e. gave *one/some* to each pupil).

give up (tr or intr) = abandon an attempt, cease trying to do something:

I tried to climb the wall but after I had failed three times I gave up/gave up *the attempt*/gave *the attempt* up/gave *it* up.
A really determined person never gives up/never gives up trying.

give up (tr) = abandon or discontinue a habit, sport, study, occupation:

Have you given up drinking whisky before breakfast?
He gave up *cigarettes*/gave *them* up.
He tried to learn Greek but soon got tired of it and gave it up.

give oneself up (object before **up**) = surrender:

I'm tired of being chased by the police; I'm going to give myself up.
He gave himself up to despair.

go

go ahead (intr) = proceed, continue, lead the way:

While she was away he went ahead with the work and got a lot done.
You go ahead and I'll follow; I'm not quite ready.

go away (intr) = leave, leave me, leave this place:

Are you going away for your holiday? No, I'm going to stay at home.
Please go away; I can't work unless I am alone.

go back (intr) = return, retire, retreat:

I have left that hotel and I'm never going back to it. It is a most uncomfortable place.

go back on (tr) = withdraw or break (a promise):

He went back on his promise to tell nobody about this (i.e. he told people about it, contrary to his promise).

go down (intr)

a = be received with approval (usually of an idea):

I suggested that she should look for a job but this suggestion did not go down at all well. She said that it was up to her relations to support her at home, now that she was a widow.

b = become less, be reduced (of wind, sea, weight, prices &c.):

During her illness her weight went down from nine stone to seven stone.
The wind went down and the sea became quite calm.

go for (tr) = attack:

The cat went for the dog and chased him out of the hall.

go in for (tr) = be especially interested in, practise; enter for a competition:

This restaurant goes in for vegetarian dishes (specializes in them).
She plays a lot of golf and goes in for all the competitions.

go into (tr) = investigate thoroughly:

'We shall have to go into this very carefully,' said the detective.

go off (intr)

a = explode (of ammunition or fireworks), be fired (of guns usually accidentally):

As he was cleaning his gun it went off and killed him.

b = be successful (of social occasions):

The party went off very well (i.e. everyone enjoyed it).

c = start a journey, leave:

He went off in a great hurry.

go on (intr) = continue a journey:

Go on till you come to the cross-roads.

go on (intr), *go on with* (tr), *go on* + gerund = continue any action:

Please go on playing; I like it.
Go on with the treatment. It is doing you good.

go on + infinitive:

He began by describing the route and went on to tell us what the trip would probably cost (= he continued [his speech] and told us &c.).

go out (intr)

a = leave the house:

She is always indoors; she doesn't go out enough.

b = join in social life, leave one's house for entertainments &c.

She is very pretty and gay and goes out a lot.

c = disappear, be discontinued (of fashions):

Crinolines went out about the middle of last century.

d = be extinguished (of lights, fires &c.):

The light went out and we were left in the dark.

go over (tr) = examine, study or repeat carefully:

He went over the plans again and discovered two mistakes.

go round (intr)

a = suffice (for a number of people):

Will there be enough wine to go round?

b = go to his/her/your &c. house:

I said that I'd go round and see her during the weekend.
I think I'll go round tonight (i.e. go to her house).

go through (tr) = examine carefully (usually a number of things. **go through** is like **look through** but more thorough):

There is a mistake somewhere; we'll have to go through the accounts and see where it is.
The police went through their files, to see if they could find any fingerprints to match those that they had found on the weapon.

go through (tr or intr) = suffer, endure:

No one knows what I went through while I was waiting for the verdict (i.e. how much I suffered).

go through with (tr) = finish, bring to a conclusion (usually in the face of some opposition or difficulty):

He went through with his plan although all his friends advised him to abandon it.

go up (intr)

a = rise (of prices :

The price of strawberries went up towards the end of the season.

b = burst into flames (and be destroyed), explode (used of whole buildings, ships &c.):

When the fire reached the ammunition store the whole ship went up (= blew up).
Someone dropped a cigarette end into a can of petrol and the whole garage went up in flames.

go without (tr) = do without. (But it only applies to things. 'Go without a person' has only a literal meaning i.e. it means 'start or make a journey without him'.)

grow

grow out of (tr) = abandon, on becoming older, a childish (and often bad) habit:

He used to tell a lot of lies as a young boy but he grew out of that later on.

grow up (intr)

a = become adult:

'What are you going to do when you grow up?' I asked. 'I'm going to be an acrobat,' said the boy.

b = develop (of customs):

The custom of going away for one's holiday has grown up during the last thirty years.

hand

hand in (tr) = give by hand (to someone who need not be mentioned because the person spoken to knows already):

I handed in *my resignation* (i.e. gave it to my employer).
Someone handed *this parcel* in this morning/handed *it* in.

hand on/down (tr) = bequeath or pass on (traditions/information/possessions):

This legend has been handed down from father to son.

hand out (tr) = distribute:

He was standing at the door of the theatre handing out *leaflets* (handing *leaflets* out/handing *them* out).

hand over (tr or intr) = surrender authority or responsibility to another:

The outgoing Minister handed over *his department* to his successor (handed *his department* over/handed *it* over).

hand round (tr) = give or show to each person present:

The hostess handed round *coffee and cakes* (handed *them* round).

hang

hang about/around (tr or intr) = loiter or wait (near):

He hung about the entrance all day, hoping for a chance to speak to the director.

hang back (intr) = show unwillingness to act:

Everyone approved of the scheme but when we asked for volunteers they all hung back.

hang on to (tr) = retain, keep in one's possession (coll.):

I'd hang on to that old coat if I were you. It might be useful.

hold

hold off (intr) = keep at a distance, stay away (used of rain):

The rain held off till after the tennis party.

hold on (intr) = wait (especially on the telephone):

Yes, Mr Pitt is in. If you hold on for a moment I'll get him for you.

hold on/out (intr) = persist in spite of, endure hardship or danger:

The survivors on the rock signalled that they were short of water but could hold out for another day.
The enemy besieged the town but we held out for six weeks.

hold up (tr)

a = stop by threats or violence (in order to rob):

The bandits held up the train and robbed the passengers.
Masked men held up *the cashier* and robbed the bank (held *him* up).

b = stop, delay (especially used in the passive):

The bus was held up because a tree had fallen across the road.

join

join up (intr) = enlist in one of the armed services:

When war was declared he joined up at once.

jump

jump at (tr) = accept with enthusiasm (an offer or opportunity):

He was offered a place in the Himalayan expedition and jumped at the chance.

keep

keep somebody back (object before **back**) = restrain, hinder, prevent from advancing:

Frequent illnesses kept him back (i.e. prevented him from making normal progress).

keep down (tr) = repress, control:

What is the best way to keep down *rats*? (keep *them* down).
Try to remember to turn off the light when you leave the room. I am trying to keep down *expenses*/keep *expenses* down.

keep in a schoolboy = oblige him to remain at school after school hours as a punishment:

The master kept Tom in/kept him in because he had been inattentive.
Some boys would rather be beaten than be kept in after school.

keep off (tr or intr) = refrain from walking on, or from coming too close:

'Keep off the grass' (park notice).

keep on (often followed by gerund) = continue:

I wanted to explain but he kept on talking and didn't give me a chance to say anything.

keep out (tr) = prevent from entering:

My shoes are very old and don't keep out the *rain* (keep *the rain* out/keep *it* out).

keep out (intr) = stay outside:

'Private. Keep out' (notice on door).

keep up (tr) = maintain (an effort):

He began walking at six miles an hour but he couldn't keep up *that speed* and soon began to walk more slowly (he couldn't keep *it* up).
It is difficult to keep up a conversation with someone who only says 'Yes' and 'No'.

keep up (intr), *keep up with* (tr) = remain abreast of someone who is advancing; advance at the same pace as:

A runner can't keep up with a cyclist.
The work that the class is doing is too difficult for me. I won't be able to keep up (*or* to keep up with them).
It is impossible to keep up with the news unless you read the newspapers.

knock

knock off (tr or intr) = stop work for the day (colloquial):

English workmen usually knock off at 5.30 or 6.0 p.m.
We knock off work in time for tea.

knock out (tr) = hit someone so hard that he falls unconscious:

In the finals of the boxing championship he knocked out *his opponent*, who was carried out of the ring (knocked his *opponent* out/knocked *him* out).

lay

lay in (tr)= provide oneself with a sufficient quantity (of stores &c.) to last for some time:

Because she expected a shortage of dried fruits she laid in a large supply.

lay out (tr) = plan gardens, building sites &c.

Lenôtre laid out *the gardens* at Versailles (laid *the gardens* out/laid *them* out).

lay up (tr) = store carefully till needed again (used of ships, cars &c.):

When petrol rationing started many people laid up *their cars* (laid *them* up).

be laid up (of a person) = be confined to bed through illness:

She was laid up for weeks with a slipped disk.

lead

lead up to (tr) = prepare the way for, introduce (figuratively):

He wanted to borrow my car, but he didn't say so at once. He led up to the subject by talking about his holidays.

leave

leave off (usually intr) = stop (doing something):

He was mowing the grass but I told him to leave off because the neighbours were complaining about the noise.

leave out (tr) = omit:

We'll sing our School Song leaving out the last ten verses.
They gave each competitor a number; but they left out *No. 13* as no one wanted to have it (left *No. 13* out/left *it* out).

let

let down (tr) = lower:

When she lets *her hair* down it reaches her waist (lets down *her hair*/lets *it* down).
You can let a coat down (i.e. lengthen it) by using the hem.

let someone down (object before **down**) = disappoint him by failing to act as well as expected, or by failing to fulfil an agreement:

I promised him that you would work well. Why did you let me down by doing so little?
He said he'd come to help me; but he let me down. He never turned up.

let in (tr) = allow to enter, admit:

They let in the *ticket-holders* (let *the ticket-holders* in/let *them* in).
If you mention my name to the door-keeper he will let you in.

let someone off (object before **off**) = refrain from punishing:

I thought that the magistrate was going to fine me, but he let me off (**I got off** see page 221).

let out (tr)

a = make wider (of clothes):

That boy is getting fatter. You'll have to let out *his clothes* (let *his clothes* out/let *them* out).

b = allow to leave, release:

He opened the door and let out *the dog* (let *the dog* out/let *it* out).

listen

listen in (intr) = listen to the wireless:

I only listen in if there is a good concert.

live

live down a bad reputation = live in such a manner that people will forget it:

He has never quite been able to live down a reputation for drunkenness which he got when he was a young man/live it down.

live in (intr) = live in one's place of work (chiefly used of domestic servants):

Advertisement: Cook wanted. £8 a week. Live in.

live on (tr) = use as staple food:

It is said that for a certain period of his life Byron lived on vinegar and potatoes in order to keep thin.

live up to (tr) = maintain a certain moral or economic standard in keeping with one's ideal, position &c.:

He had high ideals and tried to live up to them (i.e. he tried to act in accordance with his ideals).

lock

lock up a house (tr or intr; usually intr) = lock all doors:

People usually lock up before they go to bed at night.

lock up a person or thing = put in a locked place i.e. box, safe, prison:

She locked up *her diamonds* every night (locked *her diamonds* up/locked *them* up).

look

look after (tr) = take care of:

Will you look after my parrot when I am away?

look ahead (intr) = consider the future so as to make provision for it:

Everyone should look ahead and save a little money each year for when he retires.

look at (tr) = regard:

He looked at the clock and said, 'It is midnight.'

look back (intr), *look back on* (tr) = consider the past:

Looking back, I don't suppose we are any worse now than people were a hundred years ago.
Perhaps some day it will be pleasant to look back on these things.

look back/round (intr) = look behind (literally):

Don't look round now, but the woman behind us is wearing the most extraordinary hat.

look for (tr) = search for, seek:

I have lost my watch. Will you help me to look for it?

look out for (tr) = keep one's eyes open so as to see something (usually fairly conspicuous) if it presents itself:

I am going to the party too, so look out for me.

look out (intr) = be watchful, beware:

(to someone just about to cross the road) 'Look out! There's a lorry coming!'

look forward to (tr) = expect with pleasure (often used with gerund):

I am looking forward to her arrival/to seeing her.

look in (intr) = pay a short (often unannounced) visit = call in):

I'll look in this evening to see how she is.

look into (tr) = investigate:

There is a mystery about his death and the police are looking into it.

look on . . . as (tr) = consider:

Most people look on a television set as an essential piece of furniture.
These children look on their teachers as their enemies.

look on (intr) = be a spectator only, not a participator:

Two men were fighting. The rest were looking on.

look on (tr), *look out on* (tr) (used of windows and houses) = be facing:

His house looks on to the sea (i.e. from his house you can see the sea).

look over (tr) = inspect critically, read again, revise quickly (**look over** is similar to **go over** but less thorough):

Look over what you've written before handing it to the examiner.
I'm going to look over a house that I'm thinking of buying.

look through (tr) = examine a number of things, often in order to select some of them; turn over the pages of a book or newspaper, looking for information:

Look through your old clothes and see if you have anything to give away.
Look through these photographs and try to pick out the man you saw.
He looked through the book and decided that he wouldn't like it.

look through someone = look at him without appearing to see him, as a deliberate act of rudeness:

She has to be polite to me in the office but when we meet outside she always looks through me.

look up an address/a name/word/train time/telephone number &c. = look for it in the appropriate book or paper, i.e. address book/directory/dictionary/time-table &c.:

If you don't know the meaning of the word look *it* up (look up *the word*/look *the word* up).
I must look up the time of your train (look for it in the time-table).

look somebody up can mean **visit**. The person visited usually lives at some distance. **look up** is therefore different from **look in**, which implies that the person visited lives quite close:

Any time you come to London do look me up (come and see me).
I haven't seen Tom for ages. I must find out where he lives and look *him* up (look *Tom* up/look up *Tom*).

look up (intr) = improve (the subject is usually *things/business/world affairs/the weather*, i.e. nothing very definite):

Business has been very bad lately but things are beginning to look up now.

look someone up and down = look at him contemptuously, letting your eyes wander from his head to his feet and back again:

The policeman looked the drunk man up and down very deliberately before replying to his question.

look up to (tr) = respect:

Schoolboys usually look up to great athletes.

look down on (tr) = despise:

Small boys usually look down on little girls and refuse to play with them.
She bought a television set because she was afraid that her neighbours would look down on her if she didn't have one.

make

make for (tr) = travel towards:

The escaped prisoner was making for the coast.

make off (intr) = run away (used of thieves &c.):

The boys made off when they saw the policemen.

make out (tr)

a = discover the meaning of, understand, see, hear &c. clearly:

I can't make out *the address*, he has written it so badly (make *the address* out/make *it* out).
Can you hear what the man with the loudspeaker is saying? I can't make it out at all.
I can't make out why he isn't here yet.

b = state (probably falsely):

He made out that he was a shipwrecked sailor. We later learnt that this wasn't true at all.
The English climate isn't so bad as some English people make out.

c = make out a cheque = write it:

Customer: Who shall I make it out to?
Shopkeeper: Make it out to Jones and Company.

make up one's mind = come to a decision:

In the end he made up his mind to go by train.

make up a quarrel/make it up = end it:

Isn't it time you and Ann made up *your quarrel*/made *it* up?

make up a story/excuse/explanation = invent it:

I don't believe your story at all. I think you are just making it up.

make up (tr or intr) = use cosmetics:

Most women make up/make up *their faces*/make *their faces* up.
Actors have to be made up before they appear on the stage.

make up (tr) = put together, compound, compose:

Take this prescription to the chemist's. They will make it up for you there.
Notice in tailor's window: Customers' own materials made up.
The audience was made up of very young children.

make up for (tr) = compensate for (the object is very often **it**):

You'll have to work very hard today to make up for the time you wasted yesterday *or* to make up for being late yesterday.
We aren't allowed to drink when we are in training but we intend to make up for it after the race (i.e. to drink more than usual then).

miss

miss out (tr) = leave out ('leave out' is more usual).

mix

mix up (tr) = confuse:

He mixed up the addresses so that no one got the right letters/mixed them up.

be/get mixed up with = be involved (usually some rather disreputable person or business):

I don't want to get mixed up with any illegal organization.

move

move in (intr) = move self and possessions into new house, flat, rooms &c.

move out (intr) = leave house/flat &c., with one's possessions, vacate accommodation:

I have found a new flat. The present tenant is moving out this weekend and I am moving in on Wednesday.

move on or *up* (intr) = advance, go higher:

Normally in schools boys move up every year.

order

order somebody about (object before **about**) = give him a lot of orders (often regardless of his convenience or feelings):

He is a retired admiral and still has the habit of ordering people about.

pay

pay back (tr), *pay someone back* (tr or intr) = repay:

I must pay back *the money* that I borrowed (pay *the money* back/pay *it* back).
I must pay back *Mr Pitt* (pay *Mr Pitt* back/pay *him* back).
I must pay Mr Pitt back *the money* he lent me.
I must pay him back *the money*. I must pay *it* back to him.

pay someone back/out = revenge oneself:

I'll pay you out for this (i.e. for the harm you have done me).

pay up (intr) = pay money owed in full:

Unless you pay up I shall tell my solicitor to write to you.

pick

pick out (tr) = choose, select, distinguish from a group:

Here are six diamonds. Pick out *the one you like best* (pick *it* out).
In an identity parade the witness has to try to pick out *the criminal* from a group of about eight men (pick *the criminal* out/pick *him* out).
I know that you are in this photograph but I can't pick *you* out.

pick up (tr)

a = raise or lift a person or thing, usually from the ground or from a table or chair:

He picked up *the child* and carried him into the house/picked *the child* up.
She scatters newspapers all over the floor and I have to pick *them* up.

b = call for, take with one (in a vehicle):

I won't have time to come to your house but I could pick you up at the end of your road.
The train stops here to pick up *passengers*, but only if passengers arrange this in advance (pick *passengers* up/pick *them* up).
The crew of the wrecked yacht were picked up by helicopter.

c = receive (by chance) wireless signals:

Their S.O.S. was picked up by a ham radio operator, who informed the lifeboat headquarters.

d = acquire cheaply, learn without effort:

Sometimes you pick up wonderful bargains in these markets.
Children usually pick up foreign languages very quickly.

point

point out (tr) = indicate, show:

As we drove through the city the guide pointed out *the most important buildings* (pointed *the buildings* out/pointed *them* out).

pull

pull down (tr) = demolish (used of buildings):

Everywhere elegant old buildings are being pulled down and mediocre modern erections are being put up. (pull down *houses*/pull *them* down.)

pull off (tr) = succeed (the object is normally **it**):

Much to our surprise he pulled off *the deal*/pulled *it* off (= sold the goods/got the contract).

pull through (intr or tr) = recover from illness/cause someone to recover:

We thought that she was going to die but penicillin pulled her through (tr).
He is very ill but he'll pull through if we look after him carefully (intr).

pull up (intr) = stop (of vehicles):

A lay-by is a space at the side of a main road, where drivers can pull up if they want a rest.

put

put aside/by (tr) = save for future use (usually money). **put aside** often implies that the money is being saved for a certain purpose:

He puts aside *£5 a month* to pay for his summer holiday (puts *it* aside).
Don't spend all your salary. Try to put *something* by each month.

put away (tr) = put tidily out of sight (usually in drawers, cupboards &c.):

Put *your toys* away, children; it's bedtime (put away *the toys*/put *them* away).

put something back = replace it where you found it/where it belongs:

When you've finished with the book put it back on the shelf.

put back a clock/watch = retard the hands: *put the clock back* is sometimes used figuratively to mean *return to the customs of the past*:

Mother: Your father and I will arrange a marriage for you when the time comes.
Daughter: You're trying to put *the clock* back. Parents don't arrange marriages these days! (put back *the clock*/put *it* back).

put down (tr)

a = the opposite of **pick up**:

He picked up the saucepan and put it down at once because the handle was almost red-hot (put *the saucepan* down/put *it* down).

b = crush rebellions, movements:

Troops were used to put down *the rebellion* (put *the rebellion* down/put *it* down).

c = write:

Put down *his phone number* before you forget it (put *the number* down/put *it* down).
Customer to shop assistant: I'll take that one. Please put it down to me/to my account (= enter it in my account).

put something down to (tr) = attribute it to:

The children wouldn't answer him, but he wasn't annoyed as he put it down to shyness.
She hasn't been well since she came to this country; I put it down to the climate.

put forward a suggestion/proposal &c. = offer it for consideration:

The older members of the committee are inclined to veto any suggestions put forward by the younger ones (put *a suggestion* forward/put *it* forward).

put forward/on clocks and watches = advance the hands. **put forward** is the opposite of **put back**:

At the beginning of summer people in England used to put *their clocks* forward/on an hour. When summer time ended they put them back an hour.

put in a claim = make a claim:

He put in a claim for compensation because he had lost his luggage in the train crash.

put in for a job/a post = apply for it:

They are looking for a lecturer in geography. Why don't you put in for it?

put in (intr) used of ships = call (at a port):

Ships going to Australia usually put in at Genoa/put in here.

put off an action = postpone it:

Some people put off making their wills till it is too late.
I'll put off *my visit* to Scotland till the weather is warmer (put *my visit* off/put *it* off).

put a person off

a = tell him to postpone his visit to you:

I had invited some guests to dinner but I had to put them off because a power cut prevented me from cooking anything.

b = repel, deter him:

I wanted to see the film but the queue put me off.
Many people who want to come to England are put off by the stories they hear about English weather.

put on clothes/glasses/jewellery = dress oneself &c. The opposite is take off:

He put on *a black coat* so that he would be inconspicuous (put *a coat* on/put *it* on).
She put on her glasses and took the letter from my hand.

put on an expression = assume it:

He put on an air of indifference, which didn't deceive anybody.

put on a play = produce/perform it:

The students usually put on a play at the end of the year.

put on a light/gas or electric fire/wireless = switch it on:

Put on the light (put the light on/put it on).

put out any kind of light or fire = extinguish it:

Put out *that light*/(put *the light* out/put *it* out).
Put someone out = inconvenience him.
He is very selfish. He wouldn't put himself out for anyone.

be put out = be annoyed:

She was very put out when I said that her new dress didn't suit her.

put up (tr)

a = erect (a building, monument, statue &c.):

He put up *a shed* in the garden to keep tools in (he put *a shed* up/put *it* up).

b = raise (prices):

When the importation of foreign tomatoes was forbidden, home growers put up *their prices* (they put *their prices* up/put *them* up).

put someone up (object usually before **up**) = give him temporary hospitality:

If you come to Paris I will put *you* up. You needn't look for an hotel.

put someone up to something (usually some trick) = give him the idea of doing it/ tell him how to do it:

He couldn't have thought of that trick by himself. Someone must have put him up to it.

put up with (tr) = bear patiently:

We had to put up with a lot of noise when the children were at home.

ring

ring up (tr or intr) = telephone:

I rang up *the theatre* to book seats for tonight. (I rang *the theatre* up/rang *them* up).
If you can't come ring up and let me know.

ring off (intr) = end a telephone call by putting down the receiver:

He rang off before I could ask his name.

round

round up (tr) = drive or bring together (people or animals):

The sheepdog rounded up the sheep (= collected them into a group) and drove them through the gate.
On the day after the riots the police rounded up *all suspects*/rounded *them* up (= arrested them).

rub

rub out (tr) = erase pencil or ink marks with an india-rubber:

The child wrote down the wrong word and then rubbed *it* out. (He rubbed *the word* out/rubbed out *the word*.)

rub up (tr) = revise one's knowledge of a subject:

I am going to France next month; I must rub up *my French*/rub *it* up.

run

run after (tr) = pursue (see example below).

run away (intr) = flee, desert, one's home/school &c., elope:

The thief ran away and the policeman ran after him.
He ran away from home and got a job as a cabin boy.

run away with (tr) = become uncontrollable (of emotions), gallop off out of rider's control (of horses):

My tongue ran away with me and I said things that I afterwards regretted.
His horse ran away with him and he had a bad fall.

run away with the idea = accept an idea too hastily:

Don't run away with the idea that I am uncharitable.

run down (tr) = disparage, speak ill of:

He is always running down his neighbours.

run down (intr) = become unwound/discharged (of clocks/batteries &c.):

This torch is useless, the battery has run down.

be run down (intr) = be in poor health after illness, overwork &c.:

He is still run down after his illness and unfit for work.

run in (tr) = drive slowly initially to avoid straining engine (necessary with new or reconditioned engines):

I can't go more than 35 miles an hour as this is a new car and I am still running *it* in (I am running in a *new car*/running a *new car* in).
Notice on the back window of a new car: 'Running in. Please pass.'

run into (tr) = collide with (of vehicles):

The car skidded and ran into a lamp-post (= struck the lamp-post).

run into/across someone = meet him accidentally:

I ran into my cousin in Harrods recently (I met him).

run out of (tr) = have none left, having consumed all the supply:

I have run out of milk. Put some lemon in your tea instead.

run over (tr) = drive over accidentally (in a vehicle):

The drunk man stepped into the road right in front of the oncoming car. The driver couldn't stop in time and ran over him.
He fell in the road and was run over by a small car, and taken to hospital with a broken leg.

run over (tr or intr) = overflow:

He turned on both taps full and left the bathroom. When he came back he found that the water was running over (*or* running over the edge of the bath).

run over/through (tr) = rehearse, check or revise quickly:

We've got a few minutes before the train goes, so I'll just run through your instructions again.

run through (tr) = consume extravagantly, waste (used of supplies or money):

I laid in a good stock of provisions but he ran through it all in a couple of weeks.

run up clothes = make them quickly:

Do you like this blouse? I ran it up myself this afternoon.

run up bills = incur them and increase them by continuing to buy things and put them down to one's account:

Her husband said that she must pay for things at once and not run up bills.

run up against difficulties/opposition = encounter them/it:

If he tries to change the rules of the club he will run up against a lot of opposition.

see

see about (tr) = make inquiries or arrangements:

I must see about getting in coal for the winter.

see somebody off = accompany an intending traveller to his train/boat/plane &c.:

The station was crowded with boys going back to school and parents who were seeing them off.

see somebody out = accompany a departing guest to the door of the house:

When guests leave the host usually sees them out.
Don't bother to come to the door with me. I can see myself out.

see over a house/a building = go into every room, examine it, often with a view to buying or renting (this combination is chiefly used in the infinitive):

I'm definitely interested in the house. I'd like to see over it as soon as possible.

see through (tr) = discover a hidden attempt to deceive:

She pretended that she loved him but he saw through her, and realized that she was only after his money. (= he wasn't taken in by her/by her pretence; for **take in** see page 241).

see to (tr) = make arrangements, put right, repair:

If you can provide the wine I'll see to the food.
That electric fire isn't safe, you should have it seen to.

sell

sell off (tr) = sell cheaply (what is left of a stock):

Assistant: This line is being discontinued so we are selling off *the remainder* of our stock; that's why they are so cheap (sell *the rest* off/sell *it* off).

sell out (intr) = sell all that you have of a certain type of article:

When all the seats for a certain performance have been booked, theatres put a notice saying 'Sold out' outside the booking office.

send

be sent down (intr) = be expelled from a university for misconduct:

He behaved so badly in college that he was sent down and never got his degree.

send for (tr) = summon (the person summoned may be in the building already):

One of our water pipes has burst. We must send for the plumber.
The director sent for me and asked if I could explain what had happened.

send in (tr) = send to someone (who need not be mentioned because the person spoken to knows already):

You must send in *your old driving licence* with your application for a new one (= send it to the authority concerned) (send *your old licence* in/send *it* in).

send on (tr) = forward, send after a person:

If any letters come for you after you have gone I will send *them* on (I'll send on *your letters*/send *your letters* on).

set

set in (intr) = begin (a period, usually unpleasant):

Winter has set in.

set off (tr) = start (a series of events):

That strike set off a series of strikes throughout the country.

set off/out (intr) = start a journey:

They set out/off at six and hoped to arrive before dark.

'for' is used when the destination is mentioned:

They set out/off for Rome.

set out + infinitive (often **show/prove/explain** or some similar verb) = begin this undertaking, aim:

In this book the author sets out to prove that the inhabitants of the islands came from South America.

set up (tr) = achieve, establish (a record):

He set up *a new record* when he ran a mile in under four minutes (he set *a new record* up/set *it* up).

set up (intr) = start a new business:

When he married he left his father's shop and set up on his own (i.e. opened his own shop).
When he had finished his training he returned to his native town and set up as a jeweller.

settle

settle down (intr) = become accustomed to, and contented in, a new placc, job &c.:

He was unhappy when he first went to school but he soon settled down and liked it very much.

settle up (intr) = pay money owed:

Tell me what I owe you at the end of the week and I'll settle up with you then.

shout

shout down (tr) = make a loud noise so as to prevent a speaker from being heard:

He tried to make a speech defending himself but the crowd wouldn't listen to his explanation and shouted *him* down.
The angry members shouted down *all the moderate speakers* (shouted *the moderate speakers* down).

show

show off (tr or intr) = display (skill, knowledge &c.) purely in order to win notice or applause:

Although Jules speaks English perfectly, my cousin spoke French to him all the time just to show off (i.e. to impress us with her knowledge of French).
He is always picking up very heavy things just to show off his strength.

shut

shut down (tr or intr) = close down (see p. 215).

sit

sit back (intr) = relax, take no action, do no more work:

I have worked hard all my life and now I'm going to sit back and watch other people working.

sit out (tr or intr) = remain seated with one's partner instead of dancing:

I can't dance the Samba; let's sit *this one* out (sit out *this dance*).

sit up (intr) = stay out of bed till later than usual (usually reading, working, or waiting for someone):

I was very worried when he didn't come in and I sat up till 3 a.m. waiting for him.
She sat up all night with her sick dog.

stand

stand by (someone) (tr) = continue to support and help him:

No matter what happens I'll stand by you, so don't be afraid.

stand for (tr) = represent:

The symbol 'x' usually stands for the unknown quantity in mathematics.

stand for Parliament = be a candidate for Parliament, offer yourself for election:

Mr Pitt stood for Parliament five years ago but he wasn't elected.

stand up for (tr) = defend verbally:

His father blamed him, but his mother stood up for him and said that he had acted sensibly.

stand up to (tr) = resist, defend oneself against (a person or force):

This type of building stands up to the gales very well.

stand out (intr) = be conspicuous, be easily seen:

She stood out from the crowd because of her height and her flaming red hair.

stay

stay up (intr) = remain out of bed till later than usual ('stay up' is practically the same as 'sit up', the only difference being that 'sit up' usually implies work, study, or waiting, while 'stay up' may be for pleasure only):

Children never want to go to bed at the proper time; they always want to stay up late.

step

step up (tr) = increase rate of, increase speed of (this usually refers to industrial production):

This new machine will step up production/step it up.

take

be taken aback (intr) = be surprised and disconcerted:

When she told me that she was going to ride the horse herself in the race I was completely taken aback and at first couldn't think of anything to say.

take after (tr) = resemble (one's parents/grandparents &c.):

He takes after his grandmother; she had red hair too.
My great-grandfather was terribly forgetful and I take after him; I can never remember anything.

take back (tr) = withdraw (remarks, accusations &c.):

I blamed him bitterly at first but later, when I heard the whole story, I realized that he had been right and I went to him and took back my remarks.

take down (tr) = write, usually from dictation.

He read out the names and his secretary took *them* down (she took down *the names*/took *the names* down).

take for (tr) = attribute wrong identity or qualities to someone:

I took him for his brother. They are extremely alike.
Do you take me for a fool?

take in (tr)

a = deceive:

At first he took us in by his stories and we tried to help him; but later we learnt that his stories were all lies.

b = receive as guests/lodgers:

When our car broke down I knocked on the door of the nearest house. The owner very kindly took *us* in and gave us a bed for the night.
People who live by the sea often take in *paying guests* during the summer (take *paying guests* in/take *them* in).

c = understand, receive into the mind:

I was thinking of something else while she was speaking and I didn't really take in *what she was saying.*
I couldn't take in *the lecture* at all. It was too difficult for me (I couldn't take *it* in).

d = make less wide (of clothes):

I'm getting much thinner; I'll have to take in *my clothes* (take *my clothes* in/take *them* in).

take off (tr) = remove (when used of clothing 'take off' is the opposite of 'put on'):

He took off *his hat* when he entered the house and put it on again when he went out. (He took *his hat* off/took *it* off.)

take off (intr) = leave the ground (of aeroplanes):

There is often a spectators' balcony at airports, where people can watch the planes taking off and landing.

take on (tr)

a = undertake work:

She wants someone to look after her children. I shouldn't care to take on *the job.* They are terribly spoilt (take *the job* on/take *it* on).

b = accept as an opponent:

I'll take *you* on at table tennis (= I'll play against you).
I took on *Mr Pitt* at draughts (took *Mr Pitt* on/took *him* on).

take out (tr) = remove, extract:

Petrol will take out *that stain* (take *the stain* out/take *it* out).
The dentist took out two of her teeth.

take somebody out = entertain them (usually at some public place):

Her small boy is at a boarding school quite near here. I take him out every month (and give him a meal in a restaurant).

take over (tr or intr) = assume responsibility for, or control of, in succession to somebody else:

We stop work at ten o'clock and the night shift takes over then.
Miss Smith is leaving to get married and Miss Jones will be taking over the class/Miss Jones will be taking over from Miss Smith (see **hand over**).

take to (tr)

a = begin a habit. There is usually the impression that the speaker thinks this habit bad or foolish, though this is not necessarily always the case. It is often used with the gerund:

He took to drink (= began drinking too much).
He took to borrowing money from the petty cash.

b = find likeable or agreeable particularly at first meeting:

I was introduced to the headmistress. I can't say I took to her.
He went to sea (became a sailor) and took to the life like a duck to water.

c = seek refuge/safety in:

When they saw that the ship was sinking the crew took to the boats.
After the failure of the rebellion many of the rebels took to the hills and became bandits.

take up (tr)

a = begin a hobby, sport or kind of study (there is no feeling of criticism here):

He took up *golf* and became very keen on it (took *it* up).

b = occupy (a proportion of time or space):

He has a very small room and most of the space is taken up by a grand piano.
A lot of an M.P.'s time is taken up with answering letters from his constituents.

talk

talk over (tr) = discuss:

Talk *it* over with your wife and give me your answer tomorrow (talk over *my suggestion*/talk *my suggestion* over).

think

think over (tr) = consider:

I can't decide straight away but I'll think over *your idea* and let you know what I decide (I'll think *your idea* over/think *it* over).

throw

throw away/out (tr) = jettison (rubbish &c.):

Throw away *those old shoes*. Nobody could wear them now. (Throw *the shoes* away/throw *them* away.)

throw up (tr) = abandon suddenly (some work or plan):

He suddenly got tired of the job and threw *it* up (he threw up *the job*/threw *the job* up).

tie

tie someone up = bind his hands and feet so that he cannot move:

The thieves tied up *the night watchman* before opening the safe (they tied *the man* up/tied *him* up).

try

try on (tr) = put on (an article of clothing) to see if it fits:

Customer in dress shop: I like this dress, could I try *it* on? (could I try *this dress* on/try on *this dress*).

try out (tr) = test:

We won't know how the plan works till we have tried *it* out.
They are trying out *new ways of preventing noise in hospitals* (trying *them* out).

turn

turn away (tr) = refuse admittance to:

The hotel porter turned away *anybody who wasn't wearing a collar and tie* (turned *men* away/turned *them* away).

turn down (tr) = refuse, reject an offer, application, applicant:

I applied for the job but they turned *me* down/turned down *my application* because I didn't know German.
He was offered £500 for the picture but he turned *it* down (turned down *the offer*/turned *the offer* down).

turn into (tr) = convert into:

I am going to turn my garage into a playroom for the children.
She turned the silver candlestick into an electric lamp.

turn in (intr) = go to bed (used chiefly by sailors/campers &c.):

The campers usually turned in as soon as it got dark.
The captain turned in, not realizing that the icebergs were so close.

turn on/off (tr) = switch on/off (lights, gas or electric fires, radios, taps &c.).

turn up/down (tr) = increase/decrease the pressure, force, volume (of gas or oil, lights, fires, or of radios):

Turn up the gas; vegetables should be cooked quickly.
I wish the people in the next flat would turn down *their wireless*. You can hear every word (turn *the wireless* down/turn *it* down).

turn out (tr)

a = produce:

That creamery turns out two hundred tons of butter a week (turns *it* out).
Public schools are sometimes accused of turning out rather snobbish boys.

b = empty, evict:

i turn a person out = evict him from his house/flat/room:

At one time if tenants didn't pay their rent, the landlord could turn them out.

ii turn out one's pockets/handbags/drawers &c. = empty them, usually when looking for something:

'Turn out your pockets,' said the detective.

iii turn out a room usually means clean it thoroughly, first putting the furniture outside:

A good housewife turns out one room every month.

turn out (intr)

a = assemble, come out into the street (usually in order to welcome somebody):

The whole town turned out to welcome the astronaut.

b = develop:

I've never made Yorkshire pudding before so I am not quite sure how it is going to turn out.
Marriages arranged by marriage bureaux often turn out very well.

c = be revealed. Notice the two possible constructions: *it turned out that . . .* and: *he turned out to be . . .* :

He told her that he was a bachelor but it turned out that he was married with six children (= she learnt this later).
Our car broke down half way through the journey but the hiker we had picked up turned out to be an expert mechanic and was able to put things right.

Note the difference between **turn out** and **come out**. With **turn out** the fact revealed is always mentioned and there is no implication that the facts are discreditable. With **come out** we are told only that certain facts (usually discreditable) are revealed; we are not told what these facts are.

turn over (tr) = turn something so that the side previously underneath is exposed:

He turned over *the stone*/turned *the stone* over/turned *it* over.
The initials 'P.T.O.' at the bottom of a page mean 'Please turn over'.
'Turn over a new leaf' = begin again, meaning to do better.

turn over (intr)

a = turn upside down, upset, capsize (used of vehicles or boats):

The car struck the wall and turned over.
The canoe turned over, throwing the boys into the water.

b = (of people) change position so as to lie on the other side:

It is difficult to turn over in a hammock.
When his alarm went off he just turned over and went to sleep again.

turn up (intr) = arrive, appear (usually from the point of view of someone waiting or searching):

We arranged to meet at the station but she didn't turn up.
Don't bother to look for my umbrella; it will turn up some day.

wait

wait on (tr) = attend, serve (at home or in a restaurant):

He expected his wife to wait on him hand and foot.
The man who was waiting on us seemed very inexperienced; he got all our orders mixed up.

wash

wash up (tr or intr) = wash the plates &c., after a meal:

When we have dinner very late we don't wash up till the next morning.

watch

watch out (intr) = look out.

watch out for (tr) = look out for (see p. 230).

wear

wear away (intr) = gradually reduce; make smooth or flat; hollow out (used mostly of wood or stone. The subject is usually the weather, or people who walk on, or touch the stone &c.):

It is almost impossible to read the inscription on the monument as most of the letters have been worn away (by the weather).

wear off (intr) = disappear gradually (can be used literally but is chiefly used for mental or physical feelings):

These glasses will seem uncomfortable at first but that feeling will soon wear off.
When her first feeling of shyness had worn off she started to enjoy herself.
He began to try to sit up, which showed us that the effects of the drug were wearing off.

wear out (tr or intr)

a = (tr) use till no longer serviceable; (intr) become unserviceable as a result of long use (chiefly of clothes):

Children wear out *their shoes* very quickly (wear *their shoes* out/wear *them* out).
Cheap clothes wear out quickly.

b = (tr) exhaust (used of people; very often used in the passive):

He worked all night and wanted to go on working the next day, but we saw that he was completely worn out and persuaded him to stop.

wind

wind up (tr or intr) = bring or come to an end (used of speeches or business proceedings):

The headmaster wound up by saying that the school had had a most successful year (wound the meeting up/wound it up).

wink

wink at (tr) = ignore purposely, pretend not to notice (an error, breach of regulations):

He always goes abroad with far more currency than the regulations permit and the authorities always seem to wink at it.

wipe

wipe out (tr) = destroy completely:

The epidemic wiped out *whole families* (wiped *whole families* out/wiped *them* out).

work

work out (tr) = find by calculation or study, the solution to some problem or a method of dealing with it; study and decide on, the details of a scheme:

He used logarithms to work out *the problem*/work *the problem* out.
Tell me where you want to go and I'll work out a route.
This is the outline of the plan. We want the committee to work out the *details* (work *them* out).

299 Nouns and verbs formed by combinations listed in 298

Note that some of these compounds are hyphened and some are not; also that the verb may be the first or last part of the compound word. Definitions will normally not be given as they have been given in **298**.

break

outbreak (noun):

At the outbreak of war the children were evacuated to the country.

breakout (noun):

There has been another prison breakout. Five men got away and are still at large.

breakdown (noun):

He had a nervous breakdown last year and spent some months in a mental hospital.
A breakdown in the middle of a desert might be fatal for the driver of the car.
A breakdown of these figures would give us a lot of useful information.

bring

upbringing (noun):

An adult's personality is said to be the combined result of inheritance, environment and upbringing.

call

call-up (noun):

Some young men go abroad at the age of 18 to avoid call-up.

come

outcome (noun):

The directors have been discussing this matter, but we don't yet know the outcome of these discussions (what they have decided).

do

overdo (verb):

It's a good thing to be polite but you needn't overdo it. I don't expect you to stand up every time I come into the room.
This steak has been overdone; there's no nourishment left in it.

fall

fall-out (noun) = radio-active dust resulting from an atomic explosion:

Scientists arranging an atomic explosion always maintain that the fall-out will be negligible.

hold

hold-up (noun):

Hold-ups quite often take place in daylight in a crowded street, but everything is done so quickly that the thieves get away before the passers-by realize what has happened.

uphold (verb): = support or approve:

The magistrate sentenced him to a year's imprisonment. He appealed, but the court of appeal upheld the magistrate's verdict.

keep

upkeep (noun):

The upkeep of a house costs more every year, for builders and decorators keep raising their charges.

lay

layout (noun):

The new owners of the paper changed the layout completely.

outlay (noun):

The initial outlay will be heavy as we shall have to buy and equip the factory.

let

outlet (noun):

Children living in crowded flats in towns often haven't enough outlet for their energy.

look

look-out (noun):

He's on the look-out for a new job. If you hear of anything you might let him know.

outlook (noun):

Weather report: Showers and bright intervals. Further outlook – unsettled.

overlook (verb) = fail to notice, disregard. **overlook an offence** = forgive it:

We are afraid that your order has been overlooked. We apologize for this oversight and will deal with the matter directly.
You're late, Jones. I'll overlook it this time, but see that it doesn't happen again.

overlook can also be taken literally: *His house overlooks the park.*

mix

mix-up (noun):

They sent Mr Jones's order to Mr Brown, and Mr Brown's to Mr Jones, a mix-up which lost them both customers.

make

make-up (noun):

The actress said that it sometimes took her an hour to put on her make-up.

round

round-up (noun):

Before the arrival of the visiting president the government ordered a round-up of all people likely to throw bombs at him.

run

runaway (noun, adjective):

The runaways/runaway slaves/were making for the coast.

sell

sell-out:

There was not a single copy left in any of the shops. The first edition had been a complete sell-out.

see

oversee = supervise work/workmen.

overseer = one who does this, foreman:

In the early factories overseers used to walk up and down seeing that everyone worked as fast as possible.

set

offset (verb) = balance:

The advantage of buying things cheaply in the market are sometimes offset by the terrible trouble of carrying them home.

upset (verb/noun) = knock over (usually a vessel of some kind), disarrange, distress:

That vase is top-heavy; it's very easily upset.
The canoe upset and the children had to swim to the bank.
All my plans were upset by the sudden change in weather.
She was very much upset when she heard about your accident.

outset (noun) = start:

I warned you at the outset not to trust him, and you wouldn't listen to me.

take

intake (noun) = quantity or number taken in during a given period:

This college has a yearly intake of 2000 students.

overtake (verb) = catch up with, and usually pass:

It is dangerous to overtake at a corner.
The roadsign said: No overtaking.

take-off (noun):

The aeroplane crashed soon after take-off.

take-over (noun/adjective):

The new owners say that the take-over will not be followed by any staff changes.
A take-over bid is an offer to buy a controlling number of shares in a company.

turn

overturn (verb) = capsize, upset (especially of boats):

You can overturn a kayak and right it again if you are sufficiently skilful.

turnover (noun) = amount of money received by a shop &c. from its customers in a given period; sale and replacement of stock:

He said he had a yearly turnover of £5,000, but he didn't say how much of that was profit.
I sell cheaply, aiming at a rapid turnover of stock.

turn-out (noun):

There was a good turn-out for the football match (= a lot of people came to watch it).

32 Numerals, Dates, and Weights and Measures

Numerals

300 Cardinal numbers

1 one	11 eleven	21 twenty-one	31 thirty-one &c.
2 two	12 twelve	22 twenty-two	40 forty
3 three	13 thirteen	23 twenty-three	50 fifty
4 four	14 fourteen	24 twenty-four	60 sixty
5 five	15 fifteen	25 twenty-five	70 seventy
6 six	16 sixteen	26 twenty-six	80 eighty
7 seven	17 seventeen	27 twenty-seven	90 ninety
8 eight	18 eighteen	28 twenty-eight	100 a hundred
9 nine	19 nineteen	29 twenty-nine	1,000 a thousand
10 ten	20 twenty	30 thirty	1,000,000 a million

400 four hundred
140 a hundred and forty
1,006 one thousand and six
60,127 sixty thousand, one hundred and twenty-seven
7,000 seven thousand

301 Points to notice

a When writing in words or reading a compound figure, **and** is placed before the last word:

3,713 three thousand, seven hundred *and* thirteen
5,102 five thousand, one hundred *and* two
365 three hundred *and* sixty-five

b The words **hundred, thousand,** and **million,** when used of a definite number, are never made plural:

six hundred men   two thousand and ten pounds

If, however, these words are used loosely, merely to convey the idea of a large number, they must be made plural.

Hundreds of people   thousands of birds

Note also that in this case the preposition **of** is placed after the 'hundreds', 'thousands' &c. A definite number is never followed by **of**:

Thousands *of* pounds   *but*   Three thousand pounds

c a is more usual than **one** before **hundred, thousand** &c., when these numbers stand alone:

100 *a* hundred 1,000 *a* thousand

But when other numbers are added **one** is more usual:

104 one hundred and four *or* a hundred and four
11,100 eleven thousand one hundred
1,140 one thousand, one hundred and forty

The expressions **dozen** (12) and **score** (20), follow the rules given in **b** above. **gross** (144) has no plural form, and is always followed by **of**:

a dozen eggs, six dozen two score (definite number, no **s**)
but dozens of eggs (indefinite number, with **s** and **of**) a gross of pins two gross of paper clips

302 Ordinal numbers

first	eleventh	twenty-first	thirty-first &c.
second	twelfth	twenty-second	fortieth
third	thirteenth	twenty-third	fiftieth
fourth	fourteenth	twenty-fourth	sixtieth
fifth	fifteenth	twenty-fifth	seventieth
sixth	sixteenth	twenty-sixth	eightieth
seventh	seventeenth	twenty-seventh	ninetieth
eighth	eighteenth	twenty-eighth	hundredth
ninth	nineteenth	twenty-ninth	thousandth
tenth	twentieth	thirtieth	millionth

303 Points to notice

a Notice the irregular spelling of fifth, eighth, ninth, and twelfth.

b When ordinal numbers are expressed in figures the last two letters of the written word must be added:

fir*st*	= 1st	twenty-first	= 21st
secon*d*	= 2nd	forty-second	= 42nd
thi*rd*	= 3rd	sixty-third	= 63rd
four*th*	= 4th	eightieth	= 80th

c In compound ordinal numbers the rule about **and** is the same as for compound cardinal numbers:

101st a hundred *and* first

The article **the** normally precedes ordinal numbers:

the sixtieth day the fortieth visitor

Titles of kings &c., are written in Roman figures:

Charles V James III Elizabeth II

But in spoken English we use the ordinal numbers preceded by **the**:

Charles the Fifth James the Third Elizabeth the Second

304 Dates

a *The days of the week* / *The months of the year*

Sunday	(Sun.)	January	(Jan.)	July	
Monday	(Mon.)	February	(Feb.)	August	(Aug.)
Tuesday	(Tues.)	March	(Mar.)	September	(Sept.)
Wednesday	(Wed.)	April	(Apr.)	October	(Oct.)
Thursday	(Thurs.)	May		November	(Nov.)
Friday	(Fri.)	June		December	(Dec.)
Saturday	(Sat.)				

Days and months are always written with capital letters.

Dates are expressed by ordinal numbers, so, when reading or speaking, we say:

March the tenth July the fourteenth &c.
or the tenth of March &c.

They can, however, be written in a variety of ways; i.e. March the tenth could be written:

March 10 March 10th 10 March 10th March 10th of March

b *The year*

When reading or speaking we use the term **hundred** but not **thousand**:

The year 1957 would be read as nineteen hundred and fifty-seven *or* nineteen fifty-seven.

Years before the Christian era are followed by the letters B.C. (= before Christ). These are read in either way:

1500 B.C. *would be read as* one thousand five hundred B.C. *or* fifteen hundred B.C.

Weights and Measures

305 a Weights

The English weights table is as follows:

16 ounces (oz.)	= 1 pound (lb.)
14 pounds	= 1 stone (st.)
8 stone	= 1 hundredweight (cwt.)
20 cwt.	= 1 ton
1 pound	= 0·454 kilo.
2·2 pounds	= 1 kilo.

Plurals

ounce, pound, and **ton** can take s in the plural when they are used as nouns, **stone** and **hundredweight** do not take **s**:

six pound of sugar *or* six pounds of sugar
but ten hundredweight of coal – no alternative

When used in compound adjectives these terms never take **s**:

A ten-ton lorry

b Length

The English table of length is as follows:

12 inches (in.)	= 1 foot (ft.)	1 inch = 2·54 centimetres
3 feet	= 1 yard (yd.)	1 yard = 0·914 metre
1,760 yards	= 1 mile	1 mile = 1·609 kilometres

Plurals

When there is more than one inch/mile/yard we normally use the plural form of these words:

one inch, ten inches   one mile, four miles

When there is more than one foot we can use either **foot** or **feet. feet** is the more usual when measuring heights. We can say:

or six foot tall   two foot long
six feet tall *or* two feet long

When used in compound adjectives these terms never take the plural form:

a two-mile walk   a six-inch ruler

33 Spelling Rules

Introduction

Vowels are: **a e i o u.**

Consonants are: **b c d f g h j k l m n p q r s t v w x y z.**

A suffix is a group of letters added to the end of a word:

e.g. beauty – beautiful; **ful** is the suffix.

306 Doubling the consonant

a Words of one syllable having one vowel and ending in a single consonant double the consonant before a suffix beginning with a vowel:

run + er = ru*nn*er
hit + ing = hi*tt*ing
knit + ed = kni*tt*ed

but keep – keeping (two vowels)
help – helped (two consonants)
love – loved (ending in a vowel)

b Two- or three-syllable words ending in a single consonant following a single vowel double the final consonant when the stress falls on the last syllable. (The stressed syllable is italicized):

beg*in* + er = beginner
de*ter* + ed = deterred
re*cur* + ing = recurring

but *mur*mur + ed = murmured
*an*swer + er = answerer
*or*bit + ing = orbiting

c The final consonant of kidnap, worship, handicap, bias, fuel, dial is also doubled:

kidnapper	biassed
worshipping	refuelling
handicapped	dialled

d Words ending in an **l** following a single vowel usually double the **l**:

quarrel – quarrelling	appal – appalled
signal – signalled	model – modelling
distil – distiller	repel – repellent

Note that for the purpose of the above rules **qu** is considered as one consonant:

acquit – acquitted

307 Omission of a final e

a Words ending in **e** following a consonant drop the **e** before a suffix beginning with a vowel:

love + ing = loving
believe + er = believer
move + able = movable

but *likable* can also be spelt *likeable.*

Words ending in **ce** or **ge** however sometimes retain the **e**. See **308.**

b A final **e** is retained before a suffix beginning with a consonant:

hope – hopeful engage – engagement immediate – immediately
fortunate – fortunately sincere – sincerely

But the **e** in **able/ible** is dropped in the adverb form:

comfortable – comfortably incredible – incredibly

The final **e** is also dropped in the following words:

true – truly due – duly whole – wholly (notice also the double **l** here)
argue – argument judge – judgement *or* judgment

c Words ending in **ee** do not drop an **e** before a suffix:

foresee – foreseeing, foreseeable agree – agreed, agreeing, agreement

308 Words ending in ce and ge

a Words ending in **ce** or **ge** retain the **e** before a suffix beginning with **a, o,** or **u:**

courage – courageous peace – peaceable
manage – manageable trace – traceable
outrage – outrageous replace – replaceable

This is done to avoid changes in pronunciation, because **c** and **g** are generally pronounced soft before **e** and **i**, but hard before **a, o,** or **u.**

b Words ending in **ce** change the **e** to **i** before **ous:**

vice – vicious grace – gracious
malice – malicious space – spacious

309 The suffix ful

When **full** is added to a word the second **l** is dropped:

beauty + full = beautiful (but note adverb form: beautifu*ll*y)
use + full = useful (but note adverb form: usefu*ll*y)

If the word to which the suffix is added ends in **ll** the second **l** is dropped here also:

skill + full = skilful

Note full + fill = fulfil

310 Words ending in y

Words ending in **y** following a consonant change the **y** to **i** before any suffix except **ing**:

carry + ed = carried
sunny + er = sunnier
happy + ly = happily
but carry + ing = carrying

y following a vowel does not change:

obey + ed = obeyed
play + er = player (see also **173** and **8b**).

311 ie and ei

The normal rule is that **i** comes before **e** except after **c**:

believe sieve
but deceive receipt

There are however the following exceptions:

beige	foreign	inveigle	skein	weight
counterfeit	forfeit	leisure	sleigh	weir
deign	freight	neigh	sleight	weird
eiderdown	heifer	neighbour	surfeit	
eight	height	neither	their	
either	heinous	reign	veil	
feign	heir	rein	vein	
feint	inveigh	seize	weigh	

Index